# Align Client and Provider Perspectives

Lionel Haas

# Align Client and Provider Perspectives

## Best Practices in IT Outsourcing

 Springer

Lionel Haas
Bern, Switzerland

ISBN 978-3-030-06355-9      ISBN 978-3-319-92064-1    (eBook)
https://doi.org/10.1007/978-3-319-92064-1

Printed on acid-free paper

This Springer imprint is published by the registered company Springer International Publishing AG part of Springer Nature.
The registered company address is: Gewerbestrasse 11, 6330 Cham, Switzerland

# Preface

Literature treats outsourcing from either the client side or from the provider side. It can even treat outsourcing from both sides but then with a side-by-side approach, where the client requests services and the provider supplies them through a contract. This rather technical approach may be suitable when the client outsources non-core, non-strategic IT functions which are just expected to run, but it does not address the real challenges of an outsourcing where the dynamics of change is key for the client's business.

In such a case, the traditional client–provider relation with two distinct operating models connected through loose interfaces is just not viable, and it becomes compulsory to recognise the existence of an enlarged company with a unique and integrated operating model, the ultimate aim being to have information flow seamlessly from the business users requesting the services to the service units delivering them. This is made possible by aligning the delivery organisations at the parties' interface so that individuals on both sides understand each other, standardising the communication channels so that data is exchanged in a normalised way and integrating tools so that large volumes of data can be handled without disruption in the exchange flow.

This is the target situation the parties should have in mind from the very beginning, hence the overall Offer ↷ Plan ↷ Build ↷ Run approach. The arrows in this direction unveil the adventure, starting with a picture of the future mode of operation and then shaping the deal backwards. This implies involving all key stakeholders from the operation, project and contracting units during the offering phase when designing the solution and then again during the various phases when implementing it. From each phase to the next one, only an extensive handover between the responsible teams can ensure that the deal will be executed exactly how it has been thought.

Bern, Switzerland                                                                 Lionel Haas

# Acknowledgements

Out of the many friends and colleagues who have encouraged me and supported me psychologically, I would like to express my thanks, in particular, to the following persons for their direct or indirect contribution to this book:

- Rudi Lichtenberger, former country manager of the company Electronic Data Systems. Rudi was my mentor in my early professional years. He transmitted an invaluable knowledge to me which made every year count twice. There are people who are life changers: Rudi is one of them.
- Beat Grimm, highly respected head of Bid Management at Swisscom. Beat has been my manager for the last 10 years and, undoubtedly, the best ever. He has always trusted me and provided me with maximum flexibility for organising my time and my businesses.
- Monika Efferenn, change management specialist. Monika has successfully led the organisational changes in some challenging businesses. She provided me with a lot of useful content, both from the procedural and human perspectives. She kindly gave up some of her private time for explanations and reviews.
- Tracey Nicholls, a lifetime friend who has been present since the first days of my working experience. As a native English speaker, Tracey offered to proof-read the book.
- My parents, who relieved me from numerous small to larger day-to-day obligations at a time when writing this book added itself to heavy construction work.

And last, but not least, to Franziska Schoembs for introducing me to Springer, without whom this book would not have been possible.

# About the Book

This book develops a common understanding between the client and the provider in each of the four stages of a strategic outsourcing. These stages range from discovery where the parties envision their future collaboration, planning where they lay down the ground work for the contract and the project, building where they effectively carry out the work to, finally, running where they orchestrate the relationship on a daily basis to ensure that the new, enlarged company achieves the sought results. In a simple yet direct style, it emphasises the dos and don'ts the parties should bear in mind at each stage during the process. Here, "to-the-point" is the motto.

Given the fact that it takes two parties to form an agreement, this book combines the perspectives of both the client and the provider by comparing their respective involvement at each stage of the process and considering, equally, their obligations for establishing a balanced relationship.

As is the case in any other long-term relationship, outsourcing is primarily a human issue; it places the individual at the heart of the subject. When it is not the subject itself, such as at the time of employee transfer, it is either at the forefront as the main driver sometimes of the problem and sometimes of the solution, or in the background as the agent of a complex process.

The case studies provided herein are fictional but based on general experiences and cases which generally occur in real life.

## Summary

### Discovery Phase: The Offer

*Get the big picture* Companies considering outsourcing often face multidimensional problems that ultimately come down to an inappropriate IT operating model. The delta between the notional critical mass and the actual staffing of the organisation does not allow to cope with the diversity of activities, the lack of processes does not allow to handle large volumes in a structured way, the misuse of tools leads to a suboptimal functioning when it does not put the business at risk. Only a true understanding of the underlying structural drivers and a sound assessment of the situation can provide the beginnings of a way forward.

*Figure out target sourcing model* As the combination of forms retained for providing the services, the sourcing model should depend on the company's business and strategy. From full outsourcing for companies that want to stay close to market standards, partial outsourcing for those that see a competitive advantage in keeping some operations in house, to exotic models resulting from a conscious approach or, on the contrary, from a total loss of control, the possibilities are many. Understanding the dependencies between service layers allows one to anticipate challenges and minimise dramatic consequences where inappropriate cuts may have been made.

*Gather market information* For those clients that are not familiar with the services they intend to outsource, the request for information phase is crucial. It allows the market to be explored as well as understand what characterises the services and to identify the potential providers. The research will prove successful if it enables common patterns to be determined with respect to how the market implements, operates, measures, reports and bills the services, the ultimate objective being to receive comparable offers from providers during the request for proposal phase.

*Figure out target operating model* A new sourcing model calls for a new operating model, where the operating model stands for the combination of people, processes and tools at the interface between the parties which is required to orchestrate the service delivery. Since outsourcing is about enlarging the client IT organisation to include the provider, the optimal operating model is the one that spans seamlessly from the end users requesting the services to the service units delivering them. The nature of the outsourcing sets the people dimension of the retained organisation, the complexity of the client's business sets the required level of process standardisation and the expected volume of exchanges sets the required level of tool integration.

*Request proposals* Writing a good request for proposal is both an art and a science. It requires formulating business requirements in a way that they call for appropriate technical answers and setting as precise expectations as possible regarding the identified patterns, all while leaving open at the discretion of the provider the means for delivering the services. The objective is to receive innovation proposals, the outputs of which can be compared on an equal basis. Imposing too strict a framework for the answers may force providers to twist their service model and result in non-standard services with higher costs.

*Design proposals* Developing an outsourcing proposal is a short yet intense process. The provider only has a few weeks in which they need to compile all the knowledge of the company, the market and the client into a quality offer which will serve as the basis for a pluriannual agreement. However, in a world where all services look alike, reaching the correct stakeholders with the correct messages is no easy thing. Beyond technical descriptions, standing out from the mass requires activating the emotional drivers that make people buy and then sketching a story accordingly. This is the responsibility of the temporary bid team formed for the occasion around key people from various business units. The next challenge is to have high-flying individuals with diverging objectives collaborate under pressure to produce the winning offer that addresses the unique client situation.

## Planning Phase: The Contract

*Analyse offerings and select partner*  Comparing offers against preset evaluation criteria only provides limited information about the chances of success of the contemplated outsourcing. Each offer should be considered as a unique combination between the provider and its proposal. With respect to the provider, immaterial factors such as trust, values, culture, market positioning, decision centre and corporate image are key for a successful partnership. Material factors pertain to the capacities of the company and include, for Tier II providers and below, the stability of run activities and, for Tier I providers, the flexibility towards changes. Concerning the solution, as the only remaining contact point with the services, reports are of particular importance. In addition to their form and content, how they are produced tells a lot about the level of service integration. For the transition, a close watch on the abilities of the general coordinator will limit time and cost overrun. Last, but not least, comparing offers on a mere price basis is not sufficient. Only a global business case approach considering the TCO over twice the duration of the contract is relevant.

*Formalise willingness to collaborate*  Closing the contract takes from 4 months to 1 year. When the initial positions are so far apart that negotiations could possibly collapse, the parties may first want to identify potential showstoppers through a one-pager called term sheet summarising their agreement on fundamental clauses such as guarantees, liability or termination. Thereafter, they can enter exclusive negotiations with all appertaining confidentiality through a non-binding letter of intent. Nevertheless, if they have already built mutual trust and confidence, they may want to kick off the project straight away while they negotiate the contract in parallel: this would then call for a binding early start letter ruling investments for a defined time period.

*Devise contract set*  An outsourcing contract is an aggregation of dozens of living documents coming from various business units. Sailing across such an ocean of complexity requires navigation rules as well as clear instructions to cope with unavoidable misalignment between documents and conflicting clauses. However, if bundling the documents together to form a consistent whole is already a challenge, maintaining the consistency over time brings the problem to another dimension. Here the expected dynamic of the relation comes into play. Additions, extensions, modifications and terminations are as many possibilities to hamper the overall consistency. A bulletproof contract must resist the rhythm of change.

*Negotiate contract* Negotiating an outsourcing contract is similar to executing a project whose main deliverable is the contract. With a clear goal in mind and the scope, timeline and teams set accordingly, one can expect the negotiations to run as smoothly as contractual discussions normally permit. If not, the parties will likely struggle and the negotiations will bog down. Exaggerated expectations of all kinds due to lack of experience constantly drive the parties apart from the equilibrium paradigm which should govern any mutually beneficial relationship. The structural communication misalignment between the teams on both sides due to the different roles and prerogatives of the negotiators is an additional obstacle to an already difficult progress.

*Set up project governance* The type of outsourcing determines the impact of the transition on the business which in turn determines the complexity of the governance structure needed to drive the project, where complexity stands as the combination between the number of distinct services and the number of management layers. Consequently, the higher the complexity, the greater the number of roles. For coordination between the distinct services to always take place at the lowest possible level, roles should be defined in a way to empower people. Once roles are defined, they must be filled with the right persons. Here, it is the context that drives the selection. Whereas skills and experience are obviously important, soft factors such as acquaintance, personality, resilience, flexibility, culture and language sometimes make all the difference.

*Plan the project* An outsourcing transformation makes no exception to the golden triangle scope/time/cost that characterises any other project: services are assembled along a schedule for a given cost. However, this is only half of the issue. The transformation affects, if not completely changes, the client operating model characterised by the organisation/processes/tools tryptic. Planning the project is thus defining a comprehensive transition concept which considers both the technical and operational dimensions and provides for a progressive ramp-up that minimises business impacts. In outsourcing terminology, this changeover from one equilibrium regime to another is called shifting from the present mode of operation to the future mode of operation.

## Building Phase: The Project

*Execute the project* As outlined earlier, what characterises the transformation is the duality between the construction of the target environment and the concurrent transformation of the source. This would not be such a problem if the source was fixed. The fact is that it is not. During the transformation, the client continues doing business—generally at the same pace as before. This results in changes in the source and as many potential changes in the target. When these happen at the beginning of the project, they may only affect the plans. As the project progresses, the likelihood that they also affect the systems already built increases. This dynamic requires an infallible change process to track down all deviations from the contract, with the consequences documented, explained and enforced. The corollary is the need for a solid common governance structure along with permanent contacts between the parties at all levels.

*Operate systems during the project* The instantaneous switch from the project where systems are built to operations where they are run works for simple transformations, but it does not for complex information systems involving a progressive ramp-up because it is simply impossible to change the state of dozens of new services from not supported to fully operational overnight. During that phase, which can last months, some systems may already be used productively while the project has not been accepted yet, hence the question of which contractual and operational states the systems are in. The answer lies behind the introduction of a transitory regime called operations during project aiming at maintaining the systems in a reasonable state of operationality, but freed from all legal consequences.

*Accompany organisational change* Any change is stressful. It moves people out of their comfort zone and, by doing so, pulls them back to their natural behaviour. This exacerbates the differences and harms an already fragile equilibrium. The change in the ways of working is one part of the problem. Resistance to change is the other. The consequence is that the productivity drops during the project. With appropriate supporting measures, it is back to normal a few months after the end of the project. Without such supporting measures, the recovery can take much longer if the relation has not already died. By raising awareness, fuelling desire, developing knowledge and developing ability, change management supports the process of transformation. It helps individuals to overcome their resistances progressively and turn down opponents into ambassadors.

*Transfer personnel* What happens with the personnel during and after the outsourcing is a question that must be answered from the very start of the analysis, not only because it is the duty of any respectable employer to care for its people, but because it has multiple implications on the viability of the deal. Beware that some countries set a strict legal framework and force the transfer on the provider. Personnel being the first budgetary item in service-sector companies, the financial consequences may weigh heavily in the business case. The timing of the transfer also influences the deal. Depending on when it happens, it leaves the client without staff for running its current operations and thus calls for a temporary operations contract. This boosts the overall level of complexity and risk.

*Enforce operational governance* Governance is the human interface between the parties used to steer the contract and ensure that information is properly relayed on both sides. It is a symmetric arrangement relying on roles, bodies and rules. While simple outsourcings are satisfied with direct communications between identified interlocutors, more complex outsourcings require a more rigid framework and a higher level of formalism. However, whether simple or complex, no governance is no option. Cutting back on governance costs is not a good investment either. Inexperienced clients do not realise a priori to what extent it is needed. On the other hand, even experienced providers can get caught by surprise with demanding clients exercising a level of control sometimes inversely proportional to their level of trust.

*Handover to operations* Handing over to operations is the process for shifting services from project to operations and transferring the responsibility to the corresponding teams with the goal to reach the so-called business as usual mode. For each service, the process happens in two successive handshakes: between the client and the provider first and then within the provider organisation between the project and operation teams, occasionally in reverse order. These handshakes are carried based on acceptance tests calibrated in a way to not leave room for interpretation. Handing over complex services such as the service desk requires a specific on-boarding procedure with a longer preparation and is considered a sub-project in itself.

## Running Phase: The Operations

*Drive outsourcing* No matter how fluid the relation is, an outsourcing will never be as flexible as an internal IT. For the operation to fulfil its promise, the client needs to operate a profound shift of paradigm, from reactive to proactive, where proactive means anticipating the evolutions of the information system to the extent possible. Anticipating is made possible by properly managing the sources from where the evolutions emanate, i.e. the management, the users and the IT itself, and managing these sources is made possible by installing an appropriate internal communication structure between the IT and each source. The most efficient structure is the one that stands as a natural extension of the outsourcing governance and connects the persons from each side at the right level.

*Manage multiple providers* Whether desired or not, working with multiple providers always calls for special attention. Depending on where the cuts between the services are made, the attention can range from keeping an eye on the interfaces to actively managing them. The higher the dependencies between the outsourced services on the run and change axes, the higher the level of management required. In such a case, the client shall not only manage each distinct provider but ensure the coordination between them. This requires a global operating model with adequate organisation, processes and tools that seamlessly integrates the individual operating models enforced with each provider.

*Terminate relationship* There are a few other situations where the contract becomes as important as at the end of the relationship, when the parties do no longer expect anything from a common future. Since all contracts end one day, it would be a risky bet to fly over the reversibility clause during the negotiations. In addition to transfer and run-down services which apply in all cases, post-contract services may have to be delivered way after the termination date. If these are inherent to a complex technical situation and cannot be avoided, fair enough. If they result from a lack of anticipation, this is inexcusable. Data that must be transformed before being remitted, physical assets that are returned without their configuration and intellectual property preventing the transfer of key functions are three topics for which the consequences can be dramatic if not properly foreseen.

## Limitations

In *The Spirit of Laws*, Montesquieu says that the diversity of histories, people, cultures and climates lead to the same diversity of political regimes and concludes that there are few universal laws that apply to all countries. By analogy, few universal recipes can be applied to all outsourcing situations. Although the book addresses the problematics that are most likely to arise and details the corresponding responses that are most likely to work, it is not the ultimate answer to all contexts.

This book begins with the client already having decided to outsource and, therefore, having overcome the corresponding barriers, and hence it does not include all the preliminary strategic and tactical thoughts which lead up to the decision.

Even if this book addresses international aspects of outsourcing, it does not treat the peculiarities of offshoring where distance, culture and language constitute the real hurdles.

Nor does it fully apply to public or GATT/WTO offers which, by nature, impose their own strict set of rules.

Finally, readers will find in this book many tips to make things clearer between the parties, but will not find any tricks with which to fool the other party.

## Main Target Groups

The book is not a crash course in outsourcing fundamentals. It is primarily intended for experienced people in the private sector called upon to deal with complex outsourcing situations who are looking for the small or bigger differentiators that will comfort their decisions and actions. Since to-the-point is the motto, they may flip to any chapter and easily find precise answers without having to go through all the chapters.

Target audiences include, on the client side, COO, CIOs, lawyers, procurement managers, outsourcing consultants and IT service managers and, on the provider side, account managers, bid managers, outsourcing project managers, operation managers and service managers.

It can also be used by anybody who is directly or indirectly involved in an outsourcing and seeks to develop a global understanding of the main processes and roles upstream and downstream the chain.

# Contents

**1 Introduction** . . . . . . . . . . . . . . . . . . . . . . . . . . . . . . . . . . . . . . . . 1
IT Service Stack . . . . . . . . . . . . . . . . . . . . . . . . . . . . . . . . . . . . . . . 1
Service Coverage Acronyms . . . . . . . . . . . . . . . . . . . . . . . . . . . . . . 1
Sourcing Models . . . . . . . . . . . . . . . . . . . . . . . . . . . . . . . . . . . . . . 3

**2 Discovery Phase: The Offer** . . . . . . . . . . . . . . . . . . . . . . . . . . . 5
Get the Big Picture . . . . . . . . . . . . . . . . . . . . . . . . . . . . . . . . . . . . 6
Figure Out Target Sourcing Model . . . . . . . . . . . . . . . . . . . . . . . . 18
Gather Market Information . . . . . . . . . . . . . . . . . . . . . . . . . . . . . . 27
Figure Out Target Operating Model . . . . . . . . . . . . . . . . . . . . . . . 33
Request Proposals . . . . . . . . . . . . . . . . . . . . . . . . . . . . . . . . . . . . 44
Design the Proposal . . . . . . . . . . . . . . . . . . . . . . . . . . . . . . . . . . . 53

**3 Planning Phase: The Contract** . . . . . . . . . . . . . . . . . . . . . . . . 69
Analyse Offerings and Select Partner . . . . . . . . . . . . . . . . . . . . . . 70
Formalise Willingness to Collaborate . . . . . . . . . . . . . . . . . . . . . . 79
Devise Contract Set . . . . . . . . . . . . . . . . . . . . . . . . . . . . . . . . . . . 84
Negotiate Contract . . . . . . . . . . . . . . . . . . . . . . . . . . . . . . . . . . . . 93
Set Up Project Governance . . . . . . . . . . . . . . . . . . . . . . . . . . . . . 107
Plan the Project . . . . . . . . . . . . . . . . . . . . . . . . . . . . . . . . . . . . . 116

**4 Building Phase: The Project** . . . . . . . . . . . . . . . . . . . . . . . . . 123
Execute Project . . . . . . . . . . . . . . . . . . . . . . . . . . . . . . . . . . . . . 124
Operate Systems During the Project . . . . . . . . . . . . . . . . . . . . . . 133
Accompany Organisational Changes . . . . . . . . . . . . . . . . . . . . . . 138
Transfer Personnel . . . . . . . . . . . . . . . . . . . . . . . . . . . . . . . . . . . 152
Enforce Operational Governance . . . . . . . . . . . . . . . . . . . . . . . . . 160
Handover to Operations . . . . . . . . . . . . . . . . . . . . . . . . . . . . . . . 166

**5   Running Phase: The Operations** ............................ 175
     Drive Outsourcing ..................................... 176
     Manage Multiple Providers .............................. 184
     Terminate Relationship ................................. 192

**About the Author** ....................................... 199

**Index** ................................................ 201

# Abbreviations

| | |
|---|---|
| AM | Application Management |
| AO | Application Operation |
| ASP | Application Service Provider |
| BaaS | Business-as-a-Service |
| BaU | Business as Usual |
| BPO | Business Process Outsourcing |
| BSP | Business Service Provider |
| CAB | Change Advisory Board |
| CAPEX | Capital Expenditure |
| CAT | Client Acceptance Tests |
| CtB | Change-the-Business |
| DB | Database |
| DRP | Disaster Recovery Plan |
| ERP | Enterprise Resource Planning |
| ESL | Early Start Letter |
| FMO | Future Mode of Operation |
| FTE | Full-Time Equivalent |
| GDPR | General Data Protection Regulation |
| HaaS | Housing-as-a-Service |
| HCD | Human-Centred Design |
| IaaS | Infrastructure-as-a-Service |
| ISAE | International Standards for Assurance Engagements |
| ISO | International Standard Organisation |
| IT | Information Technology |
| ITIL | Information Technology Infrastructure Library |
| IMACD | Install Move Add Change Dispose |
| ITO | IT Operations |
| KPI | Key Performance Indicator |
| LAN | Local Area Network |
| L-1 | First-Level Support |
| L-2 | Second-Level Support |
| LoI | Letter of Intent |
| MA | Master Agreement |

| MPM  | Multi-provider Management    |
|------|------------------------------|
| MRC  | Monthly Recurring Charge     |
| ODP  | Operations During Project    |
| OLA  | Operating-Level Agreement    |
| OPEX | Operation Expense            |
| OS   | Operating System             |
| OTC  | One-Time Charge              |
| SAP  | Service Access Point         |
| PaaS | Platform-as-a-Service        |
| PMO  | Present Mode of Operation    |
| RCA  | Root Cause Analysis          |
| RfI  | Request for Information       |
| RfP  | Request for Proposal         |
| RfQ  | Request for Questions        |
| RPO  | Return Point Objective       |
| RtB  | Run-the-Business             |
| RTO  | Return Time Objective        |
| SLA  | Service-Level Agreement      |
| SME  | Subject Matter Expert        |
| SaaS | Software-as-a-Service        |
| SPOC | Single Point of Contact      |
| T&M  | Time & Material              |
| TCO  | Total Cost of Ownership      |
| TCV  | Total Contract Value         |
| TMO  | Transition Mode of Operation |
| TOM  | Target Operating Model       |
| UAT  | User Acceptance Tests        |
| WBS  | Work Breakdown Structure     |
| WPL  | Workplace                    |

# Introduction

1

**Abstract**

This chapter introduces the concepts and representations widely used throughout the book, namely the IT service stack with the various layers that constitute an information system, the most common groupings of layers and corresponding forms of service provisioning, the most common sourcing models.

## IT Service Stack

Figure 1 represents the main service layers that constitute an information system. The service layers are further grouped into service categories that represent the most common forms of outsourcing combinations.

The layers are arranged in a way to best support the explanations and simplify the illustrations. Their position in the stack does not always signify that they bear upstream or downstream dependencies with the next consecutive layers.

## Service Coverage Acronyms

Figure 2 represents the acronyms most commonly used on the market to describe the coverage of services in terms of layers. These are:

- HaaS stands for Housing-as-a-Service: provision of data centre facilities, including or not connectivity and security.
- IaaS stands for Infrastructure-as-a-Service: provision of computing power, including or not the management of operating systems. As the base of cloud computing services, it is the most widely spread form.
- PaaS stands for Platform-as-a-Service: IaaS with added-value services such as middleware and database management. The service is deemed application-ready.

© Springer International Publishing AG, part of Springer Nature 2018

L. Haas, *Align Client and Provider Perspectives*,

https://doi.org/10.1007/978-3-319-92064-1_1

| Category | Service layer | Description | Added-value |
|---|---|---|---|
| Workplace | Devices procurement & deployment | Procurement of end-user devices and on-site installation | Medium |
| Workplace | Application packaging & distribution | Packaging, distribution and release mgmt. of software packages | Medium |
| Workplace | Base image management | Design and maintenance of end user devices, profiles and base image | Medium |
| Business | Business process operation | Execution and control of business transactions and operations | High |
| Business | Business process analysis | Analysis of business logic and processes | High |
| Business | Business process parameterisation | Design, implementation, optimisation of workflows and parameters | High |
| Application | Application development | Development, integration and configuration of applications and interfaces | High |
| Application | Application maintenance | Management of incidents, problems, releases, changes, deployments | High |
| Application | Application operation | Monitoring of applications and interfaces, management of batches | Medium |
| Infrastructure | Database management | Management of table spaces, objects, rights, backups | Medium |
| Infrastructure | Middleware management | Monitoring, patching and optimisation of intermediate application layers | Medium |
| Infrastructure | System management | Monitoring, patching and house keeping of operating systems | Medium |
| Infrastructure | Data storage, backup and archiving | Monitoring, patching and house keeping of data repositories | Medium |
| Infrastructure | Hardware life-cycle mgmt. | Provisioning and life-cycle mgmt. of physical infrastructures | Low |
| Infrastructure | Data centre facilities | Provisioning of space floor, racks, electricity, air conditioning, security | Low |
| Connectivity | I/O Data centre, security | Provisioning of I/O connections with data centre, central security | Low |
| Connectivity | LAN / WLAN/ Telco management | Management of switches, routing, ports, access points, telephone centrals | Low |
| Connectivity | Internet | Provisioning of local and/or central Internet breakouts, proxies | Low |
| Connectivity | WAN / MAN | Provisioning of communication links between data centres and offices | Low |

(End-user support services (level-1))

**Fig. 1** IT service stack

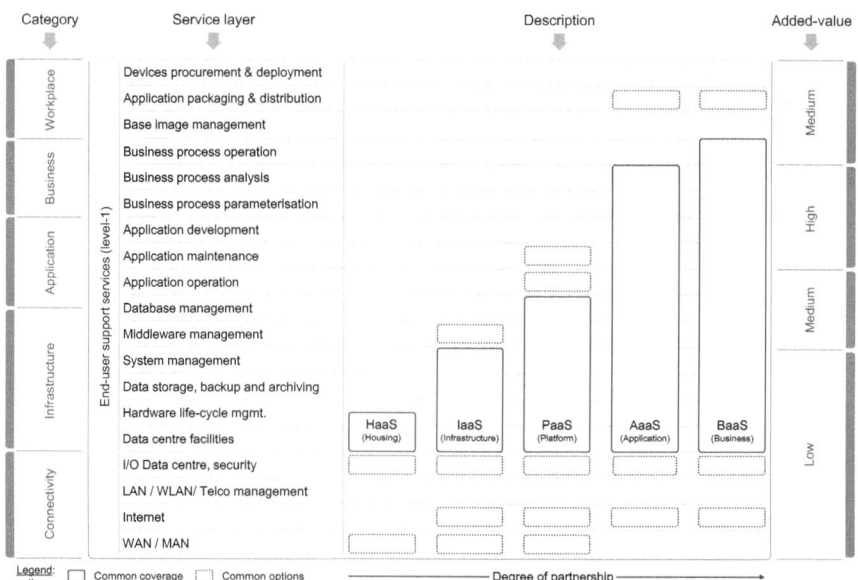

**Fig. 2** Service coverage acronyms

- AaaS stands for Application-as-a-Service: provision of software application, normally through the Internet, including the complete stack of services required. Is also referred to as Software-as-a-Service (SaaS). The provider of such model is referred to as Application Service Provider (ASP).
- BaaS stands for Business-as-a-Service: AaaS including standard business services. The provider of such model is referred to as Business Service Provider (BSP).

## Sourcing Models

Figure 3 represents the four most common forms of sourcing and the corresponding service coverage with respect to:

- The provision of human resources.
- Their instruction as regards the services to be delivered.
- The design and maintenance of the processes ruling the delivery.
- The tools used to render the services and coordinate their delivery.
- The hardware and software assets used to develop and render the services.
- The topology and arrangement of the various elements constituting the services.
- The coordination of the service delivery.

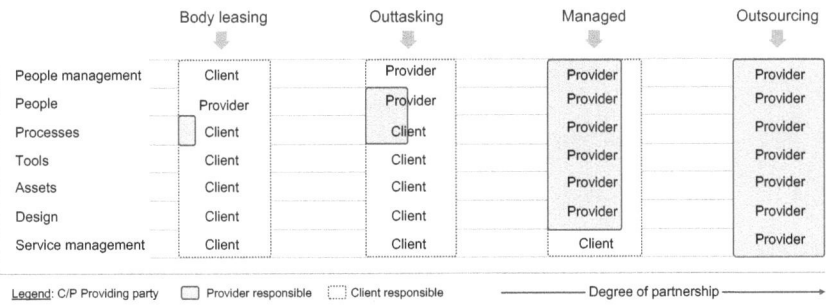

|  | Body leasing | Outtasking | Managed | Outsourcing |
|---|---|---|---|---|
| People management | Client | Provider | Provider | Provider |
| People | Provider | Provider | Provider | Provider |
| Processes | Client | Client | Provider | Provider |
| Tools | Client | Client | Provider | Provider |
| Assets | Client | Client | Provider | Provider |
| Design | Client | Client | Provider | Provider |
| Service management | Client | Client | Client | Provider |

Legend: C/P Providing party   ☐ Provider responsible   ⸽⸽⸽ Client responsible   ———————— Degree of partnership ————————▶

**Fig. 3** Sourcing models

# Discovery Phase: The Offer

**2**

**Abstract**

In this chapter, you will learn the main effects of an inadequate operating model; how to lay down the desired combination of sourcing forms for providing the services; how to explore the market offering for the sought sourcing model and services; how to define the organisation, processes and tools needed on the client side at the parties' interface; how to invite providers to submit firm offers based on standard patterns; and, finally, how to design the winning offer that will set the base for a multi-annual outsourcing agreement.

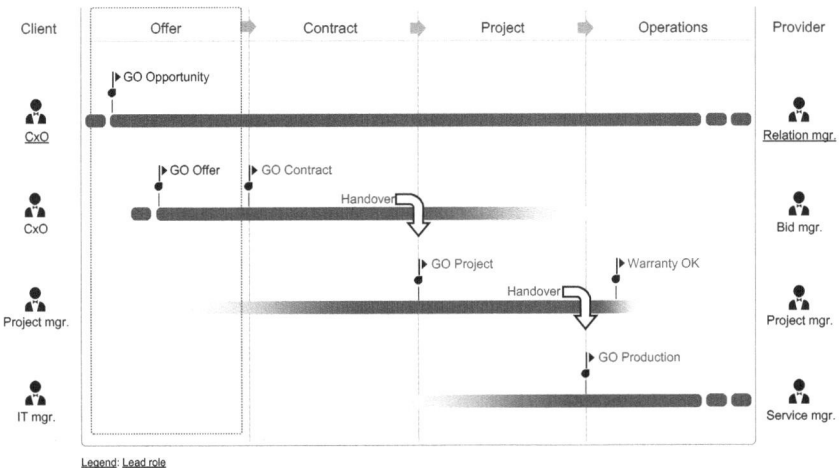

**Fig. 4** Discover phase in the outsourcing life-cycle

© Springer International Publishing AG, part of Springer Nature 2018
L. Haas, *Align Client and Provider Perspectives*,
https://doi.org/10.1007/978-3-319-92064-1_2

## Get the Big Picture

Attention which each party should pay to this topic: Client: ●●● Provider: ●●○

## Objective

Understand the main effects of an inadequate operating model.

This chapter points out the most frequent structural problems that are early signs of outsourcing and analyses them under the angle of a concept extensively developed throughout the book: the operating model.

## Positioning

An efficient IT department serves the business effectively and manages itself effectively. Determining how efficient an IT department is may follow the simple macro-micro approach below:

- Position the IT in relation with the business, where business means the market in which the company operates and, by extension, the internal users who interface with it, the point being to assess whether it promotes the same values as those of the company (e.g. if the company built its reputation on the confidentiality of its services, then the IT shall guarantee maximum security of the installations) or whether it supports adequately the business model (e.g. if the company built its business on market reactivity, then the IT shall deliver changes at the corresponding rate).
- Determine if the IT is adequately structured to cope with all its duties at a fair price. From the two examples above, the IT could truly guarantee maximum security at all times, but to the detriment of important enhancement projects because it lacks resources to both run and change the systems at once.

Once the current situation is understood, confront it with the contemplated future situation by following the same approach. The aim is to determine how the expected evolution of the business will increase or release the pressure on current IT challenges. For example, the company may plan to downsize, which could allow IT to redistribute internal roles in a more effective way to better handle changes. Conversely, the company may plan to grow vertically, which would require IT to broaden its skills to cope with more diversity, or grow horizontally, which would require IT to ameliorate its processing capacity to absorb higher volumes.

## Prerequisites

Figuring out the root of the challenges and thereon the possible solutions is a multi-faceted undertaking that exceeds mere technical analysis.

As outlined in the introduction, there are few universal recipes applicable to all companies. However, there are some common patterns one should always consider bearing in mind that although they may not always be sufficient, they are necessary. These are the three pillars to any IT operating model: the organisation, the processes and the tools.

Figure 5 shows the impact of each pillar on the costs and functioning of the IT. Consider the graphic in light of the following:

- *Organisation.* Adding more people has negative, long-term effects on costs. If the IT is not adequately staffed both qualitatively and quantitatively, very little can be done to improve the situation. Therein, changing the processes or the tools can only bring limited improvements.
- *Processes.* Re-engineering processes may be extremely complex and costly, but the bulk of the cost happens only once. Thereafter, the IT may experience meaningful improvements in the way it operates. Conversely, wrong processes can be downright obnoxious for the productivity.
- *Tools.* Changing tools may also be extremely complex and costly, especially when they touch core applications. Nevertheless, in such cases, the positive effects on costs and functioning come less from the installation of the tool itself than from the implementation of the proper business processes and parameters therein. Replacing tools without touching the business logic has normally limited effects on costs and functioning.

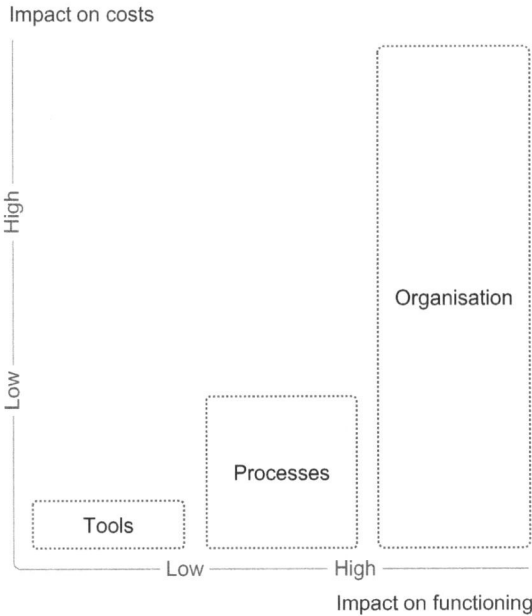

**Fig. 5** The three pillars of a sound assessment

## Practical Analysis

### Organisation

The first step of the analysis is to observe the organisational component and more specifically the gap between the notional critical mass and the current staffing of the IT.

One defines the critical mass, measured in persons, as the number of different profiles required times the whole number of occurrences of each profile. The number of different profiles determines the capacity of the organisation to handle the diversity of the activities and the number of occurrences needed to handle the workload. The critical mass determines the threshold beyond which operations can be delivered optimally in quality and quantity and, conversely, below which operations experience deficiencies in skills and/or workload capacity.

---

**Example**

A provider launches a new service that needs five engineers with different skills. Each engineer is expected to work 20% of their time. The critical mass is five persons, but the effective workload only one person ($5 \times 20\%$).

The client that wants to run the same service internally has basically two choices: either bear the cost of the five persons or distribute the workload over existing staff members with miscellaneous skills and train them reasonably on their new duties. The first option is financially inefficient because of the partial use of resources; the second is risky because of the gap of expertise and the reduction of attention on other activities.

On the provider side, it is a fact that an IT operations (ITO) outsourcing of a certain complexity involves at least 50 different profiles[1] in recurring operations and between 100 and 150 for the initial transition. Adding application operation (AO) and application maintenance (AM) for a business environment counting 25+ complex business applications can easily double or triple the figures. Obviously, the provider does not use all profiles full-time for a given client. It even involves some of them only an extremely small fraction of their time, e.g. compliancy. It is the capacity of the provider to keep all profiles busy with a wide client base that allows it to bill clients only the needed cost fraction of the critical mass. On the client side, only big organisations with large IT departments and corresponding volumes reach the critical mass. For all others, it is quite common to notice that providers and clients may deliver identical services with identical number of full-time equivalents (FTE) and roughly at the same cost, but following a different risk distribution.

This difference between the fraction of cost a provider can bill thanks to the full usage of resources on one side, and the full cost the client should bear because of the

---

[1]Various levels of engineers, technical experts, audit, compliance, security, process specialists, quality managers, etc.

partial usage of resources on the other, and the subsequent cost versus risk arbitrage the client must constantly make, is the root cause of most challenges clients face.

The gap between actual and critical mass may manifest in different ways. It turns out to be difficult to unravel sometimes with the result that drawing incorrect conclusions leads to implement incorrect solutions. Below are the three main situations observed on the market and their consequences.

## Job Roles and Role Allocation

Figure 6 compares how a provider having the critical mass and a client not having it respectively operate a system spanning several layers of the service stack:

The provider works on the horizontal axis and allocates as many specialists as required in each layer. The client works on the vertical axis and allocates a limited number of generalists who span several layers. While concentrating vertically the responsibility over a whole system through a reduced number of roles may alleviate investigations upon incidents and reduces coordination efforts, it has major drawbacks:

- *Ambiguous job descriptions.* Individual persons cover a wide range of layers, sometimes of different nature, e.g. Technology versus Business, which usually do not match in terms of hard skills. This makes the persons difficult to replace when they leave and creates a dependency on named individuals rather than on standard roles.

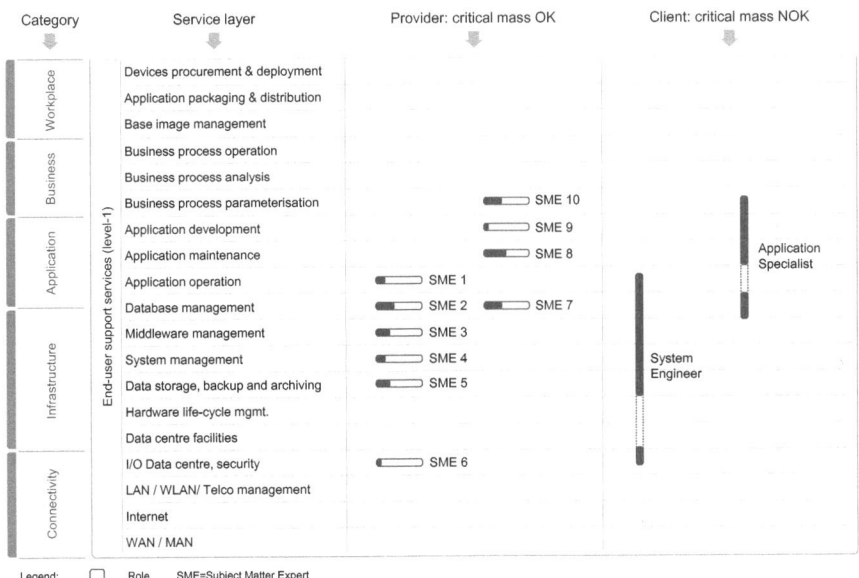

**Fig. 6** Critical mass versus role allocation

- *Lack of expertise.* Each layer does not benefit from the finest configuration and functions below optimum efficiency. The combination of suboptimal layers between them may lead to erratic behaviour in the systems.
- *Non-segregation of duties.* The same persons accessing at the same time business data, data media, and security parameters, a misconduct of a single individual may result in loss of confidentiality, integrity, or availability of data.

### Run-the-Business (RtB) Versus Change-the-Business (CtB)

Figure 7 shows how the provider and the client cope with small changes and bigger projects.

The provider assigns the responsibility of changes to a dedicated project team aside from the operations team. The client allocates the same responsibility to the existing operations team. While having the same persons implementing and, thereafter, operating a solution slightly eases the handover to production and reduces coordination efforts, it does have major drawbacks:

- *Ambiguous job descriptions.* Individual persons cover roles of different natures in the plan-build-run chain which usually do not match in terms of hard nor soft skills. This makes them not best suited for one or the other function.
- *Constraint on workload.* The same individuals absorbing an additional workload—sometimes for a long period of time, it results in both project delays (incidents and mandatory maintenance prevail) and production problems (proactive maintenance operations are left behind).

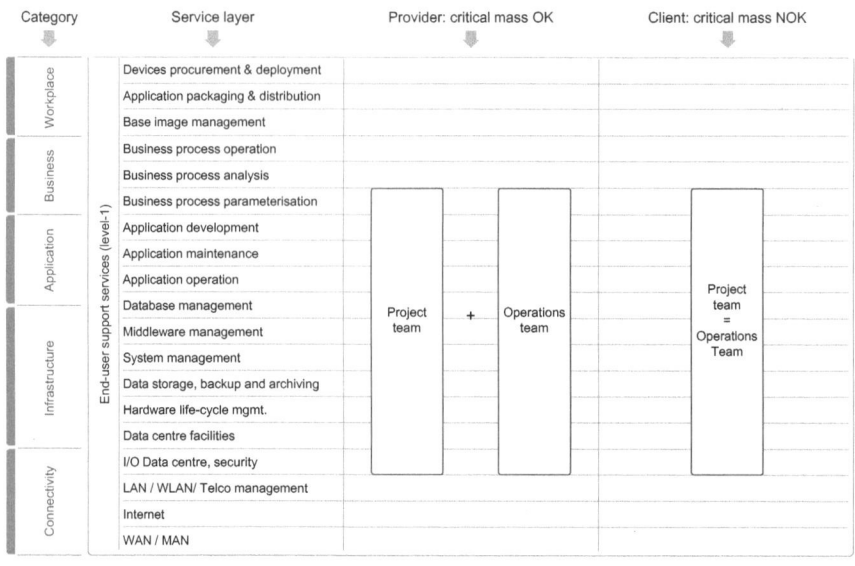

**Fig. 7** Critical mass versus RtB and CtB

- *Non-segregation of duties.* The persons who design systems may develop specific knowledge about the systems' internals, and the persons who build them have access to specific tools. The concentration of knowledge and authorisations on single individuals who have access to business data in production may result in loss of confidentiality, integrity, or availability of data.
- *Quality issues.* The workload pressure leads operation teams to take shortcuts on system testing and documentation.

## Internal Transfer of Workloads

Figure 8 shows how the provider and the client maintain the balance between back-end (IT internal) and front-end (user-facing) services:

By allocating the right experts in quantity and quality in each layer, the provider limits incidents to the minimum. By experiencing qualitative and quantitative deficiencies in operations, the client generates more incidents and involuntarily transfers workloads from the operations to the service desk. This has the following consequences:

- *Pressure on L-1.* Less proactive maintenance leads to more incidents. Consequently, the size of the service desk becomes disproportionate in relation with the number of incidents and requests that the environment should generate.
- *Pressure on L-2.* More incidents lead in turn to more L-2 analyses. Consequently, the operation team spends more time on fixing bugs than on proactive maintenance activities.

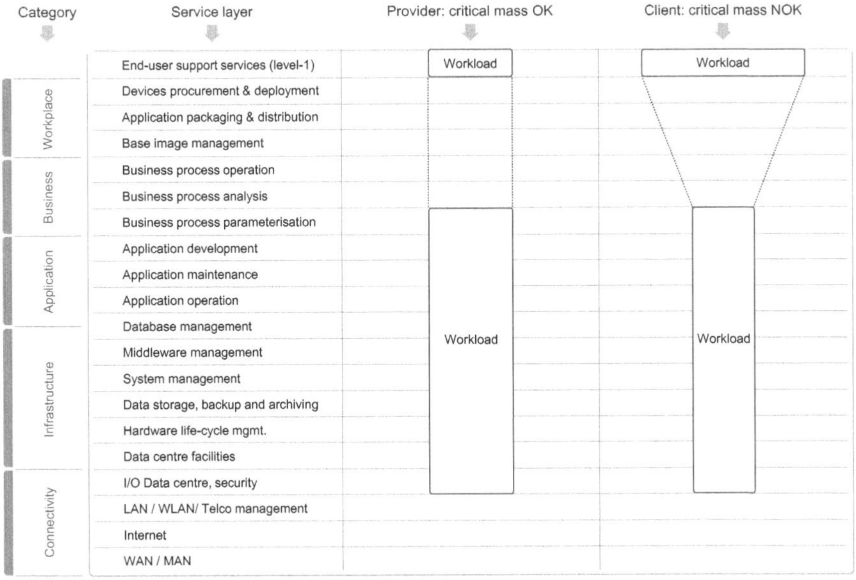

**Fig. 8** Critical mass versus internal transfer of workloads

- *Competence levelling.* Service desk agents face more complex problems and thus gain knowledge about the environment beyond their job description. Over time, this leads them to take over additional responsibilities not limited anymore to restoring services in their current state, like performing L-2 analysis or installing applications, and, subsequently, becoming key IT members.
- *Ambiguous job descriptions.* The levelling of competence leads agents to cover roles of different nature which usually do not match in terms of soft skills (support = people oriented, engineering = machine oriented). This makes them not best suited for one or the other function in addition to making them difficult to replace when leaving.

The overexposure of the service desk to complex situations transforms agents into engineers and makes the whole function too efficient compared to what it should be. Not surprisingly, all users receive VIP treatment and greatly appreciate it. This shall, under no circumstance, avoid the issue that the service desk is in fact part of a pyromaniac firefighter organisation.

## Processes

The second step of the analysis is to recognise the importance of processes and to what extent missing or suboptimal processes can affect the functioning of the organisation. Whereas the critical mass allows to handle complexity, processes allow the handling of volumes in a structured way. These are processes which permit transforming a craft production organisation into a mass production organisation. Indeed, as long as the volumes remain within the limits that a small team can absorb and commit to memory, working on the items' content will continue to be possible. However, when the number of items to be processed begins to increase at a rate faster than that at which the team can process them, it becomes necessary to increase the level of organisation, beginning with the introduction of automatic rules. Considering that the handling of an activity is based on an input upstream and that it triggers several outputs downstream, it becomes clear that the general coordination of the activities is more down to the application of industrialised processes than to individuals.

---

### Case study: how processes allow to enable large volumes

The client outsourced the bulk of its IT but kept internally the service desk that acts as a single point of contact (SPOC) for incidents and user requests. The service desk comprises 6 persons who handle overall 30 incidents per day each.

The client undertakes a major change in its core application and main satellites with the support of the supplier. As is often the case in complex migrations, there are only a few possible cutover dates possible during the year, usually an end-of-quarter falling on a long weekend to permit extensive testing. The project already missed a cutover date and cannot afford missing another one without cascaded business consequences. Although it knows it did not properly test the new systems, the client still decides to go live. By doing this, it anticipates the workload increase with organisation and procedural measures.

The go-live happens and the number of incidents rises from 30 to 90 per day and agent. After a few weeks, the number decreases but is still much higher than the regular load. The situation is finally back to normal after 12 months.

There is no question that the client suffered disorders, but it limited the damages by appropriate measures. It reinforced the organisation with four additional agents and adjusted workflows to ensure incidents would flow seamlessly from the users upstream to the service units of the provider in charge of their correction downstream. Without it, the number of incidents per day would have been higher than the number of incidents dispatched, and it would have created a backlog subject to an endemic growth.

Weaknesses or deficiencies in processes leave an impression of chaos. Since the organisation cannot count on preset rules to fulfil the work in a structured way, it relies on heroes, i.e. a few bright individuals who stand out from the others and who are empowered with special prerogatives accordingly. Heroes know they are heroes though, and they tend to protect their knowledge, which represents their survival asset. When they leave, they take with them this knowledge, which partly belongs to the organisation that fostered its development. This is a major characteristic of empirical organisations: they are not only inefficient, they cannot learn, neither from their mistakes nor from their successes.

With the publishing of the Principles of Scientific Management in 1911, Fredrick Taylor was one of the earliest thinkers on how best to coordinate action within an organisation and capitalise on skills. His most prominent theories include:

- *Knowledge transfer.* Capture the knowledge of people into a system to reduce dependency vis-à-vis individuals and make the organisation become knowledgeable.
- *Reduce complexity.* Break down activities into smaller units and attribute them to different people or other processes.
- *Ensure reproducibility.* Sequence activities by determining the relations between inputs and outputs and making sure identical conditions trigger identical processing rules.
- *Increase productivity.* Reduce floats between tasks and optimise the time required to process inputs and create outputs.
- *Applying best practices.* Figure out the most efficient way to achieve the objective out of different possible paths.
- *Limit conflicts.* Ensure that similar inputs processed by different rules or different people produce the same outputs to reduce conflicts between people and interferences between systems.

Albeit some processes like human resources management are rather generic and may apply to most organisations with minor changes only, processes linked to production units are specific to the business of the organisation they are meant for.

In IT organisations, the most common process referential is ITIL v3.[2] The section "Figure Out Target Sourcing Model" delineates succinctly the main processes referenced by ITIL and how they apply given the outsourcing model decided by the client. The consequences of not implementing a robust process framework in an IT company are countless. It is unfortunate because even a light implementation can bring significant improvement, as illustrated by the following example.

**Example: what cascaded consequences a single missing process can have**

Whereas Tier I providers manage user workplace environments following strict packaging, distribution, and release management processes, many clients still install applications directly on users' workstations without analysing the impact upstream nor coordinating the deployment downstream. Mapped with Taylor's theories, the most noticeable consequences are:

- *Knowledge.* The application matrix is not mastered. The client has no clear view of which application run on which workstation and for which user. After several installations and deinstallations of the same application, the environment is no longer in line with software licencing agreements and the client could become subject to penalties if audited.
- *Reproducibility.* The service desk cannot restore workstations to their original state automatically after an incident. A restore generates more than one intervention until the workstation is complete again. Equipping a new user with a workstation calls for several distinct actions that can eventually be processed in parallel but are almost assuredly aggregated manually.
- *Complexity.* Deploying applications on a large user audience generates a massive workload. Workstations not connected to the network cannot be deployed. When they finally join the network again, the deployment of the latest release may not function properly because the existing versions are outdated and reject the installation.
- *Best practices.* Since applications are installed on a case-by-case basis, they do not necessarily include the best set of parameters, especially those providing for compliance with company policies. For example, the automatic document saving feature of office applications should be always redirected to the servers of the company whereas by default files are stored locally. In case of hardware breakdown, the user may lose data.
- *Productivity.* Application installations, bug fixing and workstation regenerations keep the service desk busy, whereas in a fully managed environment, the corresponding effort is marginal.
- *Conflicts.* Incompatible applications are installed on the same workstations, generating erratic behaviours difficult to locate. Conflicts are solved by deploying different versions of the same application on different

---

[2]Now normalised within ISO 20000.

workstations. After a few years, dozens of application versions coexist in the landscape, resulting in hundreds when not thousands of distinct software components disseminated in the environment.

## Tools

The third step of the analysis is to have a closer look at the tools[3] the client uses, misuses or totally lacks. Whatever the form they take, from rudimentary to complex, tools shall always be considered as a natural extension of processes, never as substitutes. Let us see the main forms they can take and how their misuse may affect the organisation.

### Off-the-Shelf, Full-Featured

These tools serve a given set of functions (e.g. ticketing tool to handle incidents) and come with preconfigured processes known as workflows. They allow changing parameters and sometimes modifying existing workflows or creating new ones. These types of tools embark with them the knowledge to process the market-standard function they serve.

If they are not properly implemented, these tools can hinder the general functioning of the organisation. For example, an ambiguous categorisation of incident types during the initial set-up would lead users to lose more time than needed when opening online tickets, the service desk to route tickets to the incorrect service units and, at the end of the chain, the IT to draw statistics based on incorrect input data.

### Toolboxes

These are frameworks meant to give the client the possibility to serve almost any type of function, e.g. implement a complete ITIL chain like incidents-problems-change-release-deployment. They provide all the features to design, code and test complex workflows. Herein, it is the full responsibility of the client to reflect in the tool the knowledge to process the desired functions. Non-expert knowledge implemented in these tools can hamper the productivity.

---

**Case study: why continuous improvement is only achievable with processes**

The client recognises the need to enforce a minimum set of processes to manage incidents and service requests. It allocates for this a tight budget.

Against a discount on licence costs, the company that developed the framework also wins the implementation and thereafter appoints on the project non-experts, namely IT developers with a sensibility for processes.

The developers instantiate the target configuration from a previous implementation and tune it with new client requirements arriving daily, until the budget envelope is exhausted and the system is de facto considered final.

---

[3]Refers to technical tools, not business applications.

The end of the budget envelope leaves behind critical processes such as configuration management and knowledge management, which constitute the basis for continuous improvement. The client experiences a slight jump in productivity after the introduction of the tool, but the curve stabilises itself thereafter. Not only the tool executes suboptimal processes, but it has not set the basis for the organisation to become a learning system.

### Development Tools

They offer the highest grade of flexibility and, consequently, present the highest deviance risks. The client which uses off-the-shelf business products generally uses development tools to create missing business functions that are too small or too specific to justify buying a product, create interfaces between business applications or create support functions aimed at helping users to automate repetitive tasks. Initially called quick wins, the accumulation of non-managed developments can quickly turn into a nightmare. Lack of documentation and source code control are usual drawbacks. The real problem is, however, their lack of consideration as real applications in the change and release management processes, with consequences of system upgrades being discovered on the fly.

Text processors and spreadsheets also need to be mentioned for the risk they involve. Albeit more rudimentary compared to real development tools, the accumulation of macros can put the client in a difficult situation at the time of a major upgrade. It is common to see entire business departments relying on a single spreadsheet populated daily with critical data by a macro that runs on its own and whose developer, a business user, left the company long ago.

Development tools result in off-radar functions which constitute a whole unofficial yet critical environment called shadow IT.

---

**Case study: how shadow IT can put an organisation at risk**

The client developed 200 document templates with the macro engine of a text processor to automate the production of documents generated by the ERP. Years after, the ERP produces daily hundreds of documents that reach final clients without any human intervention. The functionality does not generate any incident at all and has become as natural as critical. It is the perfect quick win.

The client decides to upgrade its workplace environment by renewing end-user devices. New devices come with a major release of the operating system and, consequently, with a major release of user applications.

The client tests the new application releases, including the text processor, but not the macro engine of the latter. The day of the go-live, the client does not report any major issue with the text processor itself. But, a few days after, it starts receiving dozens of scrambled documents back from unhappy clients. It then enters a crisis mode and stops all written communications with clients. From this moment on, it has 48 hours to rework the source code of the most critical templates and little more than a few days for the others.

## Dos and Don'ts

Although understanding the current situation is an obvious concern of the client, the 2-h window of opportunity the provider would have to join the thinking process is worth the two attention bullets granted in the introduction. It is nearly impossible for a client non-expert in IT matters to point out alone the root causes of the challenges it faces. The provider can help to inquire about the situation by asking specific questions and then attribute the answers by order of importance to any of the three main pillars, namely the organisation first, thereafter the processes and finally the tools. Together, the parties can project the target expected situation and determine the gap.

The following questionnaire provides a basic set of essential questions per category:

Organisation

- *Job roles.* Does the IT face ever-increasing challenges proceeding from topics like innovation, digitalisation, internationalisation? In other terms, can the IT cope sustainably with the corresponding broadening of skills?
- *Job roles.* Are duties strictly segregated and control mechanisms in place to prevent massive loss of data confidentiality or integrity? In other terms, do single individuals cumulate rights on sensible service layers like application, database, storage and backup?
- *Job roles, RtB versus CtB.* Does the IT face challenges proceeding from an ever-reducing time-to-market? In other terms, can it mobilise the variety of skills within the times specified without incurring risks on other activities?
- *RtB versus CtB.* Can the IT execute in quality and in quantity all supposed RtB and CtB activities? In other terms, can it cope with the current pace of changes without inducing risks on production activities?

Processes

- *Knowledge.* Are all IT activities described in the form of procedures to be executed by generic roles or do some of them depend on named individuals?
- *Knowledge.* Does the IT capitalise on its knowledge and improve over time? For example, do incidents and problems follow a downward-sloping trend or remain unchanged?
- *Reproducibility.* Can the IT really guarantee the services? For example, in case it needs to execute the disaster recovery plan (DRP), does it have at hand the very latest configuration of the systems or does it mainly have to rely on the knowledge of named individuals to restore the services?
- *Reproducibility.* Do the internal and/or external auditors systematically point out deficiencies in existing processes of the internal control system?
- *Reproducibility.* Does your information system sometimes suffer from erratic behaviour and non-identifiable malfunctions?
- *Reproducibility.* Do you have an audit trail? In other terms, are you able to trace any action performed on or in the systems?

- *Reduce complexity.* Do some complex, but nonetheless repetitive tasks, call for skilled personnel in order to be executed?
- *Best practices.* Does the IT comply with any of the following standards: ISO 9001 (quality), 20,000 (operations), 27,000 (security)? Are the project managers certified?

Tools
- *Off-the-shelf, toolboxes.* Do incidents and service requests flow seamlessly from end users to the service units responsible for processing them or do they require manual processing?
- *Off-the-shelf, toolboxes.* Do the tools allow you to draw advanced statistics? Do you analyse such data, perform trend analysis and further optimise the processes and the tools?
- *Development.* Can you certify having an exhaustive view on all pieces of software, including macros, developed internally either by the IT or end users?

## Figure Out Target Sourcing Model

Attention which each party should pay to this topic: Client: ●●● Provider: ●●○

## Objective

Lay down the desired combination of sourcing forms for providing the services.

## Description

The sourcing model is the combination of sourcing forms wanted by the client to deliver the IT function to end users It is about deciding which service categories and single managed services are candidates for outsourcing and, for the service layers staying in-house, which ones shall internal staff provide and which ones will need the support of third parties.

## Prerequisites

Failing to define a consistent service model may have consequences ranging from minor to dramatic, depending on whether the inappropriate cuts concern standardised, stand-alone services such as LAN management (low impact) or tailored, integrated services such as business process parameterisation (high impact).

The case study contained in the section "Manage Multiple Providers" in Chap. 5 gives an example of the consequences when the cut happens between the ITO and AO layers.

| Functional view ➡ | Corporate services | | | | | Business Applications | | | | | | | Support Applications | | | | |
|---|---|---|---|---|---|---|---|---|---|---|---|---|---|---|---|---|---|
| Technical view ⬇ | Telephony | e-mail, FAX | Conferencing | Printing | ⋮ | ERP | Invoicing | Application 2 | Application 3 | Application 4 | Application 5 | ⋮ | Office tools | Client app 1 | Client app 2 | Client app 3 | ⋮ |
| Devices procurement & deployment | ● | ● | ○ | ○ | ● | ● | ● | ● | ● | ● | ● | ● | ● | ● | ● | ● | ● |
| Application packaging & distribution | * | * | * | * | | * | * | * | * | * | * | * | * | * | * | | |
| Base image management | - | ● | ● | ● | | ● | ● | ● | ● | ● | ● | ● | ● | ● | ● | | |
| Business process operation | - | - | - | - | | ● | ○ | ● | ● | ● | ● | ● | ● | - | - | | |
| Business process analysis | - | - | - | - | | - | ○ | - | - | - | - | - | - | - | - | | |
| Business process parameterisation | - | - | - | - | | ○ | ○ | ● | ● | ● | | - | - | - | * | | |
| Application development | - | ○ | ○ | ○ | | ○ | ○ | ○ | ○ | ○ | | - | - | - | * | | |
| Application maintenance | - | ○ | ○ | ○ | | ○ | ● | ● | * | * | * | | * | - | * | | |
| Application operation | - | ○ | - | ? | | ○ | ○ | ? | ? | ? | ? | ? | ? | - | - | | |
| Database management | - | ○ | - | ● | | ○ | ○ | ● | ● | * | * | * | ● | - | ● | | |
| Middleware management | - | ○ | - | - | | ○ | ○ | - | - | - | ? | ? | ? | - | - | | |
| System management | - | ○ | ○ | ○ | | ○ | ○ | * | * | * | * | * | ● | - | - | | |
| Data storage, backup and archiving | - | ○ | ● | ○ | | ○ | ○ | ● | ● | ● | ● | ● | ● | - | ● | | |
| Hardware life-cycle mgmt. | ● | ● | ○ | ○ | | ○ | ○ | ● | ● | ● | ● | ● | ● | - | ● | | |
| Data centre facilities | ● | ● | ● | ● | | ○ | ○ | ● | ● | ● | ● | ● | ● | ● | ● | ● | ● |
| I/O Data centre, security | - | ● | ● | ● | | ● | ● | ● | ● | ● | ● | ● | ● | ● | ● | ● | ● |
| LAN / WLAN/ Telco management | * | * | * | * | * | * | * | * | * | * | * | * | * | * | * | * | * |
| Internet | ○ | ○ | ○ | ○ | ○ | ○ | ○ | ○ | ○ | ○ | ○ | ○ | ○ | ○ | ○ | ○ | ○ |
| WAN / MAN | ○ | ○ | ○ | ○ | ○ | ○ | ○ | ○ | ○ | ○ | ○ | ○ | ○ | ○ | ○ | ○ | ○ |

Row groupings (left axis): Workplace, Business, Application, Infrastructure, Connectivity — all under *End-user support services (level-1)*.

Legend:  ● In-house   ○ Outsourcing or maintenance contract   * Outtasking or body-leasing   - Not needed   ? Needed but not provided

**Fig. 9** Example of service model assessment matrix

Before entering a detailed analysis of viable service models, the client should assess its current situation. A simple yet effective way to do it is by drawing the service matrix shown in Fig. 9. List service layers of the IT service stack on the vertical axis and business functions brought to the users on the horizontal axis. At each cell intersection, identify the sourcing form used to provide the service and, subsequently, the entity which provides it.

## Practical Implementation

Finding out the best service model does not rely on any scientific method. It is primarily a matter of understanding the client's business and the strategic positioning of the IT. It requires a well-rounded knowledge of all layers of the service stack and, ideally, an outsourcing experience of models that work and those that do not, along with a good dose of common sense.

The following subsections describe the main characteristics of three of the most commonly seen outsourcing models out of an infinite variety of possible combinations.

## Full IT Outsourcing

Figure 10 shows a set-up where the client outsources the whole stack of services to one provider and keeps the analysis and operation of its business processes in-house.

This model is best suited for companies that want to stay close to market standards in terms of business parameterisation and that have a low to medium appetite for change. The way the model is implemented is optimal: the client focuses on business results only and delegates to the provider the entire IT function with clear, limited interface points.

### Example

The client is a small mortgage bank with 20 employees. It built its reputation on that of its associates and the relations of trust the latter developed over years with the local community. It has no differentiating factor. It only needs a standard banking platform that it could not afford operating on its own.

The main characteristics of this set-up are:

*Operations* The provider is solely responsible for the execution of all IT operations and the coordination between the various service layers.

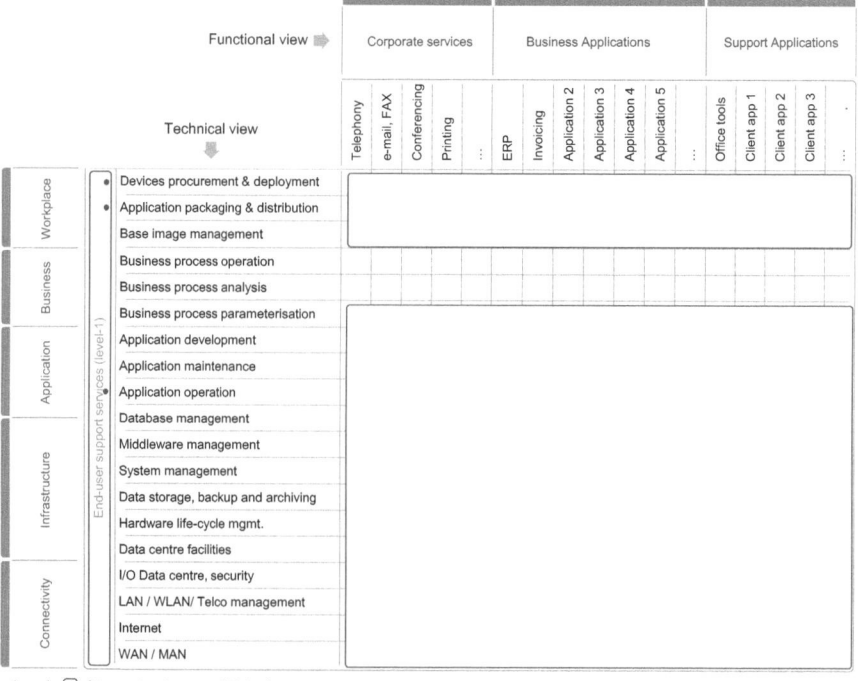

**Fig. 10** Example of full outsourcing service model

*Incidents* The provider handles all levels of support from L-1 to L-3 without the client's intervention, and involving the client's third parties as needed.

*Business continuity* In case of a major disaster, the provider executes the disaster recovery plan (DRP) which guarantees an application- or business-ready restoration of the information system.

*Changes* Upstream, the client formalises business needs and transforms them into service requirements through service-oriented orders, free of technological requirements, and, downstream, the provider introduces the new services with the support of the client.

## ITO Outsourcing

Figure 11 shows a set-up where the client outsources all base IT functions, namely IT operations (ITO) and workplace (WPL), to one provider and keeps the responsibility of the application and business layers in-house. It is supported by third parties through maintenance and out-tasking contracts for specific applications or activities.

This model is best suited for companies which see a competitive advantage in tailoring application and business processes and/or those that have a medium to high appetite for change. Given the above and accepting the higher costs on the client side

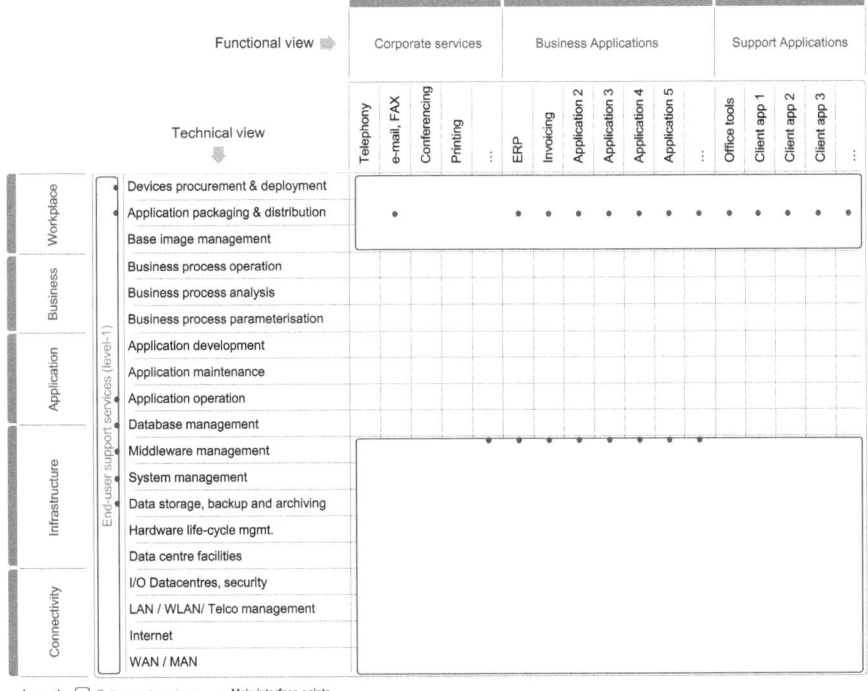

**Fig. 11** Example of ITO outsourcing service model

due to less industrialisation in exchange of more flexibility, the way the model is implemented is perfectly viable. It needs a lot more technical attention from the client, however, which will now also focus on urbanisation and production matters.

**Example**

The client is an air navigation services company. It guides civil and military airplanes in a perimeter of 150 km around two airports for which it is responsible. It has a complex information system encompassing highly specialised applications specific to this domain of activity that no provider could reasonably operate in an industrialised way. The client can delegate the lowest IT layers to gain in efficiency, but needs to keep in-house the application and business layers. It is the application vendors themselves that support the client through appropriate software maintenance and service contracts.

The main characteristics of this set-up are, per service layer:

*Database management* The provider makes the infrastructures on which the applications run available, up to the lower tier of the database for which it guarantees that it runs as expected and the data is properly backed up; through the applications or direct interventions, it is the client who manipulates the higher tier of the database, namely the data model and database objects. This interface point requires previously agreed-upon operating procedures between the two actors on each side, especially in the presence of two providers.

*Application operation* This layer is mission critical for complex information systems with interconnected applications that rely on each other's data to function. It is mainly about application monitoring and batch scheduling, processing and controlling. Whether it is an application that fails or a batch that stops, incidents call for quick reaction and possibly the involvement of the provider when they originate in an infrastructure breakdown. Here again, this interface point requires close coordination between the parties and strict operating-level agreements (OLA) between the ITO and AO teams.

*Application maintenance and above* The client installs, configures and tests new releases of the business applications to correct bugs or enhance functionalities. For obvious reasons of service guarantees, the client may only perform these activities on non-productive environments. It is then the provider, through semi-automated procedures, that install those releases onto productive environments which, thereafter, require subsequent testing. All this mechanics requires tight interaction between the parties.

*End-user support (incidents)* Either the client or the provider is declared the SPOC and handles L-1 support for all users. It routes incidents pertaining to the other party to L-1 of that party, preferably through automated procedures and tools (see section

"Figure Target Operating Model"). In the most efficient set-ups, where both organisations are tightly integrated and trained accordingly, the SPOC can assign incidents directly to L-2 of the other party. In case of a major disaster, restoring the IT function in a business-ready state would be more than ever a common endeavour. Half of the challenges would come from the chaos due to the circumstances, the other half from the lack of vertical integration given the horizontal split of responsibilities.

*End-user support (request management)*  The client is by default the SPOC for user requests as most changes originate in the business. Supported by automated procedures and tools, the client takes, prioritises, decides, assigns and follows up on service orders which they dispatch internally to the provider. Large client organisations can generate dozens of work orders daily, hence the need to have in place robust execution workflows spanning both organisations to reduce manual processing and avoid bottlenecks.

## Multi-sourcing

Cloud and managed services of all kinds have invaded the market and make internal ITs hard to compete against in many ways. On-demand provisioning, pay-per-use, operational expense (OPEX) only, unbeatable price-quality ratio, automatic life cycle, etc.: the advantages are many. Even the most traditional organisations shift from full in-house to managed services by going away from hard commodities and refocusing key staff on activities of higher added value. If this proceeds from a clear IT strategy and the organisation is fully conscious of all the consequences, an exotic set-up may bring an added value. If it just results from a succession of opportunistic decisions in response to challenges that the client faced over time and without a solid governance structure in place responsible to make all pieces of the puzzle fit together, the situation can get completely out of control.

Figure 12 shows an example of a set-up in which the client outsources the communications and workplace layers to two distinct providers; outsources the messaging and printing functions in PaaS mode to two other providers; outsources two core business functions respectively in AaaS and BaaS modes to two additional distinct, specialised vendors; uses IaaS services on which run the servers needed for the applications from a seventh provider; and out-tasks the management of the servers' operating systems to an eighth provider.

This model may be suited for companies which see a competitive advantage in mastering the general topology of their information system and how the business, application and infrastructure layers interact. Typical clients are small to large corporations operating in high-added-value markets that can afford the price premium induced by higher IT governance costs and duplicate IT functions.

The consequences and orchestration possibilities of this model are discussed in the section "Manage Multiple Providers" in Chap. 5.

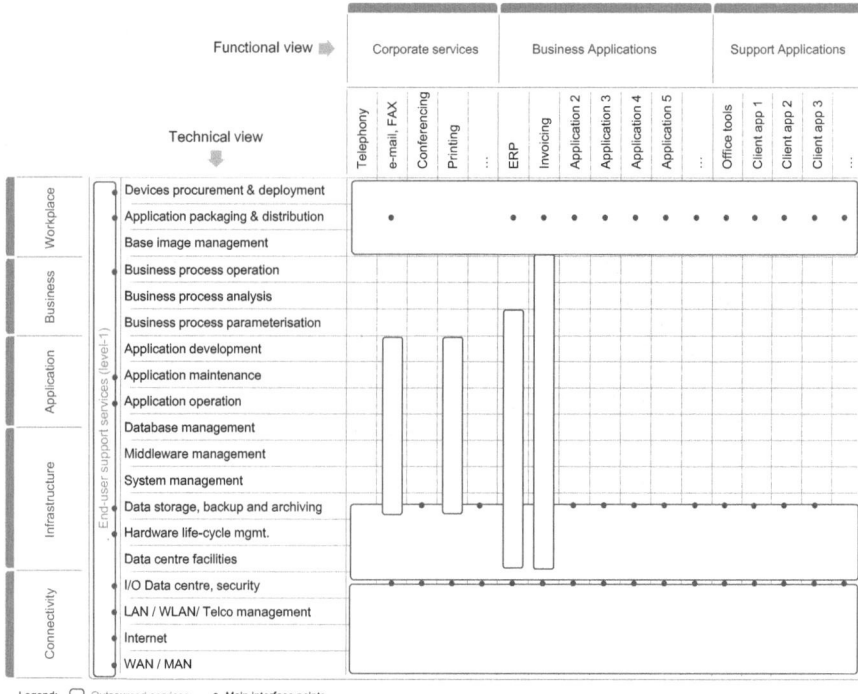

**Fig. 12** Example of multi-sourcing model

---

### Case study: why accumulated managed services do not equal outsourcing

The client is in business with a provider, but for telecommunications services only. The bulk of the services are delivered by the internal IT.

The departure of staff members one after another along with a permanent hiring freeze lead the client to progressively entrust an increasing number of services to the provider. Within 5 years, the IT completely transforms itself. It now comprises only five persons and is almost fully operated by the provider. Systems, networks, messaging, printing, etc.: it is some 12 distinct managed services that have accumulated. The client pays an annual amount of 2 million euros for the services.

The parties enjoy a trustful relationship, but the client is globally unsatisfied. It considers the costs as rather high with regard to quality, although it cannot describe precisely where the issues lie. It depicts a situation where all services are concentred under one roof but do not seem to be delivered by the same provider. With a number of interlocutors on the provider side inversely proportional to the level of integration of the services, it is often the client's governance team that ends up coordinating the provider's services. The client asks the provider to come up with proposals for improvements.

The provider forms a small team of outsourcing experts and launches an assessment. Quickly, the latter points out the deficiencies of the model due to the accumulation of managed services: no SPOC for incidents and service requests, no central coordination in case of ping-pong incidents, no problem management, no single service management, no integrated change process, no unified reporting. To remedy the situation, the operations architect proposes to enforce transverse integration layers crossing all services to manage uniformly incidents, major incidents, service requests, service management and reporting. This would call for a special organisation, additional processes and interfaces between tools and result in a 15% annual cost increase for the client.

At the same time, the team works along a second track: rebuilding entirely the client environment on the provider's outsourcing service stack, which offers native integration between layers. This alternative would call for a profound, one-time transformation valued 1 million euro, but would then bring down the annual price to 1.7 million euros.

The business case is clear: over 5 years outsourcing is almost 20% more efficient than managed services from a financial perspective. Figure 13 opposes the bolt-on versus built-in approaches, with, on the left, the various managed services which are independent from each other and require ad hoc horizontal integration to create a whole consistent and, on the right, the same services redistributed horizontally on standard, natively integrated outsourcing layers.

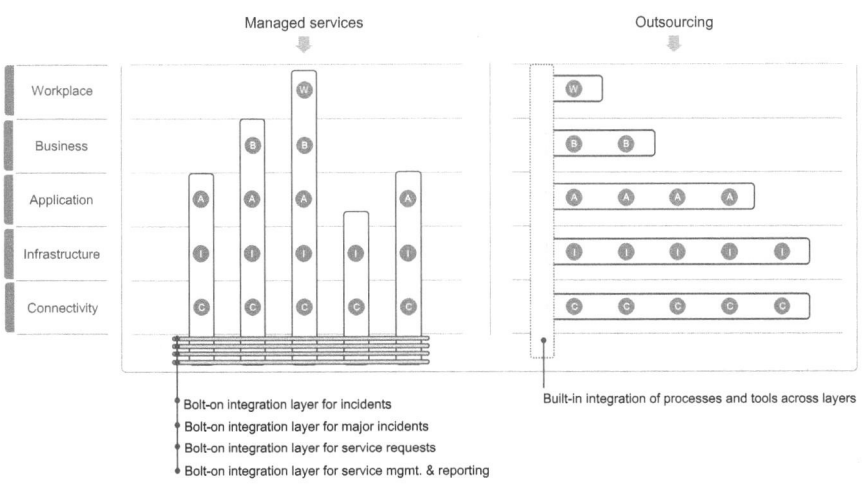

**Fig. 13** Process integration for managed services versus outsourcing

## Dos and Don'ts

The client should:

- Consider the effect of the wanted service model on the target operating model and then on the business case. Depending on the model, the variety and number of roles of the retained IT organisation becomes a key financial decision driver.
- Be knowledgeable in the areas it intends to outsource in case of multi-sourcing. They must be able to understand the dependencies with the other areas, outsourced or not, and to orchestrate the execution of operational activities for the whole information system.
- Not prevent the outsourcing of a complete service category just because they would like to keep the control over one layer. Adequate operational procedures and contractual conditions may allow to outsource while keeping a certain level of prerogatives on the services.
- Pay attention to the interaction points as much as to the services themselves. Even services running smoothly will appear chaotic without straight-through processes spanning both organisations. The more interaction points, the more people, processes and tools will be needed to manage them.
- Not outsource half layers split on the horizontal axis as, for example, handling internally the procurement of end user devices but outsourcing their management. This creates a disruption in the processing chain and generates an overhead that offsets the little gain initially sought. The horizontal split of the database layer should remain the only exception given the very different nature of services between infrastructure and application services.
- Not outsource half layers split on the vertical axis for presumed better continuity guarantees as, for example, outsourcing IT infrastructures in the primary data centre to one provider and fail-over infrastructures in the secondary data centre to another. This creates disruptions in several processing chains and generates massive overhead not offset by any gain. With respect to an alleged better allocation of risks, one should put such a conjecture into perspective with the additional complexity involved to maintain constantly in line the two providers and coordinate them in case of disaster. Clients forced to scaffold tailored constructs of this magnitude would be better off looking for a single partner that could offer the expected guarantees.
- Not consider out-tasking as a substitute for outsourcing. Unlike outsourcing which provides for the vertical integration between the layers outsourced, out-tasking is only a horizontal shift of services within a given layer and does not provide for the needed glue with the surroundings layers. It is up to the client to fill in the blanks.
- Not consider the stacking of managed services as a substitute for outsourcing. While managed services are a good solution for levelling occasional deficiencies, their accumulation proves to be overall inefficient. Not only because of the glue with the other services they call for, but more particularly because of their intrinsic structure. Managed services are like small stand-alone organisations

embarking their own set of processes and tools and do not allow for synergies between services.

## Gather Market Information

Attention which each party should pay to this topic: Client: ● ● ● Provider: ● ○ ○

### Objective

Explore the market offering for the sought sourcing model and services.

This chapter explains how to sound the market in order to receive answers that show a set of common patterns which will be used at a later stage for preparing the request for proposal (RfP).

### Description

The request for information (RfI) is the support document to collect general information about possible services in the discovery phase. It usually precedes the request for proposal (RfP) detailed in the section "Request Proposals". Whereas the RfI focuses on the client and the current situation, the RfP focuses more on the provider and the target solution.

Gathering market information allows the client to answer key questions around the services, the providers and the costs for the selected sourcing model:

- *Services.* Which types of services are available on the market for the needs? What characterises them with respect to the most common forms of provision and performance indicators?
- *Providers.* Which are the most reputable providers for these services? What would it mean for the client working with them? What consequences this would have on its organisation?
- *Costs.* What are the price benchmarks for the services? What are the existing billing models? What consequences would service increases and decreases have on costs?

### Process Overview

A situation which is described properly is a problem half solved. The better the quality of the information provided by the client, the more relevant the answers collected from providers can be. It is up to the client to give potential providers enough visibility on the context and the problem to solve while not being too prescriptive about the solution.

**Fig. 14** RfI process

This objective can easily be reached by following the five-step process presented by Fig. 14.

## Review Client Environment
The client starts by collecting internal data about the company, the users and the existing services. This part may be the trickiest depending on the fragmentation of the business, the diversity of user profiles and the heterogeneity of the service model. In this respect, clients should not proceed until they reach a reasonable view of their environment such as that presented in Fig. 9.

## Identify Potential Providers
Identifying potential bidders is not a big deal, but it requires complying with a minimum number of principles for the selection to pay off. Otherwise, the compilation of the results may raise more questions than it answers.

## Prepare and Launch RfI
Big outsourcing players often have more than one service per need and several options per service. It is important for them to understand which services best fit the need. The client should give a reasonable amount of information about the context, the problematic and the expectations to give providers a chance to quote the most appropriate solution.

## Analyse Answers
Comparing function-ready services is easier than stacking up technological layers and hoping no piece is missing. The client is well advised to state, in as much depth as possible, their business-related expectations in the RfI so as not to receive technology-related answers.

## Determine Patterns
Patterns refer to the common traits that characterise each service in terms of form, content, measurement, reporting and billing. It is not only important for the client to understand how to set the right boundaries to the services to receive comparable answers at the RfP stage but also to set expectations like service levels which correspond to market standards.

## Practical Implementation

The nature and quantity of information the client should provide in an RfI does not vary much depending on the kind of outsourcing pursued. Some may argue: "why provide detailed explanations about the business context whereas the sought services are purely technical, e.g. for an ITO outsourcing"? The answer is simple: as seen in previous chapters, a successful outsourcing which is focused on the end user is about integrating vertically all services layers irrespective of which party provides the corresponding services and then integrating horizontally the processes and the tools across both organisations to ensure a smooth delivery. As such, whatever the depth of the services the providers are called to deliver, the latter will take part of a consistent whole and work hand in hand with the other producers to deliver ready-made business functions.

### Review Client Environment
The client should collect facts about the company like:

• Industry.
• Main business lines.
• Group structure, holding company, subsidiaries, affiliated companies.
• Geographical set-up, headquarters, remote offices.
• Number of employees per company, in total and per site.
• National and international regulations to which it is subject.
• Specific constraints.

There are valuable arguments that speak in favour of communicating such details. Not only will people have a better understanding of what to do when they know why they need to do it, but some services could be delivered abroad as expected for reasons like legal constraints, logistics or performance issues.

### Identify Potential Providers
Unless there are very good reasons to do so, the client should limit the selection to five providers. This is more than enough to get a clear idea of the market.

Two big reputed and two smaller players should be invited to gauge the differences between identical services. For the rest, inviting the market leader which somehow represents the benchmark is always a safe bet. Finally, the CEO certainly has a name in mind which the RfI team should feel compelled to consider. This list of six considers the likeliness that one provider does not bid.

### Prepare and Launch RfI
An RfI is a free document with no prescribed format nor formalism to comply with. Its size depends on the complexity of the matter. Consider 10 pages as reasonable for a complex ITO outsourcing. Technical appendices detailing the current environment shall be added only if the client seeks a relatively accurate price envelope in return.

With respect to the content, it should go back over the main themes described previously and present the corresponding information in a straightforward style. A typical RfI includes:

- Introduction: document positioning, purpose and instructions for responding.
- Context: company and market.
- Current situation: services, service consumers and service producers.
- Services in scope: technical description and main metrics for services x, y and z.
- Problematic: limitations of the current model and growth perspective.
- Request: information regarding the provider and the services, as further refined below:
  Provider
  - Company, market, business lines and main figures.
  - Portfolio of services.
  - Strategic positioning of the sought services within the portfolio.
  - Client references.[4]
  Services
  - Service layers considered.
  - Service outputs,[5] service descriptions and service boundaries.
  - Applicable guarantees and corresponding measurement indicators.
  - Applicable limitations and client obligations.
  - Service controls.
  - Service desk to handle incidents and change requests.

**Analyse Answers**

A first cursory reading of the proposals provides a general idea about the maturity of the providers in outsourcing services.

The relevance of the content and the quality of the form speak for themselves, but it is above all the positioning of the documents that shall draw the attention. A business-oriented RfI which receives a technology-oriented answer should immediately raise a warning signal. The RfI and the answers shall be from the same level of abstraction. If not, it will reflect the kind of structural misalignment in the communication the parties may face during the contract.

The next step is to go over the different services and check for boundaries aka service access points and then distinguish between core and ancillary features because not all providers consider them in the same way.

---

[4]Company names only.

[5]What the client really gets for the service from a business perspective.

Comparing identical services from different providers on an equal base allows to figure out the common denominators.

## Determine Patterns

Once the common denominators at the level of the services themselves are understood, it is time to figure out the service patterns, i.e. the common traits that characterise each service and affect their cost. This will allow the client to properly calibrate the expected services at the stage of the RfP to ensure it receives comparable offers. The five following patterns may not be applicable in whole to every service, but they are the most representative of IT services in general and are clearly those that shape outsourcing contracts:

Service descriptions: kinds and quantities of activities and components included

- Incident and problem management: L-2 and L-3 analysis.
- Corrective maintenance: bug fixing, emergency[6] patching.
- Progressive maintenance: minor and major releases.
- Operations execution: recurring processing[7] and ad hoc executions.[8]
- Life cycle management: components[9] provisioning and replacement.

Service guarantees: types and standard values of key performance indicators (KPI)

- Support time: hours of support during weekdays, holidays, 24/7.
- Availability: maximum downtime per reporting period.
- Continuity: return point objective (RPO), return time objective[10] (RTO).
- Performance: throughput rate, response time, latency, load time.

Service limitations: activities and components excluded

- Service boundaries: underlying, surrounding and access infrastructures.[11]
- Licences: system, application and end user licences.[12]
- Variability: technical up/down scalability, contractual flexibility.

Service controls: visibility provided over the services delivered

- Standard reports: quantities installed/used per service and period, KPIs.

---

[6]For example, security.

[7]For example, end of period batches.

[8]For example, copy from productive to test or integration environment.

[9]For example, infrastructure hardware, end-user devices.

[10]Maximum loss of data (RPO) and maximum time to recover (RTO) in case of disaster.

[11]For example, data centre, security systems, WAN lines.

[12]For example, operating systems, business applications, client access-based.

- Audit reports: pro forma regular reports,[13] audit trails.
- Compliance reports: market compliancy,[14] regulatory compliancy.[15]
- Access control: client and/or provider access lists for sensitive services.

Service support: forms and metrics retained for the service desk

- Incidents: call handling, L-1 remote support, on-site interventions.
- Changes: standard and non-standard service requests.

## Dos and Don'ts

The client should:

- Keep things simple. The longer the list of expectations, the longer the responses, the more difficult the task is to draw the real differences between the providers. Unless the provider is expected to meet very specific requirements, endless questionnaires about, for instance, how the provider implemented ISO requirements are pointless and shall be banned: an RfI is not an audit.
- Explain to providers the reasons that drive the RfI. Telling why things are being done always provides better results. Big players often have several variants, options and service-level categories for a given need.
- Not impose technologies nor ways for rendering the services. This leaves room for providers to come up with their standard service offering and avoid designing a dedicated solution.
- Welcome changes beyond the mere services. New services likely come with new service and billing models.
- Encourage out-of-the-box thinking. Transposing 1:1 the client environment into the provider services usually brings limited benefits and is not financially viable. Experience of similar market situations should allow the provider to come up with alternative solutions.

The provider should:

- Present the services in a way that the client understands how to figure out the patterns. This will make things easier at the time of responding to the RfP.
- Limit marketing content about the company and the services to the strict minimum. Clients need objective facts and adjective-free descriptions to make up their mind. Over-selling content indicates a lack of self-confidence. Well-chosen figures and experience feedback bring a lot more value to the response.

---

[13]For example, ISAE 3402.

[14]For example, ISO certifications.

[15]For example, compliancy with national telecommunications, banking or health authorities.

- Tell clients about common market practices for each service. Clients are eager to understand why and what other clients do in similar situations. It is a fact that where the RfI concerns mere commodities, clients have no reason to go off market standards.

## Figure Out Target Operating Model

Attention which each party should pay to this topic: Client: ● ● ● Provider: ● ● ○

## Objective

Define the organisation, processes and tools needed on the client side at the parties' interface.

This chapter explains how to align the parties operating models according to the selected sourcing model.

## Description

In the context of outsourcing, the target operating model (TOM) is the term referred to for describing the client's IT organisation along with the means used to coordinate the delivery of the services by the provider, namely the processes and the tools:

- *Organisation*. Represent the IT team members who have been assigned a set of responsibilities in the form of ownership of one or more processes in addition to other activities not falling directly in the scope of the outsourcing.
- *Processes*. ITIL v3 distinguishes 4+1 categories of processes which can be mapped with the phases of an information system's life cycle: service strategy (plan), service design (change), service transition (build), service operation (run) and finally continuous service improvement which closes the loop back to service strategy.
- *Tools*. It is the way in which the information flows between the parties. Tools can range from simple file exchanges to real applications. Tools can be shared (both parties use the same set of tools with a single data repository), used (one party manually inserts data already present in his own in the tool of the other) or interfaced (each party keeps its own tool which communicates through normalised technical interfaces).

Note: ITIL was originally developed to structure the management of information systems and align the services with the needs of the business. This means it involves two categories of actors: the IT on one side and the business on the other. An outsourcing dividing the IT into the client's IT and the provider, it also divides the activities within each process and allocates them to the side it pertains. Some

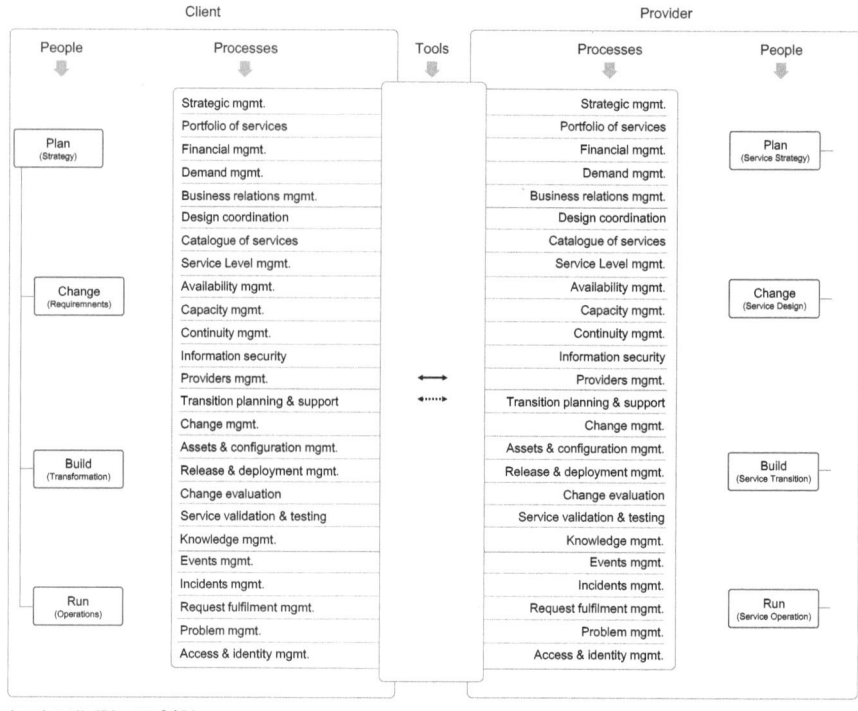

**Fig. 15**  Alignment between the parties' operating models

activities may be adequately allocated because they follow a logical flow like the request fulfilment process in which the client orders, the provider executes and finally the client validates. Some may not and shift in whole, or in part, on one side or the other. For example, business relationship management is a process with a strong business focus hence concentrated on the client side, whereas Event Management is a process with a strong technology focus hence concentrated on the provider side. For a detailed description of ITIL processes, refer to the corresponding literature.

Figure 15 puts in perspective the parties' respective operating models, and shows how processes span both organisations.

## Prerequisites

According to the Centre of Information Systems Research (CISR),[16] a corporate operating model is characterised by the level of standardisation and the level of

---

[16]From the Massachusetts Institute of Technology (MIT).

integration of its business processes. Extrapolated to the operating model of an outsourcing:

- Standardisation means that the structure of the information exchanged and the communication channels are normalised.
- Integration means that the information exchanged flows from the client to the provider automatically and without disruption.

When combined, these two dimensions form a $2 \times 2$ matrix that defines the kind of operating model:

- Diversification: low standardisation, low integration.
- Coordination: low standardisation, high integration.
- Replication: high standardisation, low integration.
- Unification: high standardisation, high integration.

The complexity of the client's business sets the level of standardisation needed. Example: once in production, the client expects to place complex change orders which require numerous fields to be filled according to a structured format to be properly executed. In such a case, one cannot envisage the parties communicating with unstructured supports such as emails.

The expected volume of exchange between the parties sets the level of integration needed. Example: once in production, the client expects to send dozens of incidents per day some of which require to be escalated to L-2 or L-3 support. In such cases, one cannot envisage the parties to handle continuous data flows with non-integrated tools.

Figure 16 positions simple and complex outsourcing on the operating model matrix. Whereas simple outsourcing may be satisfied with low levels of standardisation and integration, complex outsourcing's operating model should always be of unified type with the highest possible levels of standardisation and integration—at least for core processes. With respect to the coordination model, it does not correspond to the needs of usual outsourcing situations. Indeed, high volumes need to be handled in an industrialised way, hence the call for high standardisation.

A misalignment between the complexity of the outsourcing and the operating model either leads to unnecessary high costs, e.g. simple outsourcing does not need to be of unification type, or chaos, e.g. complex outsourcing such as multi-provider situations should not be of diversification type.

## Practical Implementation

The complexity of the target operating model is proportionate to that of the service model: the more interaction points required between the services, the more complex the overall IT operation.

**Fig. 16** Types of operating models

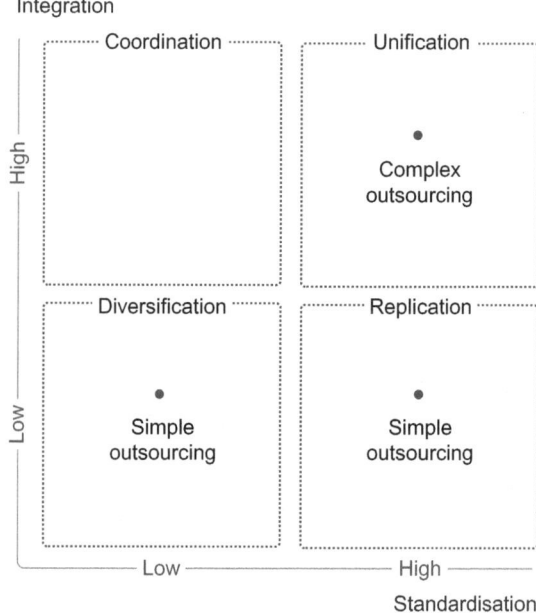

The perceived quality of the services, once in production, depends as much from the correct execution of the services than from their smooth integration between the parties. A lack of integration creates bottlenecks and gives rise to backlogs which require ad hoc responses, e.g. task forces, to be resolved until the moment a proper integration is performed.

Let us see what the target operating model[17] could look like for each of the three service models analysed in the section "Figure Out Target Sourcing Model".

Note: Processes related to service strategy are common to all outsourcing situations and are described in the section "Drive Outsourcing" in Chap. 5. All other processes play an important role, but this chapter focuses on the very essential ones given the operating model selected. They are further referenced as core processes.

## Full IT Outsourcing

### Model Type

*Unification* Both the level of process standardisation and tools integration shall be high. The limited governance structure on the client side usually does not allow other ways of operating.

---

[17]Limited to the part concerning the management of the provider and the corresponding interaction points.

## Organisation

The minimal client organisation for a full outsourcing of low complexity is two persons. The two individuals cover both RtB and CtB activities and are interchangeable to a large extent. One leads the team and probably reports to a Chief Administrative or Chief Financial Officer. Under normal circumstances, the minimal client organisation should count at least 3.5 persons as represented in Fig. 17 and described below:

- *CIO level.* One person interfaces with upper management, drives the relation with the provider at the strategic level and manages the budget. Given the small size of the team, this individual is likely to be involved in hands-on activities a significant proportion of their time.
- *CtB level.* One person interfaces with the business on one side and the provider on the other for all small and bigger changes affecting the information system. Requirements analysis, requests clarification, testing coordination, project management: the range of activities is manifold.
- *RtB level.* One person drives the relation with the provider at an operational level. The individual is usually supported by an administrative staff member who handles the flow of service requests and incidents that require further coordination with the provider.

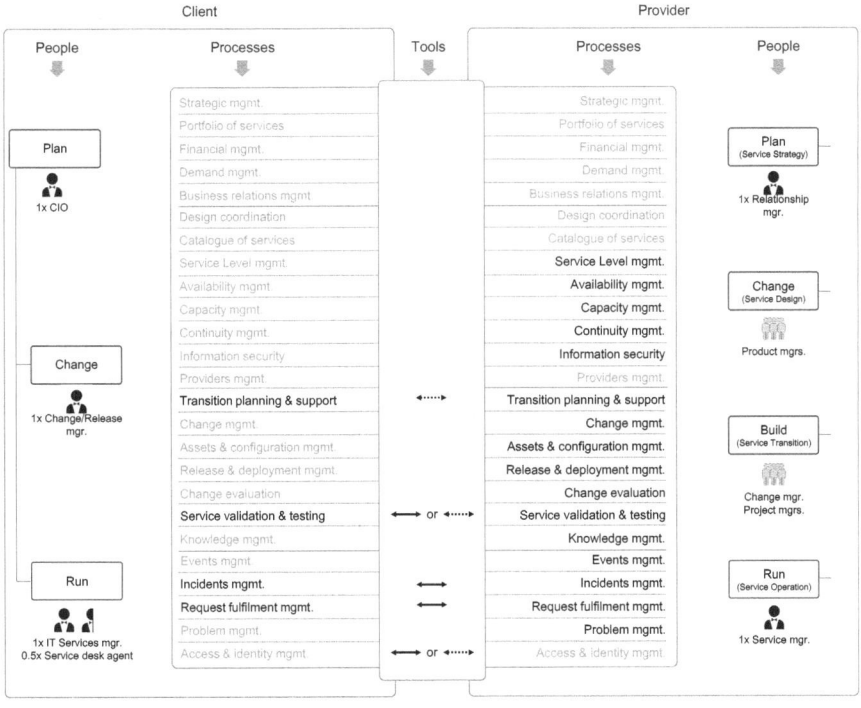

**Fig. 17** Target operating model full outsourcing

**Processes**

In this operating model, core processes are:

*Transition planning and support and validation and testing*  Respectively organise the delivery of changes and user acceptance testing. Unless the number of annual changes generates an important workload on the users for regression testing, these processes do not necessarily have to be standardised.

*Incident management*  Ensure that incidents, especially those proceeding from the introduction of new services and those returned to the client by the provider are coordinated. Incident management shall be standardised in a way that service desk agents can classify incidents according to predetermined categories and attribute them to the service units responsible for their resolution. Lack of standardisation increases resolution time because of a ping-pong effect between the service units and impairs service improvement because of suboptimal reporting capacity.

*Request fulfilment Management*  Ensure that change requests submitted by the users can be handled and, if yes, are dispatched through the corresponding channels. Request fulfilment shall be standardised at least for those requests subject to service-level agreements (SLA) and those called to occur regularly.

**Tools**

*Incident management*  Calls for a full integration which span both organisations from end users to service units with, in between, no manual interactions other than the sorting process operated by the service desk. This requires a common tool with a unique data repository. Since the service model is full outsourcing, chances are that the client does not have their own tool and uses that of the provider.

*Request fulfilment*  May benefit from a full integration from end users to service units if the expected annual number of standard requests justifies the initial investment for setting up the corresponding validation workflows[18] on the client side. If not, partial integration is perfectly acceptable. Users place their requests into an internal tool or directly into the provider's tool to the destination of the internal IT. The latter intercepts and post-processes the requests and finally enters them into the provider's tool for execution. At this moment, the orders are deemed validated and can be executed by the provider, likely after further triage operated by the service desk.

---

[18]To keep the IT budget under control, the client shall decide who in its organisation is authorised to place service requests and of which kind. This logic shall then be implemented in the tool to allow for automatic processing.

## ITO Outsourcing

### Model Type

*Replication type if simple* The parties shall follow standard processes but not necessarily integrate their tools.

*Unification type if complex* Both the level of process standardisation and tools integration shall be high to absorb the volumes generated.

### Organisation

For ITO outsourcing (application and business layers staying with the client) of low complexity, the minimal client organisation ranges from four to six persons depending on whether the client adopts a hands-off or a hands-on approach with respect to the management of its' applications. In the former case, it relies on third parties, in the latter on in-house expertise. The difference with full outsourcing is the increased complexity of the change management chain and its' integration with that of the provider. Considering a hands-on approach, the minimal target organisation may look as shown in Fig. 18 and described below:

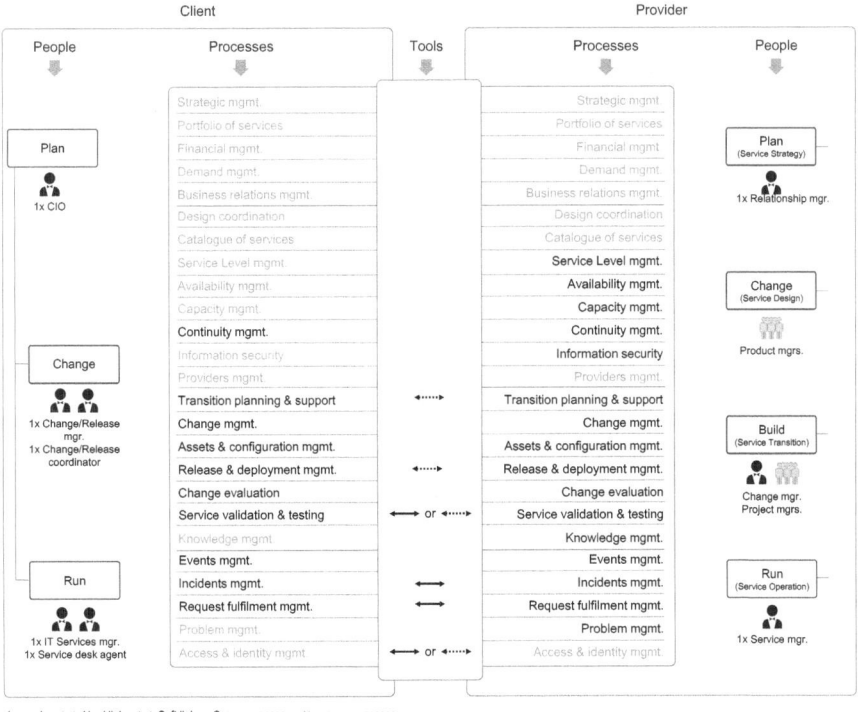

**Fig.18** Target operating model ITO outsourcing

- *CIO level.* One person who interfaces with upper management, drives the relation with the provider at the strategic level and manages the budget.
- *CtB level.* One person who interfaces with the business on one side and the provider on the other for all changes. They are seconded by one or two application specialists to absorb the introduction of new changes and cover applications operation and maintenance activities.
- *RtB level.* One person who drives the relation with the provider at operational level. They are supported by one administrative staff member who handles the flow of service requests and incidents which require further coordination with the provider. Compared with a full outsourcing, the flow of returned incidents and service requests increases very significantly.

In an ITO outsourcing of high complexity and which has a hands-on approach, the client organisation can easily grow to 10 persons or more. Here again, it is the CtB sub-organisation that has the focus. More applications induce more interfaces and thus more operational inter-dependencies, which call for additional profiles such as application architects, release managers, etc. The RtB sub-organisation directly suffers from the consequences of the increased complexity of the information system with more incidents and major incidents to handle, root causes to analyse, maintenance windows to coordinate, etc.

### Processes

An ITO outsourcing sees new processes emerging in addition to those of a full outsourcing:

*Change management* Install methods and procedures, e.g. change advisory board, to ensure that application changes do not have collateral effects when entering production. This is especially important given that infrastructure and application layers are now in different hands and that the client shall merge two production plans.

*Change evaluation* Screen all changes, categorise their importance for the business, analyse their impact on other applications (e.g. interfaces) or services (e.g. application operation) and group them into releases.

*Release deployment and configuration* Follow a consistent methodology for installing, configuring and testing the new releases. Insofar as the provider guarantees service levels on productive environments and probably restricts client accesses on them, putting the releases into production requires the collaboration of both parties.

*Assets and configuration management* Track all configuration items of the application landscape along with their dependencies within a common database. This is undoubtedly one of the most important yet most left-behind processes because of the initial and recurring workload it generates. It is critical, though, to maintain at all times a precise overview of the entire information system.

*Continuity management*  Build initially, test regularly and maintain permanently up to date the continuity plan that would allow to restore the application layer in case of a major disaster. As far as the applications may depend on specific technical implementations, continuity management can only be a collaborative work between the parties.

*Incidents management*  The cut between the services complicates the service desk model. As recommended in the section "Figure Out Target Sourcing Model", either the client or the provider should be declared SPOC and the other party integrated as secondary L-1 or, better still, L-2 support so that incidents reaching the SPOC can be forwarded without any problem to the other party. Whatever approach is used, it requires an initial integration between the parties as it touches on the process, the agents and the tools. Whenever possible, L-2 should be preferred as it removes one level in the incident processing chain. Its implementation requires more integration in the form of agent training and tool configurations.

*Problem management*  The eradication of repeated incidents requires root cause analyses (RCA), which often turn out to be long and complex. RCAs may be multicausal and cross several service layers, thus hindering the research. Unfortunately, no miracle integrated solution exists: the client and the provider need to collaborate, each time in a way determined by the circumstances as RCAs are all one of a kind.

*Events management*  If the client operates mission-critical applications which require proactive monitoring or round-the-clock interventions, this process is mandatory. Depending on the needs, the initial set-up may consist in deploying supervision agents on systems, integrating batches into a monitoring tool, automating processes and drafting the operation manual. It may be a heavy piece of work depending on the complexity of the information system and the number of interrelated systems. Recurring operations consist in running, monitoring and debugging events affecting the information system. The challenge lies here less in the skills level of the operators who carry out the operations described in the manual than in the number of operators: meeting stringent service levels on the AO layer requires at least six persons to ensure three daily shifts along with a reasonable personnel backup for absences and on-call duties. Except in very large installations, maintaining such a workforce internally is not financially viable. The client's next best option is then to include the AO layer in the ITO outsourcing.

## Tools

*Change management, change evaluation, release and deployment management and continuity management*  These processes may benefit from specialised tools but may also be perfectly satisfied with simple office-type documents and well-documented procedures.

*Assets and configuration* Provided the client has implemented the process, they shall then implement a database to store and link the configuration items they want to track. With respect to interfacing the client's and the provider's databases in order to reach a global view of the dependencies between the applications and the infrastructures, there is little chance of this happening on the grounds of data model differences and security hurdles.

*Incidents management* No tool is no option. The client can decide to keep their own tool or use that of the provider. In both cases, the parties will have to work together and implement in the tool the handling, triage and attribution workflows to reflect the mode of operation set by the process. As the latter spans both organisations seamlessly from the end users to the service units, so must the tool. Should the client decide to keep their own tool, the parties may want to consider interfacing them[19] to avoid manual double entries. The interface should preferably be in real time. If only batch processing is possible, the parties should be aware of the processing frequency of the batch and adjust their expectations accordingly with respect to the SLA.

*Event management* Standard tools included in the operating systems or basic software from the market may be sufficient. However, when it comes to automating and supervising complex production systems, proven solutions are required.

*Service validation and testing* Tools to automate non-regression tests are reserved for organisations with massive and recurring changes. The price tag for connecting the tool to the systems to be tested is massive, the price tag for developing the first set of test cases is massive and the price tag for enriching the database with new test cases after each release is massive. Nevertheless, these tools may prove cost-effective sometimes. In the end, it is simply a matter of business case and comparing the total cost of ownership of the tool versus the cost of business users constantly solicited for non-added-value tests.

## Multi-sourcing

## Model Type

*Diversification* By definition, both the level of process standardisation and tools integration are low. The client should however consider standardising the most critical processes as much as possible with each provider and integrate the tools accordingly if the expected volumes justify it.

---

[19]Most tools provide application programme interfaces (API) to exchange data.

The profusion of managed services of all kinds leads to sourcing models of all kinds which, in turn, lead to many kinds of operating models. In this context, it appears difficult to derive a unique TOM pattern.

### Organisation

The reference organisation is close to that of an internal IT because of the coordination effort it calls for. This makes the model financial suboptimal in most cases as the client cumulates internal and external costs for similar functions and services.

### Processes

Almost all processes become core, with a special focus on:

*Information security* Combining external services from different providers using different technologies raises security concerns[20] that enjoin the client to define a security policy along with security instructions applicable to personnel and rules applicable to systems.

*Providers management* Multiplying providers mechanically increases the nature and the volumes of issues to deal with. Non-aligned contractual conditions like contract duration, service levels, service support hours and maintenance windows, to name but a few, as well as multiple interface points in the operations put the client in a position of orchestra conductor.

### Tools

The multiplication of providers limits the capacity to industrialise the processes with each provider and thus to integrate the tools. If volumes become important, it is a necessity, and the client will have to consider introducing service integration layers or delegating the management of the multiple providers to a third party.

## Dos and Don'ts

The parties should:

- Consider process standardisation and tools integration from service units to end users to allow a seamless flow from the producers to the consumers. This implies considering the various use cases and implementing the corresponding workflows on both sides.
- Work on big trends once in production to improve the services. While correcting each individual incident is of course mandatory, focusing on details does not help

---

[20]Information security is not more important here than it is in other outsourcing types. The difference is that, in these other cases, the client can rely on the provider to implement default protection and safeguards based on the provider's standards.

at a corporate level. Only optimising the processes has long-term positive mass effects on the perceived quality of the services.

The client should:

- Sketch out the target operating model before requesting outsourcing proposals and request providers to include in their offer a budgetary envelope for process standardisation and tools integration. The capacity and experience of the providers to offer an end-to-end solution is a driver of the business case which is not just financial.
- Allocate the required personnel in quality and quantity for the management of the provider. This seems like knocking on an open door, but not doing so would quickly have dramatic consequences and lead to either the relation poisoning or to the client staffing a team at a cost which was not originally planned.
- Consider investing an extra amount of money up front to standardise and integrate core processes and tools according to the criticality and volumes of the environment. The outsourcing shall be an opportunity to rethink some internal modes of operation and go across their limitations.
- Address the most important processes first, but do not neglect the others. Not all processes need necessarily be industrialised, but all should be considered. For example, if the client is risk-averse and thus focuses primarily on processes which ensure a stable RtB, they should nonetheless consider some CtB processes because instability mainly comes with change. To this end, a weekly 30-min call supported by a simple spreadsheet to discuss and align on forthcoming maintenance operations may perfectly do the job.

The provider should:

- Inquire about the target operating model the client intends to enforce and anticipate situations when the client obviously did not properly consider the question. This is part of its duty to advise. When applicable, it should draw the client's attention to the obligation to enforce a minimal governance structure.

## Request Proposals

Attention which each party should pay to this topic: Client: ●●● Provider: ○○○

## Objective

Invite providers to submit firm offers for the sought services.

This chapter explains how to structure the request in a way to receive innovative yet comparable proposals.

## Description

The RfP is the requirements definition document used to collect detailed information about the sought services. It may or may not follow an RfI depending on the maturity of the client in outsourcing matters. As a reminder, the RfI focuses more on the client and the current situation, the RfP on the provider and the target solution.[21]

Soliciting firm offers from distinct providers allows the client to compare, on an equal basis, the provider's offerings, where offering stands as the combination of solution, operations, transition, costs and conditions which successfully addresses the needs:

- *Solution*. Proposed arrangement of the services in the required quantities along with the possible options.
- *Operations*. Details about the operational delivery of the services and the delivery organisation the provider intends to implement.
- *Transition*. Details about the transition from the present mode of operation (PMO) to the future mode of operation (FMO); includes at least the one-time services, the project organisation and a road map.
- *Costs*. Amounts and billing models for the one-time cost (OTC) related to the transition and monthly recurring cost (MRC) related to the operations.
- *Conditions*. Contractual provisions and other constraints applicable to the services, the relation and the prices.

## Process Overview

Amazing as it may sound, rare are the outsourcings that start only after the contract is signed. It is common practice to start the transformation straight after the selection of the provider with a simple pre-contract based on the offer. Knowing that a firm offer is a contract in the sense that, if the client accepts it, the parties are bound, it is in the client's best interest to receive offers as close as possible to the target contract.

To this end, the client can follow the five-step process presented in Fig. 19, remembering that a situation well described is a problem half solved.

While Fig. 18 shows the standard process in the case of fair competition, one cannot ignore the situation depicted in Fig. 19 where the client has already chosen their partner, but the client requests further offers in order to try and benchmark their prices. This practice is unethical, but unfortunately extremely common (Fig. 20).

### Collect Client Data
It starts with collecting the most accurate data as possible about the company, the service consumers, the service producers and the services themselves. As the base of

---

[21]If an RfI does not precede the RfP, the RfP shall also provide details about the client and the current situation.

This chapter

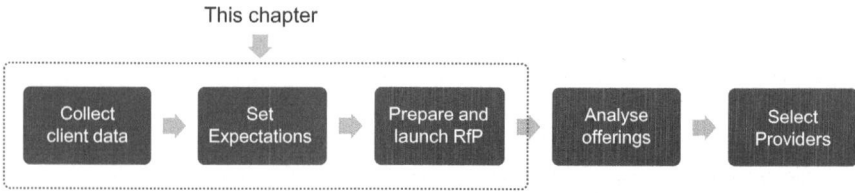

**Fig. 19**  RfP standard process

**Fig. 20**  RfP fake process

the providers' offerings, this activity is essential. The collection may be complicated if the business is fragmented, especially on an international scale. Often, the main office lacks the true understanding of all the peculiarities of the remote offices. It is further compounded by the confidentiality that usually surrounds the process, which prevents the subject matter experts from being involved.

The client should not proceed any further until they reach a reasonable view of the environment and accepts the residual risk of late discoveries.

### Set Expectations

Therein lies the hard stuff. The client sets its expectations by addressing the five dimensions of the offering. With respect to the solution, it uses the patterns determined previously, with a special focus on the content and the guarantees.

### Prepare and Launch RfP

The client sets the framework for the answers. They lay down the expectations in such a way that they call for proposals of similar structure all while leaving each provider enough flexibility to propose its own service model. It finally expresses considerations regarding the form of the bidding process.

### Analyse Offerings, Select Provider

These two steps are described in the chapter of the same name.

## Practical Implementation

The quality of the offers fully depends on each provider, but the adequacy between the offers and the needs half depends on the client. Quality in, quality out. It is the client's duty to point the providers in the desired direction while letting them express their talent. Properly setting and then formulating expectations is a key success factor of the RfP process.

## Collect Client Data

Properly setting expectations starts with collecting as precise information as possible about the context, where the context is the unique combination between the organisational context (the company and its structure), the business context (the services consumed by the end users) and the technical context (the services themselves, including how they are produced).

### Organisational Context

In the RfI phase, the client collected the following basic facts about the company:

- Industry.
- Main business lines.
- Group structure, holding company, subsidiaries, affiliated companies.
- Geographical set-up, headquarters, remote offices.
- Number of employees per company, in total and per site.
- National and international regulations to which it is subject.
- Specific constraints.

In the RfP, the client shall dive deeper into the analysis by assessing the hard and soft dependencies of the company and how these may affect the services. Such dependencies are sometimes difficult to determine, especially for entities which are part of an international group. Let us distinguish the cases where the entity that issues the RfP has the authority to decide, where it is subject to a higher authority and where there is no subordination link:

- *The entity has the authority.* The typical case is when it is the mother company of a group with remote subsidiaries. In this case, it shall inquire about the actual set-up in each remote location. Even if the headquarters already provides the bulk of the services to the subsidiaries, each remote location may run, in addition, its own set of distinct services that the head office is not aware of (any more).[22]
- *The entity is subject to a higher authority.* The typical case is when it is a subsidiary of a group. In that case, it shall anticipate group constraints. If not, these will very likely arise later in the process and jeopardise the plans to varying degrees. It is practically normal to see the mother company stepping into the deal with superseding constraints linked to security, audit, compliance and human resources, to name but a few, at the end of the process.
- *The entity has dependencies with other entities but no subordination link.* The typical case is when it shares services or facilities with other internal or external entities. For example, it profits from human resources, accounting or service desk

---

[22]Driven by history, local constraints and power politics.

services shared at group level. In those cases, it shall identify all interface points it has with these entities.

It is up to the client to decide whether to perform a sound assessment of the situation or not before launching the RfP, depending on their level of confidence in the information available and the importance of the possible consequences.

### Business Context

The client should disclose, at least:

- Who and where the internal and external consumers of the IT function are.
- What the main user profiles aka personas are.
- What business functions each persona needs to do their job.

The business context is represented by the vertical axis in Fig. 9. It materialises up-and-running business functions and thus depicts the target situation. The client is strongly advised to expose the situation to the providers to identify potential gaps between the services the provider will deliver and the services the users will receive. Predictably, even when the provider offers end-to-end services, there will always be in-between activities excluded, e.g. passive cabling in the client's facilities.

### Technical Context

The client should disclose, at least:

- Who and where the internal and external producers of the IT services are.
- What the main constituents and metrics in each service layer are.
- What the existing[23] service-level agreements (SLA) between the producers and the consumers are.

The technical context is represented by the horizontal axis in Fig. 9. It materialises the current situation and, thus, the starting point of the outsourcing transformation. Here again, whatever the type of outsourcing, the client is well advised to fully expose the situation to the providers. Things like an organisational chart of the IT department and the current sourcing model could help to avoid surprises at a later stage.

---

#### Example

The client runs the bulk of its IT with internal staff but has the management of the printers, telephone switchboard and videoconferencing system operated by third parties. The internal service desk is the SPOC for incidents and change requests

---

[23]May be explicitly documented or, as it is usually the case, implicitly agreed.

related to both internal and external services. In the latter case, it transfers the tickets to the corresponding partners and follow up regularly on their execution until completion.

The client intends to outsource all its IT but leave the already outsourced services with the existing third parties until the contracts expire. By doing so, it would do well to inform beforehand the bidders of the multi-provider situation surrounding the service desk to avoid surprises during the contracting phase or later in production. Multi-provider management is a fully fledged service that comes at an extra cost. It calls for specific on-boarding activities during the project to establish connections with the third parties and generates a recurring additional workload in production to follow up on tickets and other operational matters.

## Set Expectations

To receive quality offers, the client should request detailed explanations for each of the five dimensions. Unfortunately, all too often they position the RfP at a technical level, concentrating almost exclusively on the solution and the costs. Some RfPs even provide only for two envelopes to be opened and analysed separately. This approach tends to force providers to deconstruct their service model, which sometimes results in isolating the client from the best solution. Besides, it does not provide any information on how the parties will align their respective operating models, thus completely overshadowing the people aspect.

## Solution

Set expectations about the services with a special focus on the content and the guarantees:

Service content: types and quantities of activities and components included

- Incident and problem management: L-2 and L-3 analyses.
- Corrective maintenance: bug fixing, emergency patching.
- Progressive maintenance: minor and major releases.
- Operations execution: recurring processing and ad hoc executions.
- Life cycle management: components provisioning and replacement.

Service limitations: activities and components excluded

- Service boundaries: underlying, surrounding and access infrastructures.
- Licences: system, application and end-user licences.
- Variability: technical up/down scalability, contractual flexibility.

Service guarantees: types and standard values of key performance indicators (KPI)

- Support time: hours of support during weekdays, holidays, 24/7.
- Availability: percentage of availability or maximum downtime per reporting period.
- Continuity: return point objective (RPO) and return time objective (RTO).
- Performance: throughput rate, response time, latency, load time.


## Operations

Set expectations on how the services should be delivered in production with a special focus on the support and governance organisations:

Service controls: visibility provided over the services delivered.

- Standard reports: quantities installed/used per service and period, KPIs measured.
- Audit reports: regular pro forma reports, audit trails.
- Compliance reports: market compliancy, regulatory compliancy.
- Access control: access lists concerning the client and/or the provider users for sensitive services.

Service support: forms and metrics retained for the service desk and the operations centre

- Incidents: call handling, L-1 remote support, on-site interventions.
- Major incidents: crisis organisation, disaster recovery plan.
- Changes: standard and non-standard service requests.

Service governance: interface between the parties

- Organisation: roles, bodies and rules.
- Processes: processes to normalise the relation.
- Tools: tools to allow high volumes to flow seamlessly.


## Transition

Set expectations regarding the transition from the present mode of operation (PMO), where the client is responsible, to the future mode of operation (FMO), where the provider is in charge.

Service set-up: on-boarding of the services onto the provider's service stack

- Installation: services, systems moved or rebuilt.
- Transformation: reference system(s), standard parameterisation, gaps development.
- Migration: online data, offline data, historical data, data to transform.
- Decommissioning: current services, systems, procedures.

Project management: project execution, management of the delivery teams

- Project deliverables.
- Project road map, deployment strategy, major milestones.
- Responsibility: entrepreneur general or not; if not, role and duties of the provider.

Project governance: project control, stakeholders' management

- Organisation: roles, bodies, rules.
- Processes: project methodology, change management procedure.
- Tools: common repository for documents, testing tools, training platform.

## Costs
Set expectations about the costs of the services and the applicable billing models:

- One-time costs (OTC): amount, billing model, payment schedule for the project.
- Monthly recurring costs (MRC): amount, billing model, payment schedule for each service in scope.
- Rate cards: daily rates per competence level applicable to small changes and new projects while in production.

## Conditions
Set expectations, if any, regarding the main constraints surrounding the services:

- Relation: general obligations, confidentiality, liability.
- Contract: duration, ordinary and extraordinary terminations, bonus-malus.
- Services: decommissioning of services, benchmarking.

When the client's bid team is ready with the requirements, it must have them approved by internal stakeholders. Selecting a provider for an outsourcing is not like buying any other service and requires a full management commitment.

## Prepare and Launch RfP
An RfP targeted at the private sector[24] is a free document with no prescribed format nor special formalism. It varies in size from 20 pages to several hundreds, depending less on the complexity of the matter than on the level of prescription of the client. It usually includes detailed technical appendices.

Perhaps fearful of being pushed out of their comfort zone with unconventional answers, clients often make it far too complicated by intending to control the exact structure and format of the response in minute detail, going sometimes right down to the size and colour of the font. This results in the providers having to twist their original service model. Applying the five patterns consistently is more than enough to receive comparable offers and has the advantage of revealing each provider's

---

[24] As opposed to public invitations to tender, which shall respect a strict formalism.

maturity. Writing a good RfP is both an art and a science, the secret being to be assertive, not directive.

Here is an example of an RfP structure filled with the requirements previously determined:

Introduction

- Objective: current situation, problematic, goal.
- Scope of work.
- Bid instructions such as expression of interest, form of proposal submission, closing date, presentations.
- Communication: points of contact, questions and answers, ban on approaching the client's stakeholders during the bid phase.
- Evaluation criteria.
- Road map: deployment plan, milestones, proof-of-concept (POC), pilot installation.

Information about the context

- Company.
- Business.
- Technical.

Expression of requirements

- Solution.
- Operation.
- Transition.
- Costs.
- Conditions.

References and certifications

- Client references of similar situations.
- Certificates of compliance: quality, projects, operations, security, environment, etc.
- Supplier-related certifications for given technologies or products.
- Partnerships.

Appendices

If the RfP is confidential, the client may want to have the selected providers sign a non-disclosure agreement (NDA) before issuing the document.


## Dos and Don'ts

The client should:

- Unless they have very good reasons not to do so, limit the selection to five providers. Beyond that, the workload to analyse the proposals is not worth the gain. Worse, the overload of information may drown the essence into too many details and have controversial effects.

- Concentrate on the expression of business needs by applying the patterns consistently rather than on the solution or how the latter is produced. For example, asking providers to show proof of compliancy with standards like ISO or ISAE is sufficient. Diving into the details of how they implemented these standards is pointless.
- Be flexible with respect to the response framework. Forcing providers to twist their service model and make figures fit in cells in which they do not naturally does not set the comparison basis of an outsourcing at the right level.
- Reduce the level of prescription as the added value of the sought services increases. Complex services offer a lot more room to manoeuvre for innovation than commodities. Commodities have become commodities because they have been industrialised and optimised to the point where differentiating factors, if any, can now only make a difference with high volumes.
- Set clear expectations to external consultancy if appointed to drive the RfP. An unlimited hourly billing model could lead to an overcomplicated process with lengthy discussions.
- Involve internal stakeholders early enough in the process to collect their expectations; involve them again before issuing the RfP to review the document. Even if the effect on the hard content is not relevant, it gets their commitment and extinguishes potential resistances that may arise later.
- Have the RfP written by one person only. Some RfP resemble a patchwork of conflicting expectations.
- Organise a physical encounter with all providers to answer questions after the RfP issuance. If relevant, include a site visit.
- Refrain from requesting detailed architectural and procedural designs if these could present a value outside of the context of the offer. An RfP is not free consulting.
- Leave at least 5 weeks for the providers to answer. Responding to an RfP for complex outsourcing may involve, to a varying degree, up to 20 persons.

## Design the Proposal

Attention which each party should pay to this topic: Client: ○○○ Provider: ●●●

## Objective

Set the base for a multi-annual outsourcing agreement.

This chapter explains how best to structure a proposal from the content and form perspectives and, for the most audacious, how to get off the beaten track to surprise clients.

## Description

An outsourcing proposal is a set of documents which the provider submits to a prospective client describing its offer, where the offer stands as the combination of a solution, operations, transition, costs and conditions that successfully address the client's needs. The proposal may come as a response to an RfP when the tender is open, or can be developed jointly between the parties through an iterative process.

By default, a proposal is firm. If the client accepts it, it becomes a contract and binds the parties, hence the reason to build it as close as to what the final contract would look like. If the provider does not want the proposal to be binding, for instance if there are elements that they would like to discuss with the client before, they can make it subject to due diligence or just mention it as indicative or orientative. However, it is wise distinguishing between what the law says and what the reality is. In contrast to public tenders, where interactions between the parties are strictly framed, experience shows that a proposal in the private sector is rarely binding, especially when it concerns high-added-value services. The complexity of the matter calls for numerous interactions between the parties, which, in turn, lead to as many revisions. The flipside is also true: a proposal is never really non-binding either. Once a figure has been communicated to the client, indicative or not, it is extremely hard to step back, even if the client recognises that the scope or the conditions have changed.

## Process Overview

Developing an outsourcing proposal is a short yet intense process concentrated over a few weeks. Experienced clients that know the underlying complexity will leave 6–8 weeks to respond. Clients with less experience or little consideration for providers may leave only 3 weeks, and even 2 in most extreme cases—irrespective of the urgency of the situation.

The minimal reasonable time required to produce a quality response is 5 weeks: 1 week to qualify the opportunity and form the core team, 1 week to kick off the deal and sketch the story, 1 week to design the solution, 1 week to cost and price it and 1 week to validate and fine-tune it. Figure 21 shows the general development from an activity perspective, some activities running in parallel, e.g. writing the offer itself spans the whole timeline.

It is possible to produce a proposal in a shorter time with a reduced team, but with restrictions like requalifying the offer as non-binding. The persons who could not be

**Fig. 21**  Design proposal process

involved before issuing the proposal for the required controls and approvals would have to be involved afterwards.

### Qualify Opportunity

Responding to an RfP is costly. From proposal to contract, the sales process accounts on average for 1–1.5% of the total contract value (TCV) calculated over 5 years, i.e. approximately 350,000 € for a 30 million euros deal. Except in special circumstances, bigger deals usually cost less in proportion and smaller ones cost more. Providers should thus decide to bid only if they have a reasonable chance to win.

### Form the Bid Team

The skills set for responding to a GATT/WTO RfP with strict guidelines for a mature client differs significantly from that required to build a story from a blank page for an outsourcing newcomer. Depending on the situation, the winning bid team should either be composed of productive doers or creative thinkers.

### Sketch a Story and Design a Solution

Outsourcing is a long-term endeavour between two parties that draw different benefits but share the same goal: making the client successful. Therefore, putting the client at the centre of a common story is the only winning strategy over the long run. Once set, the story must flow naturally in the solution and in the rest of the proposal.

### Write the Proposal

A high-impact proposal shall consider four elements: the red path, around which to articulate the story; the hard content, describing the solution, operations, transition, costs and conditions; the soft content, representing the messages to address to each stakeholder; and the form, as expression of the inner content.

### Validate the Proposal

Here internal rules apply. Higher management must validate the conditions and figures. According to the deal, one or several peers' reviews can take place.

## Practical Implementation

### Qualify Opportunity

Responding to an RfP for an established client may be either an advantage or a disadvantage depending on the state of the relation. Here, the provider can only decide whether to bid or not given the circumstances.

Responding opportunistically to an RfP from a client with no established relationship is not an issue if it concerns non-critical functions. To this end, usual qualifying factors based on the solution-fit, the price-fit, the company-fit (see the section "Analyse Offerings and Select Partner" in Chap. 3) and the risk level will do. These factors are then confronted against the client's needs or the selection criteria if communicated. They are finally balanced according to the competition—known or supposed, considering the provider's unique selling proposition (USP).

This technical approach provides valuable information for most situations, but is not sufficient for high-stakes outsourcings, whichever side the stake may be. In these cases, additional parameters worth considering are:

*In-depth knowledge of the market and its systemic moves* The provider must demonstrate that they hold a solid position in the time continuum, in other words, that it was there yesterday and successfully transformed itself, that it is here today and serves the market adequately and that it will be there tomorrow thanks to the next transformation it is already preparing. Crossing time while being a key player in today's ephemeral economy is the reality that only companies with a true understanding of their market and a deeply rooted change culture can survive.

*Deep understanding of the client's internal situation* It happens that the best possible partner with the best proposal is precluded on grounds of unconvincing arguments presented by the client during the lost review. Here are a few situations that should raise warnings at the time of bidding:

- The CIO or COO is weak. He does not have an IT vision based on firm convictions and cannot abstract from details when challenged by his technical teams.
- The recommending or deciding person is risk-averse and does not want to bear the responsibility of a transformation.
- Top management requests its own internal IT to benchmark its costs against those of the provider, resulting in biased judgements.
- A powerful internal team, holding critical knowledge about legacy system internals, threatens.
- The client is fully outsourced to one provider and fears a counter-reaction upon transferring part of the services to another.
- The client outsourced only a few years ago and does not suffer a level of pain that justifies going through another (costly) transformation.
- The client follows a mono- or multi-sourcing strategy and will act accordingly, irrespective of the quality of the offering or the interest in the provider.

*Personal links with executives* Top deciders trust top deciders. They inspire each other and replicate successful strategies. If top executives on both sides know each other, it is a definite plus. If not, it is not a hurdle, but they will need to meet during the offering process. Trust is something that establishes itself between individuals, not institutions, especially during an offering phase.

## Form the Bid Team

The bid team represents the individuals selected to build the proposal. These come from different service units and are appointed temporarily for the duration of the bid.

Once the bid is over, the team is dismantled. In practice, the team remains virtual and maintains the links for a long time. If the bid was successful, the same individuals will meet again under the umbrella of the project team, responsible for the transformation.

A bid team is composed of three categories of individuals:

*Core members* The bid manager is responsible for the bid and coordinates internal activities. Depending on the situation, he also coordinates the interactions with the client, in collaboration with the account manager. He ensures the viability and the consistency of the proposal from the perspectives of both parties. He is supported by three key persons:

- The lead architect who represents the solution.
- The lead operations architect who represents the operations.
- The project manager who represents the transformation.

*Contributors* A legal representative and a financial controller are part of all bids. They make sure that the proposal is properly structured from a legal perspective and the prices of the services computed according to corporate rules. Depending on the type of proposal, service units may be involved. These are, for example:

- Security.
- Compliance.
- Audit.
- Procurement.
- Human resources.

*Reviewers/challengers* Some will always want to review the proposal, e.g. substitutes of head service lines and sales representatives. Some others may want to review it depending on the case, i.e. because they have been involved in preliminary discussions or they would inherit from the result of the proposal. Wherever they come from, reviewers should always be welcomed for the external eye they bring.

Building the winning bid team is not only a question of stacking up hard skills. The sum of bright individuals does not necessarily make a successful team. Team members must play collectively, especially if time is of essence. When under pressure, individuals instinctively go back to their natural behaviour according to their brain dominance as depicted in Fig. 26. This exacerbates the differences and hampers the collaboration. Add to this the fact that team members do not all have the same objectives nor targets. For example, sales teams are measured on the volume of new business while operations are measured on the stability of existing services. This sometimes generates discussions that consume energy and time. If they do not turn into struggles that call for arbitrage, these discussions are necessary. They allow confronting ideas and help improving the services by keeping in balance innovation and operations. Selecting persons who are used to working together and know each other's personalities should always be preferred.

## Sketch a Story and Design a Solution

People do not (only) buy things because they are useful. People buy things that empower them, i.e. things that make them feel good, look good or be part of a group. For example, when a company decides to change its ERP, it is certainly because the existing one is tired, but also possibly because the new one will open the doors to a new community. In a world where services and products look alike, successful companies get their products or services sold by placing customers at the centre of a story and empowering them—hence the reason best-selling smartphones are not necessarily those that have the most advanced technological features. This generates emotions and fuels desire. Knowing that emotions trigger 80% of an individual's actions, one easily understands that the secret of a successful proposal does not lie in endless enumerations of technical details.

Among the various possibilities to sketch a story, the actantial model, developed by semiotician Algirdas Julien Greimas, translates well to business situations. The model describes the roles, relations and corresponding acts which form the structure of the story. A character and/or the hero pursues the quest of an objective. The quest is commissioned by an originator to the benefit of an addressee. The characters, events, or objects that help the hero in his quest are called adjuvants. Those that obstruct him are called opponents. Figure 22 illustrates the model.

The hero and the objective represent the desire, the adjuvants and the opponents the strength, the originator and the addressee the communication.

---

**Example**

The client is a holding group that buys companies, make them profitable and either keeps and thus integrates them, or resells them.

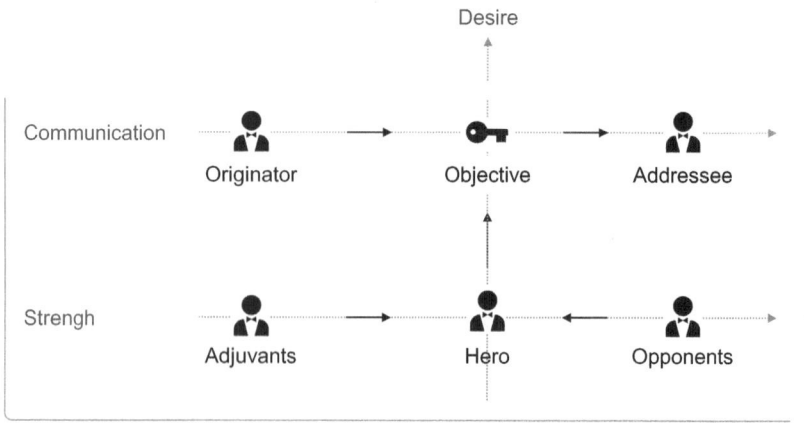

**Fig. 22** Actantial model

The COO (originator) requests the CIO (hero) to completely rethink the IT (objective) so that the group (addressee) can pursue its mergers, acquisitions and divestment mission at maximum efficiency. On his way, the CIO will face opponents: the CFO, who cannot provide enough CAPEX for hardware investments when buying a company and accelerate the depreciation of assets when selling another; the head of HR, who cannot hire and dismiss people at the velocity required; the head of digital transformation, who expects the various technologies of the companies bought to be integrated without delay; the internal and external auditors, who request detailed audit trails natively implemented in the internal control system to warrant that the data of the companies bought and sold have not been altered during their transformation.

The CIO cannot meet alone the objective: he needs support from a provider (adjuvant).

Once the story is laid down, it needs to flow in the design of the solution and in the rest of the proposal. In the example above, the keywords flexible, quick and standardised stand out. Naturally, these shall constitute the base of the proposal. They need to reflect themselves in one or another way at all stages of the development to form a consistent proposal that vehicles congruent messages, e.g. a flexible solution is useless if the costs are fixed or if the contract does not allow for changes. Where a traditional offer develops linearly, with costs and conditions determined only once the solution is designed—with possible inconsistencies between the characteristics of the solution and the service model—a development following the actantial model does not allow reaching the objective until all opponents are defeated. Practically, this means that the design shall consider natively the costs and conditions constraints. If not, it must be adjusted until it does.

## Write the Proposal

This section provides general guidance on how to shape the proposal at a macroscopic level.

## Form

Form is the expression of inner content. Under no circumstances shall it be neglected even if the RfP does not attribute any points for the quality of the proposal. Form eases or hampers the reading; it makes the proposal enjoyable or tedious.

*Approach* While a novel can be built around the story and enriched with technical details, it is recommended to build a proposal around more traditional patterns, emphasised by the most significant traits of the story—those that help to fight the opponents and meet the objective. Being too disruptive could result in a polarisation of the client's appreciation: either very positive or very negative.

*Structure* Managers read diagonally—when they read at all. The higher the position, the less they read. The ideal proposal distinguishes the information according to the audience. For example, if it is intended to reach top management, IT management and IT specialists, it should be structured in three distinct sets of documents, each providing an increasing level of detail: the summary (max 2 pages), the body (max 50 pages), the appendices (as many as required). Beyond 20 documents, include a document map as entry point.

*Content* Notwithstanding what precedes, the summary can be storyboarded using the actantial model. This enables one to visually position the parties side by side in the quest of the goal and present them as actors of the same adventure. The body should be articulated around a red path constituted by the five usual building blocks, namely the solution, operations, transition, costs and conditions. This allows the client to project into the future and show them the way to go. Follow the construction rules detailed in the dos and don'ts section below. The appendices should be in the format dictated by the best practices with respect to their content. Name the appendices adequately and reference them visually everywhere in the body where they provide detailed information.

*Appearance* While technology fundamentally changed modes of communication in the last two decades, outsourcing proposals seem to be stuck in the past on paper documents. This is the heritage of laws that, until recently, only recognised the physical signature as legally binding. When no legal constraint applies, it is highly recommended to use modern multimedia tools, at least as a complement to the traditional book format. Quoting Benjamin Franklin "Tell me and I forget, teach me and I may remember, involve me and I learn", interactive media have a greater impact than simple reading.

## Hard Content

*Positioning* Outsourcing, being a corporate adventure, it is important to position the proposal at a corporate level and have a distinct message for each stakeholder. As appropriate, focus on all aspects of the deal as represented by the jigsaw in Fig. 23.

*Scope* This is the first side of the golden triangle.[25] Correctly scoping outsourcing is far from trivial. Defining what is included versus what is not commands a thorough and systematic approach, as described below:

- For each system, identify the applicable service layers.
- For each system and applicable service layer, identify the interactions with the layers above and below (vertical axis).
- For each system, identify the interfaces with other systems (horizontal axis), especially when the interface connects systems in and out of the scope.

---

[25]Scope, time, cost.

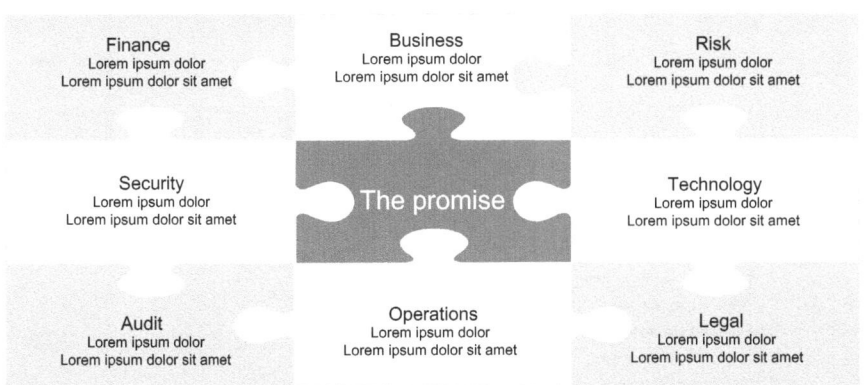

**Fig. 23** A message for each stakeholder

- For each system and applicable service layer, determine the services provided by the provider, the services to be provided by the client and the services which are not included.
- For each system, pay attention to the question of support and interactions both on the horizontal and vertical axes.
- Pay attention to services that generate joined responsibilities within a layer.

---

**Example**

Figure 24 represents what the scope of an ITO+AO outsourcing may resemble for a complex, diverse IT environment. Each number draws the attention to a specific kind of situation that would call for clarification in the proposal:

1. WAN/MAN is likely to transmit data from all systems, including those out of scope, e.g. video-surveillance, which may require network configurations like quality of service (QoS).
2. Although the scope is limited to ITO+AO, a certain level of AM services which cannot be dissociated from the rest are included.
3. The system is fully managed by a specialised third party but produces data which are stored and backed up on shared facilities foreseen in the proposal.
4. The system is fully managed by a specialised third party but includes a monitoring system installed on a server to be provided by the provider.
5. The ERP is fully provided in an ASP mode by a third party, but the system has interfaces with other systems, which will generate a few ping-pong incidents during the contract.
6. The system is fully managed by the provider, with the exception of the higher end of the database layer, which is operated by the client as part of application services.
7. The system is an appliance (black box) provided by a third party. The provider provides the facilities, storage and backup services and the monitoring of application agents.

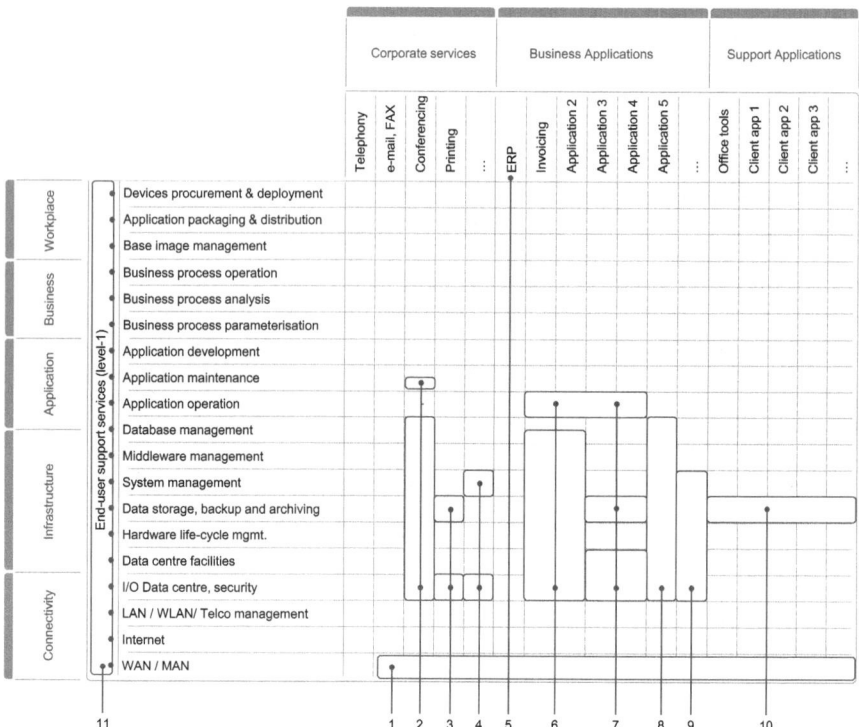

**Fig. 24**  Example of scope definition for an ITO+AO outsourcing

8. The system is market standard and fully operated, DB included, by the provider. The system does not provide any supervision agents for the application.
9. The system is operated until the OS but does not include the management of any middleware nor DB. This is the basic service of an ITO outsourcing.
10. Client applications are not managed in the context of this ITO outsourcing, but the saving directory of some applications is deviated to the shared storage facilities.
11. The solution includes an L-1 service desk, but in second line behind the L-1 provided by the client. L-2 support is included in the services themselves.

*Time*  Time management is key in outsourcing because of contract dependencies: the end of the project triggers the start of the operations. A project slippage has a direct impact on costs due to the longer time frame as well as collateral effects of various kinds such as a shorter lifetime of physical assets bought during the project, with possible consequences on the conditions of service. Since the project is calculated for a given duration, it is good practice to fix an end date. This forces the parties to reassess the overall situation in case of slippage and rebalance the golden triangle and not only the time axis. The starting date of the operation contract can be relative, triggered by the end of the project. Whatever the construct and number of imbricated contracts, it is highly recommended to analyse all scenarios of slippage with their cascaded consequences and to adjust the contractual dependencies accordingly.

*Costs* An essential cost driver in long-term contracts is the forward-costing concept. The principle is to anticipate the future cost of the services by forecasting the efficiency gains that the provider units plan to achieve through forthcoming improvement programmes. Figure 25 shows an example of a 10-year contract whose cost distribution in year 1 is as follows—server: 1 million, storage: 500,000, services: 1 million, overhead: 20%, margin: 8%, total turnover: 4.536 million. The provider plans to achieve improvements of respectively 3% and 10% per year on the servers and storage production costs but at the same time anticipates a yearly 1% rise on salaries. Overhead and margin stay equal in percentage. Forecasting the figures over 10 years leads to an average client price 9% lower than in year 1, reduced from 4.536 million to 4.304 million per year. Such calculations call for precaution when they are combined with extraordinary exit conditions before the end of the term if the provider offered the average price right from the beginning of the contract. In such a case, the client should pay an exit fee whose amount depends on the year of exit to cover the losses of the provider.

*Assumptions* Unless the impact on the price really justifies asking detailed questions, work with assumptions for the following reasons: (1) The correction between the costs envelope of the proposal and the final envelope in the contract is usually insignificant with respect to the total amount of services. (2) Once answered, the question may lead to modifying the solution in a way that would compel the provider to deviate from its standards, whereas clients are usually demanding best practices. The provider should try bringing the client into its'

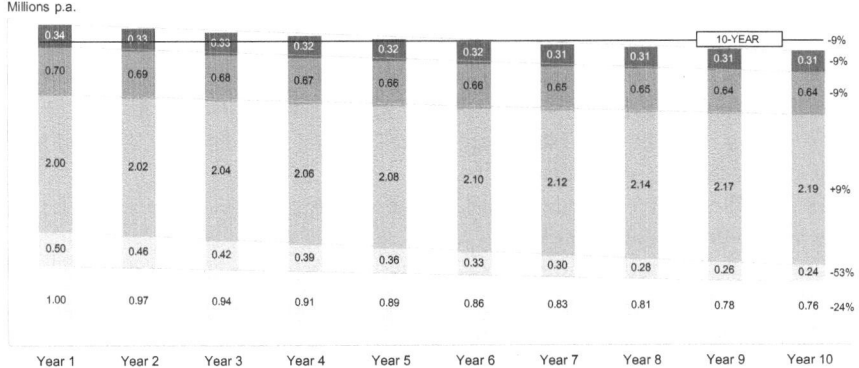

**Fig. 25** Example of forward-costing deal calculation

outsourcing model rather than reproducing the current environment. (3) Questions may raise interest in the community of competitors. (4) Questions aimed at responding to complex problematics should be reserved for face-to-face interviews during later due diligence.

## Soft Content

*Differentiator* The concept of competitive advantage is not outdated; it has just shifted from hard to softer factors. In a world where every product has become identical, differentiators are more down to emotions, surprise or attention than to the latest technical refinements as such. Surprise the client with side approaches to solving problems or by breaking prejudices they may have. For example, if the provider has a reputation for being inflexible, surprise the client during the bidding process with agile behaviour. This supposes, of course, the full support of top management and the potential consequences accepted.

*Complexity* Complicated things generate bad emotions and bad emotions are three times stronger than positive emotions. From the overall structure to the formulation of individual sentences, all aspects of the proposal should converge towards more simplicity. De-complexify things should be the motto. Beware, however, not to trivialise them. Whether de-complexifying has to do with the form and hides from the client a complexity that anyway remains—outsourcing is a complex matter—trivialising has to do with the content and breaks the internal structures between the elements. In that case, the provider takes a risk of removing important information.

*Storyline* General keywords characterising the story stand out. For each building block in the proposal, select words or expressions belonging to the same lexical field than that of the keywords. This allows conveying the same underlying message, but applied to the context. For example, if the keywords were flexible, quick and standard, the applied keywords could be:

- *Solution.* Technology agnostic (=standardised), scalable (=flexible) to allow rapid (=quick) increases and decreases.
- *Operations.* Integrated at all stages of the value chain (=standard), real-time (=quick) automated reports (=standard) available online (=flexible).
- *Transition.* Role-based (=standard), interchangeable (=standard), certified staff to allow resources variability (=flexible).
- *Costs.* OPEX type (=standardised), marginal costs of increases (=flexible), pay-per-use billing model (=flexible).
- *Conditions.* Dynamic contract (=quick), no min/max thresholds (=flexible).

*HBDI* The Herrmann Brain Dominance Instrument (HBDI) is a system developed by William Herrmann that measures and describes thinking preferences in people. Figure 26 shows the four different modes of thinking, which apply in the form of preferences of different magnitudes, nobody falling solely into one category.

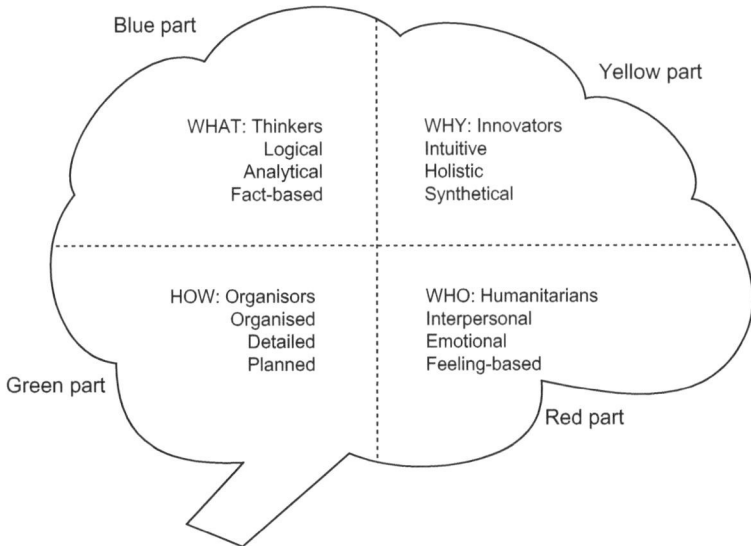

**Fig. 26** The languages of the brain

Knowing the brain preference of the persons who will analyse, recommend and decide in the client organisation may help orienting the messages for maximum impact. The brain dominance of each key stakeholder in the client should be part of the stakeholder's map of any good account manager. If the client is not known, simply formulate the important messages of the proposal in a way that they adequately reach the intended interlocutors. For example, a CFO is obviously blue-green, a COO probably yellow-blue, an HR person red-yellow, etc.

## Validate the Proposal

The review and approval process can involve from 5 to more than 20 persons, depending on the visibility of the deal.

It starts with a technical review. The persons who designed the solution, namely the members of the core bid team, perform a technical reading. They control the services, the quantities, the guarantees.

Then comes the peers' review. All the persons who have a stake in the deal are invited to read the proposal. They give their opinion on the structure, the readability, the messages. They ensure that the proposal is adequately positioned.

The process is completed by top management's formal approval. Board members formally authorises the bid team to submit the offer after reviewing the deal's fundamentals:

- Scope: service lines concerned, services in scope and out of scope, volumes.
- Timeline: project and operations contract as a minimum, other contracts.
- Costs: pricing model, financials ratio, margins per service unit.

- Service model: offer type, delivery conditions.
- Risk assessment: 360° assessment, including internal and external factors.
- Specials: asset takeover, personnel takeover, general entrepreneur, etc.

If the bid team keep the stakeholders readily informed all along the bidding phase, the final approval is simply a formality. If the deal shows any particularities which could, potentially, be subject to intense discussions or, more importantly, arbitrage, the bid team is well advised to prepare individually each stakeholder beforehand, as early as required according to the complexity of the matter.

## Dos and Don'ts

Bid team
- Appoint the core team members according to the nature of the proposal. Creative people are likely to get bored responding to a GATT/WTO RfP and may dangerously underestimate the required formalism. For their part, structured people may not know what to do with open requirements or no requirements at all and may endanger the response if not their own health.
- Beware of personal incompatibilities between key people in the core team. This is especially true for the account manager—bid manager tandem, the former being responsible for the client and the latter for the proposal. Two alpha males each wanting to take the control of the situation may lead to clashes. As professionals, they should establish their respective roles together.
- Avoid the "too many cooks in the kitchen" syndrome. Appoint a small core team with one leader per domain. For example, one lead architect for the end-to-end consistency of the solution. If additional architects are needed for specific components, it is the lead architect's responsibility to define the expected work packages and coordinate their integration with his peers. The more interlocutors, the more individual responsibilities, the less global consistency.

Story sketching and solution design
- Bring together convergent[26] and divergent[27] thinking people to confront ideas and elaborate an innovative yet operable solution. As explained earlier, in a world where every product has become identical, differentiators shall emerge from soft factors like surprise. The point here is not to revolutionise the service offering, but rather to add originality on a solid, standard base.

Proposal writing
- Comply with the rules of the RfP and address all topics raised by the client, even though they do not seem always relevant. Failing to do so will leave an

---

[26]Capacity to find a solution to a given problem; the process is rational.

[27]Capacity to find multiple different solutions to the problem; the process is intuitive.

impression of a provider difficult to manage. Whenever suitable and possible, create a variant of the requested solution or a completely alternative proposal. These have few chances to be retained as such though, but they position the provider as resourceful and thus create a small advantage.

- Consider the form as a competitive advantage. Apply all techniques that can help improving the presentation and the readability. Write the proposal with a single hand. On a macroscopic level, chunk the structure of the document and the sections with a maximum of seven topics as beyond that number, the human brain loses the overall context. On an information level, emphasise the first words of a sentence: they are the most retained. Check out the internal website of the marketing department, which certainly provides valuable advice with respect to corporate identity, design, guidelines and writing style. Make use of interactive media to improve retention.

- Create subsequent versions of the proposal by highlighting the changes with the previous revision when entering discussions with the client. As irresistible as it may be, refrain from sending explanations or worse, corrections or amendments to the proposal by email. It is common practice to reference the original offer, including all subsequent exchanges, in the resulting contract. Reconstructing a fair view of the situation after months of discussions by aggregating dozens of over-amended emails is nearly impossible.

- Position the proposal in a way that it creates the conditions of adherence at the top while limiting the conditions of rejection at the bottom. An outsourcing is a strategic decision rarely originating in the IT department. Talk to the right audience by developing the most important concept for each different stakeholder and using words drawn from the same lexical field as the key drivers of the proposal.

**Abstract**

In this chapter, you will learn how to extract the essence of each provider's offering and select the best fitting partner, how to establish the contractual bridge between the proposal and the contract or the beginning of the project, how to devise a bulletproof contractual structure that resists the rhythm of change, how to negotiate the contract and set the base for a well-balanced relationship, how to set the baselines to guide project control and execution through appropriate governance and work breakdown structures.

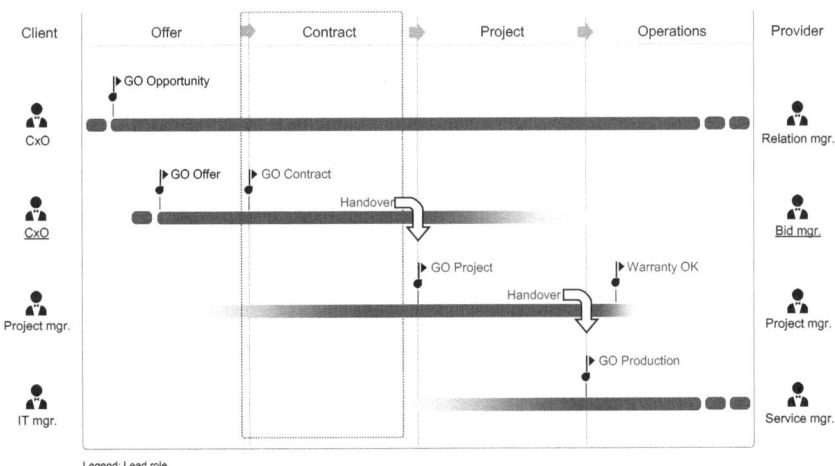

**Fig. 27** Planning phase in the outsourcing life-cycle

## Analyse Offerings and Select Partner

Attention which each party should pay to this topic: Client: ●●● Provider: ●●○

## Objective

Extract the essence of each offering and select the best fitting partner.

This chapter draws attention to the key elements of the analysis and identifies the common set of characteristics the parties should share to form a solid partnership.

## Description

It is the logical continuation and end of the request for proposal (RfP) process described earlier. The client bid team compiles the providers' offerings and compares them with the preset criteria. It then collects the feedback from the internal stakeholders and presents its recommendation to the management committee. After several iterations, the client makes their choice.

## Process Overview

If the choice of the partner is still open, then the last two steps of Fig. 28 apply as shown. If the client has already chosen its partner before or during the RfP process, then the last two steps are still likely to apply, but in the reverse order. Whatever the order, chances are that the client's management ordered the bid team to proceed with the standard process to make sure they have robust arguments for the forthcoming price negotiations with the partner. Regarding the selection of the partner, it will probably be more down to an unconscious identification process or discussions with confreres rather than to the technical application of the criteria described in this chapter. In any event, the characteristics of the selection remain the same.

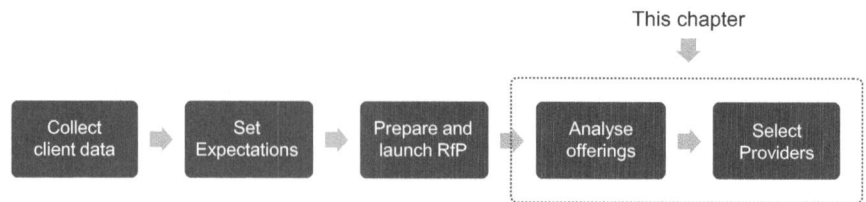

**Fig. 28** Offerings analysis and provider selection process

## Analyse Offerings

The client weighs the proposals against its evaluation criteria and does a comparison between them. They may request additional written explanations from the providers as necessary. In all cases, it should give each prospective provider a chance to present their offers and have a face-to-face exchange.

## Select Provider

If no provider clearly stands out, the client establishes a short list of three, but preferably only two, providers and refines the assessment until they are satisfied with the provider and its offering.

## Practical Implementation

### Analyse Offerings

There is a natural tendency for clients to jump directly to the price section. This is fair enough if they come back later to the services for a thorough analysis of the differences between the offerings. The competition in the IT services market is harsh, particularly in the lowest layers, and no provider can afford charging a premium price not linked to any service or added value.

### Solution

If the client used the patterns described previously, it should be able to easily map the requirements with the providers' answers. The following questions may help to point out the coverage of each solution and its key features.

*Synoptic* How does the solution look like on a synoptical level and does it fit naturally within the client's environment?

*Coverage* (1) From a functional perspective, what services are included, excluded, optional and in what quantities? (2) From a technical perspective, is the solution open enough to interface with external services, e.g. hybrid clouds from different parties? (3) From a service perspective, does the solution encompass all the components to run or is the client supposed to provide some of them? If this is the case, it may generate hidden costs.

---

**Example**

Suppose provider A offers to deliver a workplace service for 7000 users based on PCs provided by the client and provider B with its own assets for a price slightly higher. The client chooses solution A.

Both providers guarantee a replacement of desktops in 1 business day in case of breakdown, but, for this, provider A expects the client to maintain a permanent stock equivalent to 2% of the desktops. This condition represents for the client an additional cost of approximately $2\% \times 7000 \times \$1000 = \$140,000$ over the depreciation period of the assets, in addition to the human effort required to procure the stock and interface with the provider's delivery units.

*Scalability and flexibility* Is the solution based on shared services or services entirely dedicated for the client? The answer to this question sets the base for the sought scalability and flexibility. If the solution is dedicated, perhaps it is effectively scalable and flexible from a technological point of view. However, unless the provider takes upon itself all the risks, the solution is very likely to include financial or contractual restrictions.

## Operations

*Capacity to deliver* The client needs to verify the capacity of the provider to run the services. For this, a 1-day on-site assessment, including an encounter with the heads of the provider's critical service units and a comprehensive visit of the facilities, is time well invested. From all the relevant thematics, the client would want to analyse at this occasion are the front-end and back-end interfaces.

The front-end interface refers to the service desk, i.e. the interface between the users who log tickets and the production units that treat them. Key elements to verify are:

1. The level of proximity the service desk can offer in its relationship with the users, for instance through regular exchanges between key members on both sides.
2. The ability of the service desk to capitalise, over time, knowledge about the client environment, for instance thanks to specific knowledge management processes and tools. These two aspects are particularly important in case of outsourcing of the application and business layers: the L-1 (service desk) and L-2 (production units) support organisations must know the platform of the client in all its details.

The back-end interface refers to the operations centre, i.e. the interface between the production units that run the services and the client IT governance organisation. Key elements to verify are the capacity of the operation centre to:

1. Act proactively on events, thanks to the real-time monitoring of the installations.
2. Immediately set up a war organisation in case of any major incident.
3. Liaise regularly with the client's IT to keep it informed on the evolution of the situation in such a case.

*Reports* Since it is practically the only remaining point of contact with the production of the services, the client will want to verify the quality and the quantity of the reports it will receive in production. The reports serve different purposes and target different audiences. The ones which will most likely be needed are:

1. Monthly reports on services and key performance indicators; these reports target the client's IT and allow controlling the adequacy of the services with the contract.
2. Quarterly reports on advanced topics such as security, e.g. access rights of provider's personnel on the client's systems; in the present case, they target the security officer.
3. Yearly compliance reports, e.g. ISAE reports to certify the provider's internal control system; they target the client's internal and external auditors.
4. Ad hoc reports, e.g. audit trail upon modification of data by the provider on behalf of the client, or the provider's compliancy with the general data protection regulation (GDPR); in the present case, they target the client's internal audit and the client's chief data officer (CDO).

If the client contemplates entering into business with a Tier I provider, they will generally be satisfied with a presentation of the content and frequency of the reports. With smaller providers, it should not just take the word for it and should investigate further about the capacity of the provider to really keep the promises. Having a closer look at the level of process standardisation and tools integration within the provider's organisation may allow to corroborate or not the first impression about the provider's capacity to fulfil the guarantees.

---

**Case study: how the absence of processes demonstrates the existence of deficiencies**

The provider states in the offer that it guarantees the restoration of the IT function within 4 hours in case of disaster on the base of a disaster recovery plan (DRP), which it tests and updates once per year. At the same time, the analysis shows that the provider:

- Does not possess a content management database (CMDB) or other type of central repository in which it stores the configurations of the clients' systems.
- Does not manage the configuration management process and does not update in a systematic manner the systems' documentation upon changes.
- Never conducts a mass recovery test considering the overall number of clients and systems.

Conclusion: The disaster recovery plan is not operational. In the event of a major incident, operations would be carried out in a chaotic manner. Even if the provider were to succeed in restoring the systems, this would be down to the knowledge and chance availability of one or more isolated heroes rather than resulting from the plan itself.

## Transition

*Orchestration* Knowing that the bulk of activities will be executed by the provider to build the target environment, the client can reasonably expect the provider to take ownership of the project master plan.[1] Unless the client is familiar with outsourcing projects, they should either request the provider to maintain such master plan and endorse the operational duty or appoint a partner to orchestrate the transition on their behalf.

*Services* The transition will generate thousands of activities. It is obviously impossible for the client to understand all of them and make sure they are properly reflected in the contract. More important than the services themselves are the acceptance criteria that should draw the client's attention. These shall be formulated in a way that the provider compels to deliver an up-and-running solution, as described in the corresponding section of the offer, and to populate it with the client's data. Since transforming the source environment into the target solution requires the collaboration of the client, e.g. to extract the data from the systems, the client shall consider the services to be delivered by the provider, the services excluded from the scope and the client's obligations as the only consistent whole that permit defining the boundaries of the provider's services.

*Billing model* An experienced provider will offer the project at a fixed price unless the client's environment records a level of risk that cannot be reasonably mitigated.

Given the number of persons on the provider side who will contribute to the project—several hundred in complex outsourcings involving a transformation of the application landscape—the threat of an important cost slippage is very real.

*Miscellaneous* Project road map, project organisation, project governance, organisational change management, takeover of personnel, takeover of client assets, experience of such transitions: the subjects of attention and ways to distinguish the providers are many. The following sections provide further details about the best practices on how to structure and document the services related to the transition.

## Financial

*RtB costs* They represent the cost of recurring operations. This is where the bulk of cost lies. The biggest drivers are: (1) What services are included and what are excluded? (2) Is the life cycle of dedicated hardware components included, including

---

[1]Plan which aggregates all the activities from all involved parties, namely the client and its third parties—including the outgoing provider, as the case may be, the users and the provider itself. Being responsible for elaborating and maintaining the master plan does not necessarily mean being legally responsible for all parties. Such a responsibility, called general entrepreneur or prime contractor, is a specific agreement that involves a lot of risks for the provider and that, consequently, calls for a specific agreement.

the effort to renew it? (3) Which software licences are included, from technical to business applications? (4) What is the applicable billing model (normally fixed price)? (5) What are the incremental/decremental costs if volumes increase/decrease and are there any steps? Here the client can verify the capacity of the services to scale linearly. (6) What collateral effects on other services does volume increase/decrease of services have? If the client is in a growing phase, it would be well advised to ask the provider an incremental cost projection with selected scenarios to measure all impacts of an increase, e.g. licences, storage, service desk.

*CtB costs*   It represents the costs of changes which come on top of operations, from daily, small changes to enterprise-wide projects. The biggest cost drivers are: (1) What is the client's appetite for change—which can make the CtB (change-the-business) vary from a few percent of the total IT budget to 50% or more? (2) What is actually a change? What the client could consider a change may be part of recurring operations for the provider and vice versa, e.g. minor versus major releases of databases or operating systems. (3) What is the applicable billing model (usually cost-based)?

*One-time costs*   They refer to costs that normally occur outside of regular operations. The most obvious concerns are the initial transition and the contract termination. The others are more difficult to point to and are, thus, those that should retain the attention. For example, those costs potentially involved to renew hardware components that have reached their end-of-life in case of contract extension. The client should pay attention to the following elements: (1) What is the cost for the initial transition? (2) What would be the types of costs incurred in case of termination? (3) What are the assumptions, if any, on which these costs are based? (4) What are the different billing models? While the initial set-up is usually offered as a fixed price, the termination is billed on a real cost basis as it depends on the specific situation when it happens. (5) What would be the costs in case of contract renewal? Would there be any hardware or software reinvestments? For information, the cost of the project for a lift and shift IT operations (ITO) outsourcing, i.e. without application or business logic transformation, is often about the same as 1 year of RtB (run-the-business).

*Business case*   Many factors of different natures combine themselves to form the real cost of an outsourcing, hence the reason for the client to compare its current situation with the offers on a business case basis, i.e. considering the total cost of ownership (TCO) of the IT before and after the outsourcing, rather on raw RtB and CtB figures.

Figure 29 shows the four main cost categories to consider and, for each category, the most influencing drivers.

   Whether the business case comparison says which solution is the most competitive over the expected duration of the contract, it does not necessarily say which one is the most competitive over the long run. Because of intermediary one-time costs

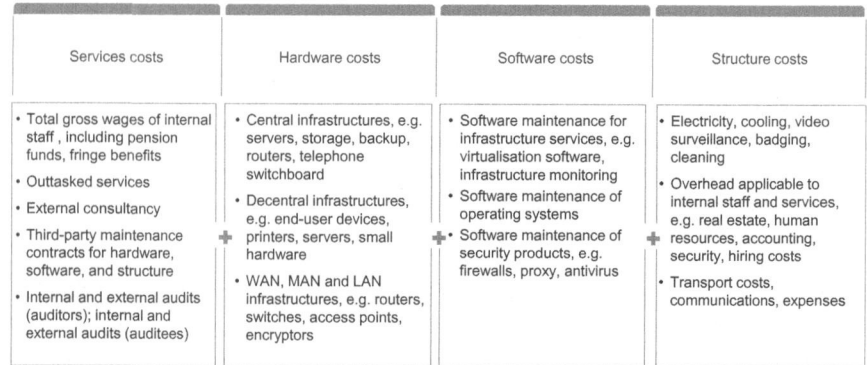

| Services costs | Hardware costs | Software costs | Structure costs |
|---|---|---|---|
| • Total gross wages of internal staff , including pension funds, fringe benefits<br>• Outtasked services<br>• External consultancy<br>• Third-party maintenance contracts for hardware, software, and structure<br>• Internal and external audits (auditors); internal and external audits (auditees) | • Central infrastructures, e.g. servers, storage, backup, routers, telephone switchboard<br>• Decentral infrastructures, e.g. end-user devices, printers, servers, small hardware<br>• WAN, MAN and LAN infrastructures, e.g. routers, switches, access points, encryptors | • Software maintenance for infrastructure services, e.g. virtualisation software, infrastructure monitoring<br>• Software maintenance of operating systems<br>• Software maintenance of security products, e.g. firewalls, proxy, antivirus | • Electricity, cooling, video surveillance, badging, cleaning<br>• Overhead applicable to internal staff and services, e.g. real estate, human resources, accounting, security, hiring costs<br>• Transport costs, communications, expenses |

**Fig. 29** Business case main cost positions

that may occur, e.g. end-of-life reinvestments, the client shall compare the offers over twice the duration of the expected contracts.

**Example**

The client compares the cost of two all-inclusive, 5-year outsourcing offers:

– Offer A shows project costs of five million, including an initial hardware investment of two million, and recurring costs of five million p.a.
– Offer B shows project costs of four million and recurring costs of 5.2 million p. a., including hardware depreciation and automatic renewal.

Over 5 years, both offers show a total contract value (TCV) of 30 million. However, over 10 years, offer A shows a TCV of 58 million[2] and offer B a TCV of 56 million.

To round the financial analysis, the client should further consider the following topics:

*Compliance* Very likely, the client faces annually costs proceeding from internal auditors, external auditors and, as the case may be, regulators. These costs may be indirect, e.g. effort spent by the internal IT to answer questions and management to liaise with the auditors and/or direct, when the auditors solicit information from the provider. The capacity of the provider to show compliancy of its services or internal control system with international norms, e.g. ISO or ISAE 3402, is a definite advantage. Check if the offers make provisions for such reports.

---

[2]Initial project (5 million) + running costs (2 × 25 million) + hardware reinvestment needed after year 5 (2 million).

*Taxes*  The client should check: (1) The effect of non-refundable value-added tax (VAT). Some types of companies like banks cannot recover the VAT paid on services. Consequently, they need to absorb it and compare the offers VAT included. (2) The effects of other special taxes applicable in some international constructs. Some countries apply taxes differently on imported products or services. Depending on how the deal is structured with respect to physical assets, e.g. sold to the client or provided as part of a service, this may affect the client's business case.

*Currency*  The effect of foreign currencies creates risk if the provider and the client's currencies differ.

*Invoicing*  Finally, as part of the financial analysis, the client may want to consider the flexibility of the provider's invoicing process if it intends to post-process the invoices for internal cost distribution. Depending on the complexity of the outsourcing, post-processing the invoices manually each month may represent a massive overhead for the client.

## Conditions

Special conditions and reserves affecting the services should be stated in the offer. These should normally be self-explanatory.

## Select a Partner

The best offering as it stands on paper may not necessarily be the best solution for the client. Like the relations among humans, an outsourcing is a long-term adventure and the success of which largely depends on a proper match between the parties. Such a match happens when the parties share a common set of characteristics.

*Trust*  Outsourcing is above all a matter of trust. No client would entrust sensitive assets like customer data, patents or other business secrets to a partner it does not trust. Trust is a feeling that first emerges from the encounter between persons, not institutions. It is only after this that the institutions take over and farm this feeling with appropriate actions. Virtually no strategic outsourcing happens without top executives on both sides looking in each other's eyes and shaking hands.

*Values*  The parties should share the same corporate values and position themselves accordingly in their respective market. This brings us back to section "Get the Big Picture" in Chap. 2 and the positioning of the IT against the business: both should form a congruent system. If the values are not aligned, at least they should not convey conflicting messages.

*Culture*  Cultural differences affect the way people, and thus companies, do business and resolve conflicts. One can easily understand that differences may arise when working with a foreign company, but the same may happen within an individual country with strong regional influences: there are a few of these in Europe and even next door when one party is constrained by the rules of an international group. An example of cultural difference is the importance of the written form to reach an agreement. An Anglo-Saxon company will give more importance to the contract (e.g. the legal terms for a North American company, the processes for a German one) than a Latin company which will rely more on its capacity to find solutions through the dialogue (e.g. from very courteous for a Portuguese company to more disputing for a French one). In this example, the parties are very likely to experience tensions during the initial contractual negotiations because of the overall pace of the discussions and the level of attention to details. In production, frustrations for every time the client requests a change that takes weeks to get delivered because of an overwhelming control process on the provider side. Cultural differences create small misunderstandings at the beginning which may turn into profound disagreements in the long run.

*Structure* It might be tempting for a client to choose a smaller provider to profit from better prices and, at the same time, be able to exercise a higher level of control. Similarly, it is tempting for this provider to bolster its reputation with a bigger client and to accept conditions it would normally not. No matter how tempting this may be for both parties, it calls for extreme caution. There is the question of the critical mass of the provider described in section "Get the Big Picture" in Chap. 2 which may affect the delivery of the services (the larger the client, the broader the expected scope of services). There is also that of the structural misalignment of the communication channels. If not of the same size, the parties should at least be able to establish communication links between executives of the same level of responsibility and prerogatives. This is less driven by the wish to protect egos at each level than by the need to adequately relay the information at the correct organisational levels. Each party needs to feel properly understood.

*Objectives* The parties should have a long-term stake in their marketplace at least when they contemplate entering business, because things can obviously change during the lifetime of a multi-annual agreement. More specifically, it signifies that the client has to make sure that the services to be outsourced form part of the provider's core business and for the provider that the client is not subject to mergers, acquisitions or divestitures. If they are contractually foreseen and their consequences accepted, such situations should normally not prevent the parties from going forward.

*Decision centre* Local and easy access to the top management of the other party is key in strategic outsourcing. Entering into relation with international players whose decision centres are located outside the country constitutes obstacles when important issues are to be addressed.

*Image* The image of the partner may have consequences on the client's interests, especially if the latter is in the business-to-business market and works with regulated institutions. The consequences may be positive with, for example, prospective institutions probably seeing the capacity of the provider to show proof of compliancy with international standards like ISO or ISAE as a safety guarantee. They may also raise issues when, for example, the client informs institutions with which it is already in business of its decision to outsource the operation of critical data belonging to them to an unknown and/or foreign company.

## Dos and Don'ts

The parties should
- Have top executives from both sides meet during the selection process such as a 1-day encounter to walk through the provider's facilities and meet heads of key delivery units.

The client should
- Request to meet key members of the providers who are not in the sales team, i.e. a project manager or a service manager, to gain more insight into the real service delivery conditions.
- Orient the analysis of the offerings according to the type of provider. Asking Tier I providers to demonstrate their capacity to meet service levels is a waste of time. It would be better for the client to concentrate their questions on pain points like reactivity and flexibility. Conversely, the capacity to handle the volumes of the production in a structured way is a central question for smaller providers, while reactivity and flexibility is inherent to their structure. In both cases, the client should enter in the details of the corresponding processes.

The provider shall
- Beware of presentations which appear too polished at the time of the offer. They tend to put the client on guard and, in some cases, place them involuntarily in a position of inferiority, which could then have negative consequences. It is heart and passion that bring people together and make the difference, not perfection.
- Identify potential cultural differences early enough and adjust the offering accordingly. For example, the provider should not expect a chaotic client to fully enter highly standardised processes. If they still decide to enter into business with this client, then they should foresee special management gates, e.g. by reinforcing the service management position.
- Draw the client's attention to the frontiers of responsibilities between the services of the provider and the obligations of the client. For the project, it means identifying who between the client or the provider is responsible for establishing the master plan and coordinating all involved parties; for the operations, it means explaining the role and duties of the retained organisation.

## Formalise Willingness to Collaborate

Attention which each party should pay to this topic: Client: ●●○ Provider: ●●○

## Objective

Establish the bridge between the proposal and the contract.

This chapter explains how to start the project straight after the selection of the provider without waiting for the contract to be finalised.

## Description

Closing an outsourcing contract takes time. On average, it takes a minimum of 4 months for organisations up to 500 users, 6 months for mid-size organisations up to 10,000 users and 6–12 months or more for organisations in an international set-up.

Whereas the decision process is almost always an arduous path, once the decision to outsource has been taken and the provider chosen, the client usually wants to kick off the project without delay. The number of times the client compels to going through the full contracting process before engaging in any action are arguably rare. This is quite understandable on several grounds. Firstly, an outsourcing is, above all, a matter of trust and the parties have no reason to think at this stage of the relationship that the project could go wrong to the point that the parties terminate the relationship. Secondly, the decision process takes longer than expected and the client is already running behind schedule. Finally, the client may no longer have any more opportunities to roll back commitments made to employees or agreements taken with external parties.

Fortunately, there are easy ways to go forward for each situation.

## Process Overview

Depending on the urgency and the level of trust, the parties may enter a preliminary agreement and sign either a letter of intent (LoI) or an early start letter (ESL). Both are pre-contracts but serve distinct purposes. Nevertheless, whatever name they are given, since these documents are not regulated, it is their content that matters.

Both are similar in that they offer moral commitment. The simple fact that the parties sign the document is a positive signal of their engagement.

### Letter of Intent

An LoI, also sometimes called memorandum of understanding, confirms the wish of the parties to enter exclusive negotiations with the aim of reaching a final agreement, usually within a limited time frame. As shown in Fig. 30, the project starts only upon

**Fig. 30**  LoI process

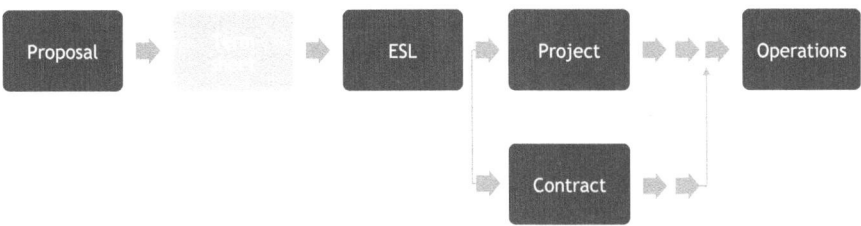

**Fig. 31** ESL process

signature of the contract, which may take months. An LoI is usually not binding, in the sense that the parties may leave the negotiations without consequence, but may bind the parties through some specific clauses such as exclusivity of negotiations.

### Early Start Letter

An ESL confirms the wish of the parties to start the project straight away on the basis of the proposal while they discuss the contract. As shown in Fig. 31, the project and the contract negotiations start upon signature of the ESL in two parallel streams.

If the parties expect particularly complex negotiations or see there may be a possibility that they do not reach an agreement, they can agree on a so-called term sheet prior to signing the ESL to agree on a limited number of key topics.

An ESL is binding.

## Practical Implementation

While an LoI could hold on one page as the expression of unique concern, in outsourcing agreements it usually takes a longer form. There, the LoI and the ESL share a common base. This common base shall be that the parties compel to negotiate in good faith.

*Preamble* This introductory statement that normally holds on one page comes before the core content itself and serves two purposes: recite the historical facts that led the parties to the agreement and set the philosophy on which the parties intend to build the relation. Because the preamble does not contain any resolution clause, some may doubt its usefulness. It is a risky bet. No matter how brilliant the persons who write the contract are, rest assured that there will be gaps. If a case reaches the court for a situation which was not foreseen or a complex situation which has become inextricable, the judge may well go back to the original intentions of the parties to base their decision.

*Contractual base* The starting point of the discussions is the proposal, including all its constituents or, at least, the set of documents on which the parties formed a common interest. The contractual base assumes more significance for the ESL because of the investments it triggers. In such a case, no contractual base means for the client to sign a blank cheque.

*Confidentiality* The parties compel to keep all discussions confidential during the negotiation phase and limit the number of involved people to the strict minimum. Leaks may have dramatic consequences, especially on the client side where key staff may resign and thus endanger current operations as well as the transition project. The parties may also not want the market to know that they are under discussions, especially if the discussions could collapse.

*Costs* Each party bears its own costs in relation with the negotiations, whatever the outcome.

*Liability* The parties assume no liability in case the negotiations collapse and reject any claim for damages except for a breach in the agreement, e.g. a breach of confidentiality.

*Duration* The parties need to set a fixed term beyond which the negotiations automatically stop and the agreement dies. In general, this fixed term is 3 months. In practice, this clause is virtually never applied. It generates instead useless paperwork for extending the agreement until the contract is signed. In the unlikely event that the negotiations actually stop, the clause may foresee that other clauses such as confidentiality or intellectual property survive the end of the agreement for a certain period of time.

*Due diligence* Going forward with the contract may be conditioned to the results of a due diligence. A due diligence is the detailed analysis requested by one or both parties to confirm that the proposal considers properly the current environment. Topics usually analysed are assumptions, metrics and complexity.

## LoI

One of the only additional conditions that characterises the LoI is the exclusivity of negotiations. Since the LoI does not provide any guarantee to the parties that the deal will happen, each party will want at least to make sure that the other party does not engage in parallel discussions in which it would find a better interest or that it could use to influence the discussions.

## ESL

The ESL requires more attention, especially from the client side. It is binding and it is the starting point of the project. In this respect, recall section "Get the Big Picture" in Chap. 2 and the number of persons that an outsourcing transformation may involve.

*Duration*  If negotiations are successful, the ESL is deemed void and the conditions negotiated are simply reintegrated in the contract. If not, the ESL ends also, but with consequences.

*Costs*  The common practice establishes that the client does not bear any cost for the duration of the ESL. If the ESL turns into a contract, then the effort the provider spent is deemed the same as the one it would have spent under the conditions of the project. The client will pay the fixed installments foreseen by the contract later. If the negotiations collapse, the client shall pay for the services delivered on a time and material (T&M) basis until the ESL is declared failed. This special condition calls for specific reporting rules, decisions for investments, definition of hourly rates, investment limits, etc., to be introduced in the ESL to give the client enough visibility on the provider's actions.

*Obligations*  The ESL shall set the respective obligations of the parties with respect to the project in addition to those for the negotiations. If the proposal adequately sets out the modalities of the transition, this section could be limited to only restating that the parties commit to appoint a project manager and set up the governance structure for the project. The provider starts delivering the services and the client pays for them (although payments are delayed).

*Delivery*  Legal conditions related to the delivery of projects, like testing, acceptance, warranty, correction of defects, intellectual property and liability, should theoretically be described, ideally through the general terms and conditions or a master agreement template attached to the ESL. If the ESL does not reference any such agreement, the law applies. Unless the parties want to enforce very specific conditions, this is definitely the best solution at this stage for a pre-contract which is not expected to last more than a few months and thus not expected to need any of these clauses.

*Appendices*  In cases where large investments are to take place during the ESL or critical milestones may be reached, additional information like investment schedules or timetable must be added.

## Term Sheet
Sometimes called heads of terms, the term sheet helps identify deal breakers at an early stage. It summarises on one page the key deal points identified as critical.

**Case study: how a one-page term sheet can set the tone of the relationship**

In a mega deal, the starting position of the client for the negotiations is to have an uncapped liability for all types of contractual infringements: gross negligence, slight negligence, loss of data, breach of intellectual property, breach of service levels, breach of confidentiality, death of personnel, etc. No provider would accept such a clause. Different causes and different consequences shall lead to different liability caps. If the client stands firm on its position, it is a deal breaker.

To judge the elasticity of this aggressive entry statement, the parties try to categorise the amounts of liability per severity. They draw a table with several columns, each column representing a cap, and then fill the cells with the causes: unlimited (death, gross negligence, loss of data), limited to the annual contract value (breach of confidentiality, breach of intellectual property), limited to 10% of the concerned individual contract (breach of service level), etc.

The parties reach an agreement on this topic as well as some others. They lay down a set of general principles, the spirit of the contract, which will serve as a base for further negotiations.

## Dos and Don'ts

The parties shall
- Keep the document short and simple. This is particularly true for the ESL, which shows a natural propensity to expand endemically given its binding nature. Two to three pages for an LoI and five to six pages for an ESL should be the maximum.
- Write the document like a contract, not an offer. Adjectives, imprecise formulations, conditional statements, etc., are not appropriate.
- Use the vocabulary that corresponds to the binding/non-binding nature of the document. What is stated as "the parties intend to" in an LoI should be stated as "the parties agree" in an ESL.
- Expressly state whether the document is binding or not.

## Devise Contract Set

Attention which each party should pay to this topic: Client: ● ○ ○  Provider: ● ● ●

## Objective

Draw a bulletproof contractual structure.

This section explains how to best structure the contract at the macroscopic and microscopic levels. It does not consider the legal aspects giving rise to the formation of the contract, nor is it intended to provide document templates.

## Description

What comes to mind when thinking about the word contract is one document. The reality is however quite different.

An outsourcing contract is a collection of dozens of documents coming from different business units, all serving the same purpose but with different perspectives: technical, operational, legal and financial, to name but a few. Not surprisingly, the assembly building is challenging. If, aside from conflicting clauses, imprecise formulations and terminology misalignments, the contract lacks a solid structure, the situation can deteriorate over time. Additions, extensions and partial or total termination to and of the contracts, etc.: the possibilities to hamper the overall consistency are many.

In light of the above, a sound structure appears to be key.

## Structure Overview

### Key Concepts
A well-defined structure must satisfy the following essential criteria:

- *Accessibility.* Without structure and navigation rules, retrieving information is like searching for a pin in a haystack.
- *Precedency.* Precise descriptions shall overrule broad descriptions even when these appear in documents of higher rank.
- *Factorisation.* The same information shall never be repeated twice throughout the whole set of documents. Similar concepts should be factorised at a higher level.
- *Modularity.* Adding or removing individual contracts must be possible without having to resign other documents.
- *Consistency.* Adding, modifying or removing services partially or totally shall not affect the consistency of the remaining documents.

### Structure Variants
Between one document of 1000 pages and hundred documents of ten pages, the possibilities to structure the contract are numerous. For the sake of simplicity, let us consider the two most common variants: per business function, represented by the vertical axis in Fig. 32, and per service layer, represented by the horizontal axis.

*Per business function* This model is well suited in case of full outsourcing where the provider supplies all services from one hand. The client gets a function-ready service. There is one main contract. Each function has its own service-level agreement (SLA) document or its own section in a global SLA that covers all functions.

Advantages. All services provided for a given application are available at a single glance. Adding, modifying or removing a function, e.g. introducing a new business application, touches only one document. The parties may easily agree on a set of KPIs to measure the entire function from end to end.

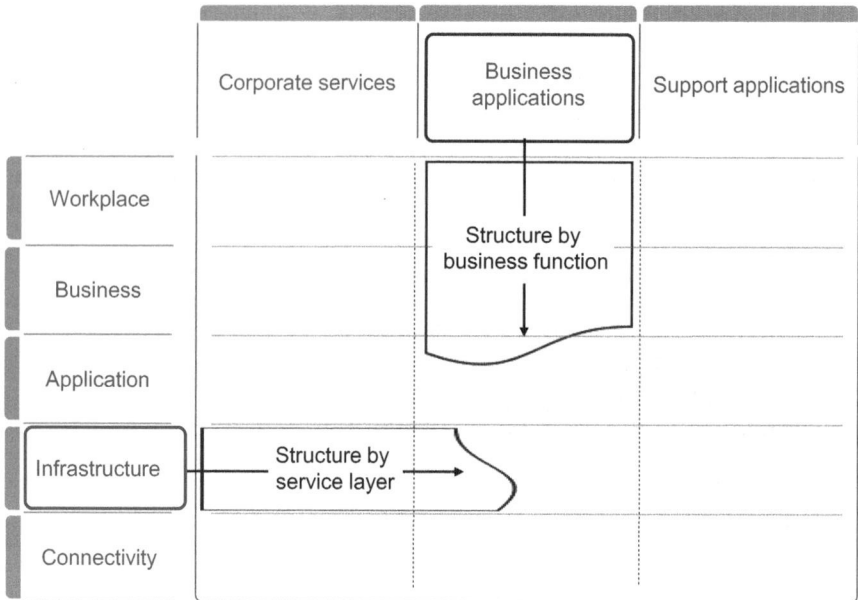

**Fig. 32**  Contract structures two most common variants

Drawbacks. The number of documents increases linearly with the number of business functions. In high-volume environments, with hundreds of applications, the contract becomes unmanageable.

*Per technical layer*  This model is well suited in case of partial outsourcing where the provider supplies only part of the services required up to delivering the business functions. The client gets a layer-ready service, e.g. DB-ready (ITO contract) or application-ready (AM contract). There are several individual contracts. Each contract has its own SLA document that encompasses all systems.

Advantages. This modular construction allows the client to attribute distinct contracts to distinct providers. It can also absorb high volumes: adding, modifying or removing multiple systems in a contract only touches one document.

Drawbacks. There is no 360° view per function; each function spans over several contracts. The service levels of a given function result from the combination of the service levels agreed in each individual contract, possibly using distinct measurement formulas if the contracts are from distinct providers. The frontiers of responsibility in each contract require more attention from the parties.

Full outsourcing being proportionally rare, the per technical layer variant is the most commonly observed. This is the one studied in the rest of the chapter.

**Fig. 33** Contract structure by service layer

## Overall Structure

The contract is a living asset that evolves at the rhythm of the CtB. In high-volume environments, several offers for new services—with as many changes affecting the contract—are agreed upon every week. Even though the parties do not modify the contract on a weekly basis (once or twice per year is sufficient if they track changes through a systematic process), the fundamental principle on which to base the structure of the contract is the ease of change. This is achieved when adding, modifying or deleting services causes minimal disturbances and requires minimal attention.

Figure 33 shows a five-level documents structure which enables such flexibility.

## Master Agreement

Layer One sets the legal framework for agreements and contracts to be agreed in the future, including the conditions in case of termination.

## Service Agreements

Layer Two sets the operational framework for contracts of similar natures to be agreed in the future. They provide for speed, by allowing the parties to focus only on deal-specific terms, and safety, by devising the applicable conditions if things go wrong.[3]

---

[3]Once in production, the parties will contract new changes at a rate of several per year, month or week. The persons who will write and validate these offers on both sides, who have little or no legal background, will concentrate on change-specific terms. It is in the parties' best interest to figure out right in the contracting phase how to deal with those unwanted situations that are most likely to occur.

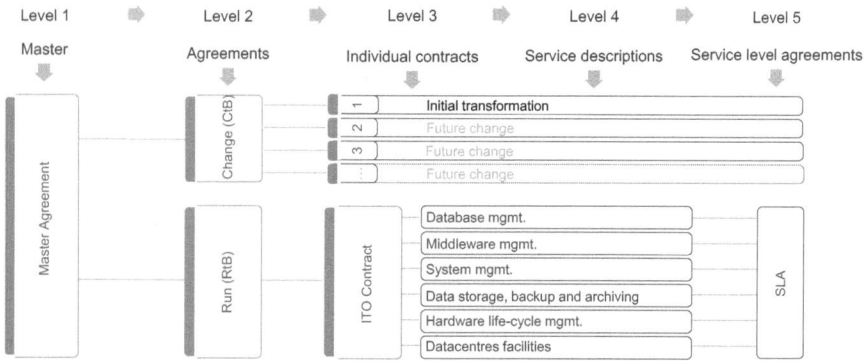

**Fig. 34**   Contract structure example for an ITO outsourcing (expanded)

## Individual Contracts

Layer Three sets the scope, time and costs of the agreed services, along with any other service-specific terms and conditions. Common practice is one contract per service category.

## Service Descriptions

Layer Four details the features and characteristics of each service constituting the individual contracts.

## Service-Level Agreements

Layer Five sets the service levels and other guarantees agreed for each service, along with bonus/malus credits, if any.

## Practical Implementation

Figure 34 shows an example of ITO outsourcing contract based on a five-level structure. Figure 35 shows the same contract based on a reduced structure with two levels only where the operating agreements have been merged and where the service descriptions and the SLAs have been integrated in the contract itself. The parties should favour the latter variant if the frame agreement and the contracts stand below 50 pages each, excluding service descriptions. Beyond, it is very likely that specific conditions inserted in the contracts could be transformed into generic conditions and moved to dedicated agreements. This would allow to maintain consistency by not repeating identical conditions with possibly diverging formulations in future contracts.

The concepts are detailed below.

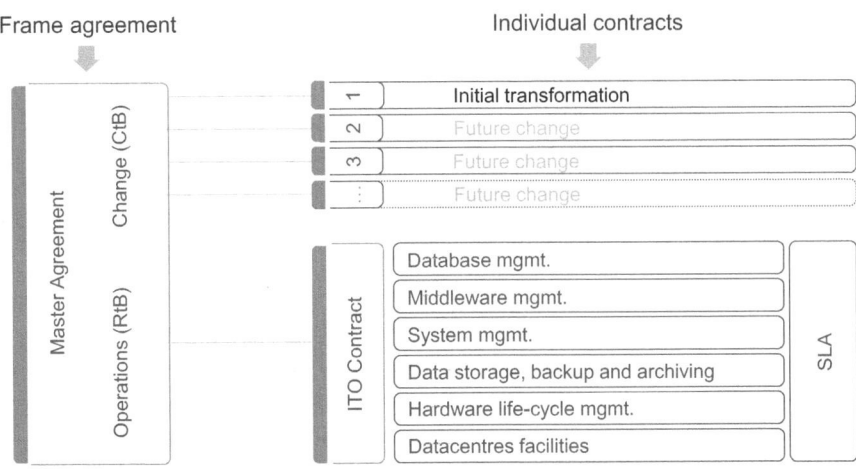

**Fig. 35** Contract structure example for an ITO outsourcing (condensed)

## Master Agreement

To meet the accessibility criterion, the master agreement (MA) shall include a map that shows the ranking of the documents in the hierarchy. To meet the precedency criterion, it shall establish the reading rules between conflicting clauses. Such rules are mandatory because conflicts, whether intentional[4] or not, are frequent. In this respect, two schools of thought oppose one another.

Companies with a strong legal focus, or with lawyers both geographically and emotionally distant from the matter, want the MA to prevail over all other documents. This approach:

1. Ensures that the main legal conditions cannot be overruled and that the corresponding corporate policies remain in force at all time.
2. Gives the legal department the visibility on all claims that could arise from the contract and simplifies the analysis in case of conflict.
3. Avoids conflicts coming from misuse of language, formulations written by lawyers being of superior quality than by technical people.

This approach has also major disadvantages:

1. In case of conflict, general descriptions overrule detailed descriptions, which is a nonsense and could lead the parties to look for more details in annexes anyway.
2. It over-inflates the MA with specific conditions, the parties wanting to rule a maximum of details at the highest level.
3. It over-involves lawyers, with negative consequences on negotiation costs and duration.

---

[4]Example: wanted exceptions to general statements.

4. It makes specific conditions thought for in the initial contract prevail over different specific conditions that could require future contracts which could, in turn, could force the parties to renegotiate the MA later on. This top-down approach is acceptable only if the MA stays light and tackles legal topics only.

Companies with a more robust technological background—and thus providers—want to have the most detailed documents prevail over the MA. Aware of the risk that inappropriately formulated clauses in future technical appendices could inadvertently overrule major clauses like liability, they either prevent or restrict the modifications to these clauses, e.g. by authorising them only if they are accompanied by an explicit reference to the modified clause. The MA plays its best role when it focuses only on general legal terms like the parties' obligations, intellectual property, liability, confidentiality and data protection, termination, ordinary and extraordinary terminations. The MA should remain in force until the last individual contract binding the parties expires.

**Service Agreements**

To meet the factorisation criterion, the contract set shall group, at the next higher level, similar conditions applying to underlying contracts. For this, the parties need to identify the common denominators of the individual contracts they intend to sign and structure them into service agreements. By default, at least two agreements factorising the conditions for services of different natures can be devised: CtB and RtB.

*CtB* This agreement describes the default conditions the parties want to apply at each stage of the change process, from submitting to receiving, assigning, quoting, executing, accepting and, finally, closing orders. Main conditions usually foreseen concern:

1. Form of delivery, obligation of means or obligation of result, and corresponding modalities.
2. Testing, accepting and authorising for production.
3. Delays and consequences.
4. Warranty and correction of defects.
5. Impact on RtB agreement.

*RtB* This agreement describes the default rules governing operational services. Main conditions usually foreseen concern:

1. Guarantees of service and applicable waivers.
2. Grace periods after the introduction of changes into production.
3. Applicable regime for the correction of defects in production, i.e. CtB warranty or RtB guarantees.
4. Bonus/malus concept.

## Individual Contracts

To meet the modularity criterion, service layers belonging to the same service category are grouped to form the individual contracts. Each contract is thereafter attached to one of the service agreements enforced at the level above to make sure the corresponding conditions apply to it. In the case illustrated in Fig. 34, the individual contract Nb. 1, representing the initial transformation, is attached to the CtB agreement; and the ITO contract, representing the services from database management to data centre facilities, is attached to the RtB agreement. The main characteristics of CtB and RtB individual contracts are described below.

*CtB* Contracts of this nature materialise projects. By definition, a project is unique. Once it is over, the contract is of historical interest only. Project contacts shall contain at a minimum the services to be delivered, the project organisation, the expected duration and the projected costs. Fixed-priced projects require additional details such as obligations of the parties, project milestones, acceptance criteria and payment schedule. For more complex projects, such as the initial transformation, the parties may want to overrule some of the general provisions in the contract foreseen in the CtB agreement, e.g. specific warranty conditions.

*RtB* Contracts of this nature materialise recurring operations. Depending on the exhaustiveness of the service descriptions, operating contracts like the ITO mentioned above may hold on a few pages, the main conditions being the start and end dates of the contract, the scope of the services and pointers to the documents describing the services and the guarantees in greater detail. If no pro forma service descriptions exist, then the contract itself shall provide for the details.

*Offers* These are hybrid documents encompassing the project and operations. When, in production, the client requests a change that affects the operations, e.g. installation of a new system, the provider can either issue a project contract along with a new SLA covering the change or an offer. In the former case, the client needs to sign both contracts at the same time or make the commitment to sign the operations contract later. In the latter case, the parties need to reintegrate the operational part of the offer in the operations contract at the next general contract review.

## Service Descriptions

To meet the consistency criterion, services must be described so as not to present any gap nor overlap among themselves, limiting their interactions through a platform contact called service interface point.

Ideally, each service should specify its outcome, input parameters, recurring activities included, exclusions, obligations of the client and reporting features.

Depending on the maturity of the provider, service descriptions may come in the form of pro forma documents, which can then be attached as appendices to the contract, or as simple text inserted directly in the contract.

**Service-Level Agreements**

KPI types and values are specific to the services delivered.

For ITO and AO/AM contracts, the most common KPI are support time (days and hours during which the client may receive support), availability (maximum downtime per period[5]) and continuity (RPO and RTO measures).

For AO/AM contracts, additional KPI in relation with batches execution, application environments cloning, data correction, to name but a few, may apply.

For BPO contracts, the most common KPI relate to the number and types of transactions handled per time unit and the error rate.

When similar KPI apply to consecutive layers, only the KPI of the highest layer is of interest.


## Dos and Don'ts

The parties should
- Pay attention, during the negotiations, to any changes in the end-to-end conditions' ruling (CtB service agreement in this chapter) in proportion to the prospected volume of changes once in production. CtB conditions are always under-represented when not totally absent, whereas CtB volumes can represent up to 50% of the annual contract turnover.

The provider should
- Structure the contract by applying the five-level tearing concept, even if these are not all physically materialised by separate documents. Implementing five separate document types is less important than properly reflecting the underlying concepts behind each level.
- Add a contract map which includes references of all documents (date, version, ID) and allow the service descriptions to be substituted by new versions over time only by changing their version in the map. This allows the parties to stay up-to-date with service improvements proposed by the factory with reduced formalism.
- Write the contract in such a way that it can be used by technical people. Avoid legal jargon further from IT reality; use real company names instead of the client/ the provider; use plain English; illustrate complex conditions with examples.

The client should
- Refrain from imposing its' own contract set,[6] particularly with respect to the description of the services and the service levels. In addition to lengthy discussions, it could lead the provider to raise its prices during the contracting phase because of non-standard services or service guarantees.

---

[5]Time interval between two service reports, usually a month.

[6]Or that of the consulting firm it appointed, on the grounds of conditions allegedly optimised over time.

## Negotiate Contract

Attention which each party should pay to this topic: Client: ●●● Provider: ●●●

## Objective

Set the base for a well-balanced relationship.

This chapter prepares the parties for the structural communication misalignments they will face during the negotiation stage and draws attention to the hottest contract topics.

## Description

Negotiating an outsourcing contract is similar to executing a project which main deliverable is the contract. Mapped with the main project management disciplines, key elements characterising the negotiations include:

*Goal* Most clients engage into negotiations because it takes a contract, more pushed by the circumstances than dragged by a goal. When they have one, it is usually defined in broad terms such as: get the best services/prices/conditions. If there is no goal, fair enough, it simply needs to go through the topics one after the other. If there is a goal, it must translate consistently into the other dimensions, particularly the scope.

*Scope* Depending on the level of confidence the client has in the quality and quantity of what they are buying, it will either fly over or dive deeply into technical descriptions. However, despite the services and the surrounding conditions obviously constituting the core of the contract, they do not embrace to their full extent the whys and wherefores of what is at stake. Business, finance, procurement, legal, audit, security, compliance and risk departments also have requirements that need to be considered. The scope further conditions the time frame and the team.

*Time* If the client sets a strict time frame, appoints the negotiation team accordingly and has the commitment from top management, the contract could be negotiated in four weeks. This would put the organisation under stress, but it would allow to create a dynamic. Without dynamics, it is almost impossible to keep a reasonable momentum and negotiating the contract then becomes a side activity, which can last from four months to over a year.

*Team* The strict minimal team on the client side is the person appointed as responsible for the mission, supported by a legal counsel. On the provider side, the couple bid manager—relationship manager is in the front line. Depending on the scope, the number of persons involved on each side can grow to ten or more. In these

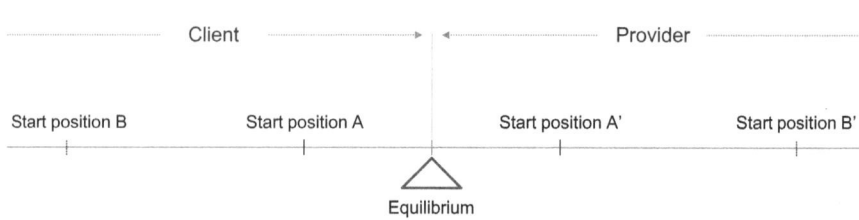

**Fig. 36** Negotiation equilibrium

circumstances, what really matters is that the leaders on both side speak with one voice and are granted enough authority to limit escalations to upper management. With respect to the timeline, backstage contributors should align their agenda with that of the negotiations to provide timely input and feedback. If not, the parties will have to put aside for later an ever-increasing number of subjects and go repeatedly through the issue list.

*Cost* Each party bears its own costs in relation to the negotiation phase. On the provider side, unless exceptional circumstances arise, these are purely internal. On the client side, it depends largely on the autonomy level acquired during similar experiences. The client that outsources for the first time will not want to take the risk to go alone without external support.

## Negotiations Paradigm

Balanced positions during the negotiations are the base for a sound contract, and a balanced contract is the base for a sane relationship. Equilibrated positions do not mean that the parties shall reach a flabby consensus on every topic. It means that each party shall preserve the matters that are important to it while making concessions on matters that are important for the other party.

What about the matters of common interest? The respective positions should be proportionated to the stake. They are in fact more often linked to the parties' internal rules. Here, the size plays its part: the bigger the company, the heavier the control processes, the higher the expectations, the more extreme the positions.

Figure 36 shows that one party entering negotiations with an extreme position leaves little choice to the other party than entering with the other extreme to expect reaching the equilibrium.

> **Case study: how an unbalanced contract can kill a relationship**
>
> The client is a mid-size institution outsourced to a Tier I provider. At a moment the market is experiencing a wave of mergers & acquisition, the 10-year contract is only half-way through when the client is bought by an international group.

All of a sudden, the provider is facing a giant with a level of internal and external control which no longer have anything to do with that of the local client. The client assumes the contract for a year or so, until finally it alleges that its internal audit has discovered deviances of great magnitude and the corresponding risk exposure.

The client then asks the provider to discuss and realign the contract with its own general terms and conditions. The provider rejects the proposal and enjoins the client to honour the contract. Over the twelve following months, the client will raise again the issue several times, but the provider holds firm its position.

The contract being presumably too risky, the client starts auditing the services and tries to have additional control mechanisms enforced at the delivery level. Quickly, the level of overhead on the provider side reaches such a point that the provider starts imposing restrictions on changes. As a counter-reaction, the client opens the contract and tries to make the provider bend. The provider reacts with the same magnitude. The situation escalates with soon several lawyers on each side. The initial request to reaching an agreement turns into a corporate fight. Over the remaining years of the contract, the parties exchange dozens of registered letters. Neither party finds sufficient grounds to leave the contract, though, and consequently have little other choice than to collaborate in a cold war ambiance until the end of the term.

## Negotiation Teams

What characterises negotiation teams on both sides is the difficulty to align roles and thus to ensure lean communication. Figure 37 shows this structural misalignment, highlighted by the dotted line. Not only do the interlocutors on both sides not talk the same dialect, they are not empowered with the same prerogatives. On the provider side, the core negotiation team nearly has full authority; on the client side, the person responsible for the deal needs to rely, downwards, on influent IT staff members who recommend and, upwards, on higher management who decides.

On the provider side, the structure is relatively invariant: three distinct lines with three clear scopes of prerogatives intervening in a controlled way, when needed, and with a straightforward escalation process.

*The front line* The bid manager–relationship manager tandem is in lead. The bid manager represents the change and is turned towards the internal structure, whereas the relationship manager represents the continuity and is more turned towards the client. The presence of the bid manager is ephemeral for the duration of the deal. As such, it is his duty to defend as firmly as possible the conditions of the contract, from taking the risk to become persona non-grata when the deal is over. In this respect, one often assists a "good guy–bad guy" role playing between these two individuals. Both represent the business; they jointly decide the terms and conditions of the deal. When decisions fall out of their scope of prerogatives, they escalate to the project

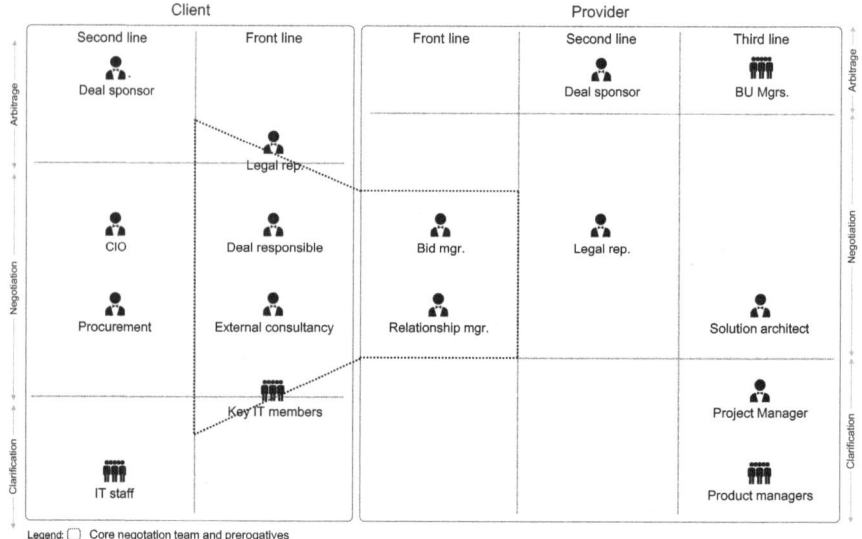

**Fig. 37** Negotiation teams structure and prerogatives

sponsor, normally a representative of top management, who liaises with his peers if the decision has a corporate-wide impact.

*The second line* The legal department—either one legal representative or several if the deal encompasses various areas of expertise—warrants the overall contract construct. Depending on the skills of the aforementioned tandem, it intervenes actively or passively in the process, respectively, from the beginning as a doer or rather towards the end as a controller.

*The third line* The experts who shaped the solution and their managers who endorse its' responsibility support the discussions at a technical level. Depending on the client's attention to detail, experts may be solicited heavily or may not be solicited at all.

On the client side, the structure is much more variable, depending on the maturity of the company and its internal organisation. If a common pattern were to be defined, it would be the absence of defined structure. Since, for the client, negotiating outsourcing contracts is not a business activity, there is no such role, and when roles are temporarily identified, there is no clear segregation of duties. Attempting to map the unofficial roles to those of the provider leads to the three following categories of interlocutors:

*The leader* Whether designated or emerging naturally, from one day to another he is appointed responsible for leading to completion a process he probably never led before. It must be a person with an all-round understanding of every IT matter and a strong business acumen. The CIO or his deputy is usually the next best choice. First, he should gather requirements from internal stakeholders representing IT, business, finance, procurement, legal, audit, security, compliance and risk and have them reflected in the contract. Then only can he engage discussions with the provider by involving key stakeholders as needed or, more likely, orchestrating internal reviews in the background. Should he have no previous experience in contracts negotiations, it is strongly recommended he seeks external support. Depending on the arrangement set out between the documents and the clauses, a contract does not necessarily equal the sum of its constituents.

*The lawyer* They come from the legal department and are specialised in the business of the company. They are appointed to warrant a major undertaking while probably being entirely foreign to the subject. Depending on their abstraction capacity, they may grab the essence and manage to focus efficiently on legal aspects, or feel overwhelmed of new information and pay attention to every detail. In the former case, the negotiations could run as smoothly as legal discussions normally permit. In the latter, they may become very tedious. If the lawyer feels uncomfortable with the new terminology, they may even completely rewrite the agreements with formulations extracted from previous contracts. Fortunately, in many cases, the company provides the funding to get external support from a legal counsel specialised in outsourcing.

*Technical persons* They come from the current IT department and obviously have a strong technological background. They are called in the discussion to ascertain that the offered solution fits within the organisational environment. As technical experts, they naturally dive into the nitty gritty of the system in order to understand how the solution has been designed, instead of focusing on what the company will get once in production. Although necessary for the client to trust the services, the involvement of the current IT staff is somehow problematic. It makes discussions much longer.

## Contract Content

The problems with contracts come less from what they contain than from what they miss out. The parties will face dozens of different situations during the relation. While many of them can be anticipated, not all can be foreseen. For these, the contract shall leave enough space for discussion, including appropriate conditions of escalation. Here is where the preamble enters the scene: missing conditions shall always be discussed with the original intentions of the parties in mind.

For the rest, here are the most relevant topics for each of the five levels on which the parties should focus.

## Master Agreement

*Liability* The company which operates its own IT is responsible for its business losses proceeding from dysfunctions. By outsourcing, it suddenly expects the provider to cover all possible types of consequences without limit and thus to profit from a double positive effect: minimise the risk and maximise the coverage. On average, services include a 2–10% risk premium on operations. Expecting a higher coverage through the liability limit is as exaggerated as usual. A limited cap set at 100% of the annual turnover of the concerned services should be the absolute limit. This excludes cases of death of persons or loss of a building which are backed by insurances: there, the liability can be unlimited. Finally, only direct damages are acceptable, although the frontier between direct and consequential may not always be obvious to determine.

*Intellectual property* By default, the intellectual property automatically goes to the party that implements, even if the other party provided detailed specifications. Intellectual property applies when developing a software like an interface. What is less well known is that it also applies when coding decision trees, implementing business logic or scheduling batches. If not carefully thought of during the negotiations, it can prove critical at the time of ending the relationship by preventing the client from leaving the contract or at a prohibitive cost. Be aware of the fact that releasing documentation or source codes does not necessarily grant the right to use or modify these. See section "Terminate Relationship" in Chap. 5 for a related case study.

*Compliance* Even if delivered in ASP or BSP form, the services are subject to changes proceeding from external factors like the regulatory environment, the business marketplace and technological evolutions. The question is then raised: which party bears the financial consequences? In general, the provider assumes the consequences of changes affecting it as service provider, e.g. the introduction of the GDPR. As provider of a specialised industry, it can also reasonably assume the consequences of changes affecting the business of the client, providing such changes apply without customisation to its other clients. When not, the client assumes them. Finally, the client usually assumes the consequences of evolution of its software and underlying technical components like operating systems, middleware and databases.

*Termination* Anything can happen that forces the relationship to end before the term. Excluding a force majeure, one distinguishes two main categories of reasons leading to an extraordinary termination: for cause, when it is linked to the non-performance of one party or other serious facts that render the pursuit of the relationship objectively impossible, and for convenience, in all other cases. Unless a strategic reason exists to maintain the relationship until its term, locking a client against their wish is pointless. In the end, everything comes down to a question of money. It is thus reasonable to give the client the possibility to leave the contract after an initial period, e.g. 3 years, by paying a lump sum of money. If the client is compelled to leave, because business conditions have changed, it should pay only the residual value of dedicated assets, non-amortised project costs and tangible losses the provider would incur. If the client leaves to go to the competition for better conditions, then they should also be subject to penalties for non-amortised pre-sales costs and unreleased gains. If one party leaves for cause, then the liability clause will likely apply. All other conditions can probably not be applied.

*Reversibility* Whatever the date and the cause of the termination, the reversibility clause will apply one day. And since the end of a contract is never happy, at least for the provider, the clause shall be precise enough to avoid any final conflict. First and foremost, the client needs to know that no contract includes financial provisions for reversibility and that they will need to remunerate the provider for all the services requested. One of the main drivers to keep costs under control at this moment is to make sure that the provider uses technologies based on open standard or commits to return the data and the systems in such formats. Extracting important volumes of data from proprietary systems and transforming them to new systems may cost millions. The provider shall commit to support, in good faith, the client in reversing the services, but for a limited period of time after the contract has expired.

*Arbitrage* At first sight, it appears clever to foresee a special process executed by a neutral person to arbitrate deadlocks. In practice, it is barely used and does not justify the investment. Topics escalated to the steering board (see section "Enforce Operational Governance" in Chap. 4) are sometimes heavily disputed, but always closed after a while. If the situation gets really bad, the parties will take the matter into their own hands. They may impose restrictions, take sanctions or, worse case scenario, engage court actions, but rarely rely on a third party.

### Service Agreements

CtB agreement. In high-volume environments, changes can represent up to 50% of the annual contact turnover. Meanwhile, the space change management is usually allocated in the contact is symbolic. Spending time to figure out how changes should fit in the target operating model is the best-invested time ever among all other topics.

*Change procedure* Figure 38 represents the change workflow. To make sure the chain does not contain weak links which could clog the whole process, the parties shall work out a solution for each individual step. The parties should:

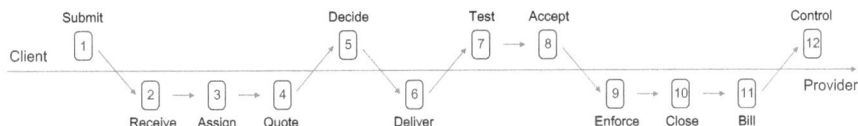

**Fig. 38** Change request process

1. Draft a requirements definition template and enjoin the client to use it for each significant change. If the client does not submit such a document, it is the duty of the provider to draft one with the client against appropriate remuneration.
2. Appoint a dedicated change manager or at least make sure that the team of pooled resources can handle the expected volumes.
3. Establish a catalogue of IMACD[7] and automate the corresponding workflows down to the service units. Pre-identify the target service units for the non-standard changes that are most likely to occur, e.g. installation of new server.
4. Consolidate price lists from productive clients in similar context. Consolidate text blocks from previous offers.
5. Define the appropriate level of authority within the governance team to authorise changes of a certain amount. Install a weekly committee with the provider to discuss open offers and take actions.
6. Agree on implementation methodology with the client and adjust the level of formalism to the complexity of the change.
7. Establish test templates and procedures. Identify key users and inform them of their new responsibility.
8. Establish acceptance protocol template. In the contract, state the rules of acceptance, including automatic acceptance in case of productive use.
9. Describe the process to put changes into production, including security aspects. The process shall apply to the client and to its suppliers, if any.
10. State how the changes are reintegrated into the contract at a later stage and how the log of changes is maintained.
11. Agree on both invoice structure and billing process to allow the client to reconcile the invoices versus the activities delivered.
12. No preliminary activity.

*Change pool*  To provide for speed for changes less than, let say, 5 days, the parties should agree on a pool hour system with reduced formalism. The pool can either be free or prepaid. If free (because the client does not know exactly on many changes it will require), the client agrees to pay the amounts incurred up to a maximum annual limit or not. If prepaid, it agrees on a minimum number of hours to spend per year and receives in exchange a discount, e.g. 10% on hourly rates.

*Warranty*  See below.

RtB agreement. Main conditions applying to RtB individual contracts include:

---

[7]Standard changes of Install, Move, Add, Change and Dispose types.

*Warranty*  The CtB agreement defines the warranty conditions applicable to changes delivered with an obligation of result. Nevertheless, when the changes lead to introducing a new system then operated under the RtB agreement, the parties shall decide whether it is the warranty of the project that applies for the correction of defects or the operative conditions. Legal and operational regimes differ. If they chose the operative conditions, it is the operations team that correct the defects. It makes things transparent, both for end users who continue calling the same service desk as usual and the provider which does not need to adjust operational processes; if they choose the warranty, then it is the project team that corrects the defects. This is usually more efficient, both from knowledge and workload perspectives; the negative issue is that it requires a special incident handling process during that phase. Besides, it costs money to maintain the project team long after the go-live date. The recommendation here is to favour the operative conditions by default and select the project warranty for a duration of 3 months beyond a certain project size or complexity.

*Grace periods*  Whatever the warranty model selected, the parties would be well advised to foresee a grace period after the introduction of changes into production during which SLAs do not apply. This is a fair practice, especially if the service embarks applications provided by the client, given the fact that clients rarely test the systems as they should. Changes of distinct natures and sizes should lead to distinct grace periods, from a few days to a few months.

*Bonus/malus*  No client understands why they should pay the full price for a service that did not meet all the guarantees and, therefore, sees the financial penalty as the ultimate answer to compensate for the harm suffered. In absolute terms, this compelling logic is indisputable but in fact is quite the opposite. First, it is one-sided. It automatically sanctions the provider for unmet SLAs, but not the client for unfulfilled obligations which are numerous: unstaffed project teams, incomplete testing, late decisions, unpaid invoices, etc. The daily accumulation of small deficiencies generates a massive overhead on the provider's side which is impossible to quantify. Second, it is costly. Penalties lead the provider to increase the risk margin and the client to globally overpay for the services. Occasional service credits do not compensate for constantly high prices. Dishonest clients come with penalties at the end of the negotiation process when prices have already been fixed. Last, but not least, it is useless. Tier I providers are structured to meet the guarantees. Bonuses or maluses for a given client do nothing to improve the services. It is only if the problem takes a corporate dimension that the provider will launch an improvement programme. If, despite the explanations given, a bonus/malus system cannot be avoided, then it should be as simple as possible. Here again, complex systems generate an important overhead on both sides for manual calculations and consequential discussions.

## Individual Contracts

CtB contracts. Out of the numerous individual contracts for changes that the parties will agree on during the lifetime of the relationship, there is one of major importance: the initial transition. Below are the main topics to be addressed.

*Services* Describing the services the provider needs to deliver is a challenge for both parties. The number of activities to be executed for outsourcing runs into the thousands, and it is impossible to list all of them. The natural tendency is to provide as precise a description as possible, but here the best is the enemy of the good. Over-prescribing activities poses real problems. First, it gives a false impression of exhaustiveness. If the parties need to find an answer, they will expect to find it in the contract. When this does not turn out to be the case, and it will happen, they will assume that the activity is not part of the scope, which may be wrong. Secondly, it relieves team members of their responsibility who will execute the contract by dictating to them the exact sequence of activities. Finally, it leads to discrepancies between the services that need to be built and those which need to be operated. For example, if the operations contract foresees the operation of a given system, but the project contract does not mention the system as needing to be built, one of the two contracts lacks information. To avoid such divergences while making things easier, both contracts must be strictly aligned. How? By stating that the main deliverable of the project is the resulting information system as described in the service descriptions. This, of course, assumes clear service descriptions, especially with respect to the frontier of each service and the duties of the client. If this formulation solves the bulk of the problem, it leads to a naked information system. To finalise the list of services, the parties need to complement it with all missing activities applicable to the context like gaps development, application parameterisation and data migration, to name but a few.

*Governance* Section "Setup Project Governance" describes the types of governance structures adapted to each type of outsourcing. For outsourcing involving a steering board, the parties should foresee in the contract a symmetric system of voting rights providing for an automatic and unquestionable way of going forward quickly. To force steering board members to join the committee—which represents the most problematic issue on the client side—the system should grant rights to attending persons only. Decisions taken within the committees shall have a value of contract if not contested within a few days after the issuance of the minutes.

*Transformation and Migration* Section "Plan the Project" broadly addresses the specificities of these two subjects according to the type of outsourcing. While going into further details about systems transformation and data migration goes beyond the scope of this book, one can say that these two subjects (1) are tightly correlated, because transforming systems may lead to transforming data, and (2) dramatically increase the risks of time and cost overrun with the number of systems and the volume of data.

*Decommissioning* At the end of the project, the client needs to decommission all legacy infrastructures, e.g. servers, user workstations and storage media. This raises a few concerns:

1. The effort is substantial, especially if the hardware is geographically spread, but the client may not have the resources any more.
2. The data must be erased according to corporate standards, which may be highly restrictive. Constraints that used to be acceptable for erasing a few machines per month before the outsourcing take another dimension when they apply to thousands of machines over a short duration.
3. Some systems shall be decommissioned but cannot be dismantled for business or legal purposes, e.g. legal archives. These shall remain accessible in read-only, either live or on demand, for years.

RtB contracts. As for CtB contracts, any kind of recurring service could turn into an RtB contract, making it impossible to derive generic conditions applicable in any circumstance. The topics below are common to all types of contracts and deserve specific conditions for the four main service categories that are ITO, AO (application operation), AM and BPO.

*Internal support* It relates to governance-type activities and processes pertaining to each individual contract and, more specifically, to the support the client needs to bring to the provider all while executing the services. If governance applies in the same way across all contracts, it calls for very specific activities according to the type of services considered. For example, an AM contract generates many more interactions between the parties than an ITO contract for incident and changes and, consequently, calls for additional support activities such as business testing. If these activities are not foreseen in the contract and therefore not implemented in the operations, they will obviously pop up in production at a critical moment.

*External support* It relates to the activities and processes ruling the interactions with third parties for the execution of the services pertaining to each individual contract. This is critical in multi-provider situations where the provider is part of an ecosystem of providers as well as in AM contracts where the provider runs the services on the basis of applications provided by software vendors of the client. For example, considering an AM contract involving 50 business applications, the client needs to communicate to the provider the relevant conditions[8] of its software maintenance agreements to allow it to access L-3 support. The client further needs to contact the software vendors, inform them of the outsourcing relationship and finally subrogate the provider in their capacity to perform in the name of the client any action permitted by the maintenance contracts. This means that the client shall:

---

[8]Number of the service desk, hours or support, access to system to log problems for bug fixing, etc.

1. Inform third parties about the outsourcing relation.
2. Transmit contract details to the provider to allow it to deliver the L-3 services, e.g. hours of service, service desk.
3. Authorise the provider to contact third parties in their name and using their credits, if any, e.g. log software defects and request bug fixing.
4. Enjoin third parties to collaborate with the provider.
5. Enjoin third parties to respect provider rules, e.g. test, acceptance and production process.

## Service Descriptions

The main pitfall for the client is to expect standard services for the price benefits they procure but request to have them customised beyond their standard possibilities. The 90-10 rule establishes that, over the duration of the contract and considering both development and maintenance costs, the 10% non-standard functionality will amount to 90% of the price. The more the provider is industrialised, the more each small deviation costs. Ideally, the client seeking efficient outsourcing should stick as close as possible to the provider's standards. By doing this, they should consider services as black boxes, where the only meaningful elements to discuss relate to the interfaces of the services.

*Service access point (SAP)*  Defines the frontier of the service: what is in versus what is out. In this respect, a small picture is worth a thousand words. Figure 39 shows an example of SAP for a storage/backup service provided to end users from the provider's data centres. The grey bubble represents the SAP and the dotted line the boundaries of the service. As shown on the picture, the service includes storage capacity mirrored across both data centres, as well as backup capacity in the first data centre only. The workstation of the end user and the connection from the client to the provider are not part of the service. It is in the best interest of both parties to scope each service with this technique and then to define the content of the service, its output and finally the client's obligations.

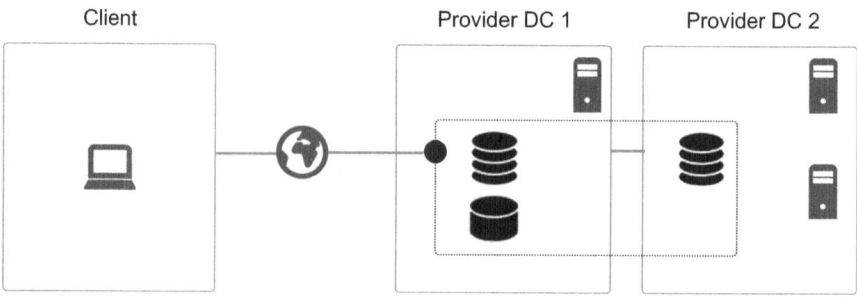

**Legend:**  ● Service Access Point (SAP)

**Fig. 39**  Example of service access point

*Reporting* It is one of the only tools available to the client to steer the services once in production, hence the reason the client should feel comfortable with the content of the reports for each service. Perhaps, more important than the content itself is how the reports are produced. This tells a lot about the provider's maturity and to what extent the client can trust what is reported. Ideally, reports should be fully automated from the production systems to the monitoring robots and the production of the final documents. Manual reports do not only generate massive overhead on the provider side, they are a source of errors. The flip side of automated reports is the cost to modify or add a report.

---

### Case study: how manual reports can distort reality

The client complains repeatedly about the number of user desktops not properly updated after the distribution of a new software release, until the moment it threatens the provider and enjoins it to launch an improvement programme to reach a better deployment rate. The provider launches a programme.

A few months go by. The provider releases statistics on the number of deployed desktops, which seems to have improved. The client analyses the report. Its eyes stop on the desktop of a person who left the company long ago. The desktop is identified as "deployed" but is not reachable on the network. The desktop is maybe connected to the network but in a different location to that it is expected.

Another few months go by, until the day the client performs an office move and discovers that the desktop was in fact broken and stored in a cabinet. The report had been arranged.

---

*Billing model* Fixed-price, pay-per-use transactions, T&M, minimum and maximum thresholds, etc.: the possibilities for billing services are manifold. This is desirable: each service should be billed according to the most appropriate model unless the client wants to avoid any risk and is ready to pay a premium for a fixed price. Beware, however, fixed prices also bear a risk for the client which is of being perfectly shaped and not leaving any room for discussion. In the end, the parties should follow the simple rule of thumb that risks should be shared and allocated per service whichever party has the best control on the service.

*Miscellaneous* Depending on the context, the following non-usual topics may have their importance:

1. Date and time of reference for the provision of the services if these are to be provided from or in different locations.
2. Effect of time zones.
3. National and regional holidays.
4. Exotic tax rules.
5. Invoicing currency, especially for long-term contracts.
6. Automatic contract price adjustments, e.g. based on inflation, or labour costs.

## Guarantees

*SLA*  Like reports, an SLA materialises the true capacity of the provider to meet expectations. They result from the proper combination of people, processes and tools and are not just simple figures on a piece of paper. Twisting the SLA of standard services without modifying one or more of the three dimensions above—and accepting the corresponding cost increase—should absolutely be proscribed for the fake impression of guarantee they would give. An SLA must be technically based and represent what the provider can really offer, not financially based and materialise what the provider is willing to pay if they miss them. Most of the time, non-standard SLAs call for non-standard solutions.

*Bonus/malus*  If, despite the warnings raised, the parties agreed to enforce a bonus/ malus system, they should at least aim for an easy one. Service credits counts, having to be processed manually, generate a substantial overhead on both sides for scoring the services and discussing the scores. For example, missed SLAs can originate in a defective service of a third party. Other sources of debate are cumulative SLA when a business function is made of technical layers each covered by a distinct SLA as well as consequential SLA when a system drags down with it a cascade of other systems.

## Dos and Don'ts

Regarding the process
- Be patient and adjust to the rhythm of the client. Negotiating an outsourcing contract takes time and pushing is counterproductive. The client may have fears and people respond differently to fear: some attack, some run away, some freeze; according to the brain dominance, they may want to go through all the details; they certainly need to follow internal processes and involve various interlocutors; finally, they may need to act in accordance with the company's culture—from dictatorship to collegiality, the decision process can vary widely.
- Keep in mind, at all times, the need to reach an equilibrium. Wanting to gain as many conditions as possible can have both short and long-term effects on the negotiation team. During the negotiations, people may feel underestimated or even humiliated and thus start behaving inappropriately, e.g. over-discussing topics which are of no importance for them. During the operations, the aggrieved party may try by all means to recover its position, the client by putting the provider in competition for each change and the provider by reducing non-visible services.
- Be careful when negotiating the prices too aggressively. The provider could be forced to cut back on internal costs. For example, if the provider has a reasonable margin, they will be able to allocate a dedicated change manager (see Fig. 38); if the margin is tight, changes submitted once in production will either fall into a

change management team with pooled resources or on any person who has the skills and the time to take care of the change. In both cases, the provider will have respected the contract.

Regarding the team
- On the client side, if possible, empower the client negotiation team with a negotiation margin to smooth and accelerate the discussions. Filter all technical questions coming from the IT staff and submit them to the provider only if they are relevant in the perspective of turnkey services. Staff a limited, but nonetheless robust, core team made of the CIO who represents both the business and the IT and two assessors: one legal and one technical. Other functions shall be called for only when required. In this respect, efficient negotiators have all experts ready at hand by chat, phone or email during the negotiations.
- On the provider side, respect the constraints of the client regarding the structure of the negotiation team, even if it seems overstaffed. Some clients have a hard time finding the person who will negotiate the contract, while some others appoint 10 people. This is obviously a question of maturity and, for big organisations, segregation of duties. This said, there is no reason for the provider to align on the client structure if one or two persons can cover all topics.

Regarding the content
- Act consistently. If standard services are discussed, refrain from imposing non-standard conditions or guarantees.
- Never start with a consensus because it is anyway where it usually ends.

## Set Up Project Governance

Attention which each party should pay to this topic: Client: ●●● Provider: ●●●

### Objective

Set the baseline to guide project control.
   This section explains how to determine the most appropriate governance structure given the type of outsourcing.

### Description

Project governance has three roles: orchestrate the construction of the new information system on the provider side, orchestrate the transition towards the new services on the client side and coordinate the two orchestras.
   The need for governance increases with the nature of the services to deliver: the more they directly touch the users, the higher the number of communication channels there are to control. A robust governance structure must be:

**Fig. 40** Project governance setup process

- Symmetric, with mirrored functions between the parties at each level to align expectations, e.g. provider experts who build versus client key users who test.
- Dynamic, with appropriate decision prerogatives at each level to favour the quick resolution of issues and limit escalations.

Unfortunately, it is a fact that clients tend to dramatically underestimate the need for governance, sometimes allocating only one person to control the project—and not necessarily full time. Figure 40 presents the process set-up.

> **Case study: how the absence of project governance can lead to a generalised drift**
>
> The client is a group of companies which grew rapidly through successive acquisitions. At a rhythm of two acquisitions per year, the group did not give itself enough time to consolidate and rationalise the systems. After 10 years, the IT had become a patchwork of centralised and decentralised systems made of different technologies.
>
> The small IT team had completely lost the control of the situation when top management decides to call for help. After a flash process of 5 months only between the diagnosis of the problem to the signature of the outsourcing contract, the transition project starts. A senior member of the management is designated responsible for the project. He is seconded by the IT manager, who acts as project leader on top of his numerous operational duties.
>
> Despite repeated requests from the provider, the client does not enforce any real governance structure. Downstream, all requests coming from the client's top management flow directly to the IT manager through unstructured coordination with the provider's team, leading the client to continue modifying the existing IT environment while the provider is building the new one. Upstream, all small and bigger complaints brought by each of the 2000 users reach directly top management, when not the owner himself, giving the impression of a constant, massive dissatisfaction whereas the bulk of the complaints are only grumbles inherent in a period of great change and could have been easily avoided trough regular communication. The false dissatisfaction turned into a real one at the time of reckoning: the project missed twice the deadline and literally burned more than 10,000 extra working hours.

## Process

### Figure Out Requirements
Recognise the type of outsourcing required to determine the potential impact on the business and then the overall level of control to apply to the project.

### Set Structure
Determine from the outsourcing type the number of distinct service categories involved and then the number of management layers required to coordinate them.

### Define Roles
Identify the various technical and managerial roles to deliver and, respectively, coordinate the work. Align the roles between the parties.

### Select Staff
Fill in the roles with the best persons for the job according to the project context. Even in process-oriented organisations, people are not always interchangeable, especially for project-related activities.

## Practical Implementation

### Figure Out Requirements
The form and content of the needed governance structure is a direct function of the potential impact of the project on the business, which is a direct function of the type of outsourcing. Let us then distinguish between the most common outsourcing types and sort them by increasing impact:

- Type One: outsourcing of a service layer. Change of technology, but no change in business processes. Limited integration tests and no user acceptance tests. Limited operational impact and easy fallback. Example: outsourcing of a LAN.
- Type Two: takeover of IT operations. No change of technology nor business processes, but change of operating processes possibly affecting the way users interact with their IT. No integration tests and no user acceptance tests. Limited operational impact. Example: outtasking of IT operations.
- Type Three: outsourcing of a service category, including transfer of applications and data. Change of technology and reinstallation of applications on new infrastructures, but no change on business processes. Heavy integration tests, but limited acceptance tests involving only key users. Significant operational impact. Example: ITO outsourcing.
- Type Four: outsourcing of several service categories including transformation of the information system and installation of new applications, but without

significant changes to the business logic. Heavy integration tests and user acceptance tests. High operational impact. Example ITO+AO+AM outsourcing.

- Type Five: complete transformation including change to the technology and core applications. Implementation of new business logic. Heavy application integration tests and user acceptance tests, including dry runs and dress rehearsals involving large number of users mobilised over one or several weekends. Fallback possible but with huge impact and only limited to one or two working days. After this, the company is forced to operate on the new information system and cope with the operational deficiencies until they are fixed.

**Set Structure**

The complexity of the governance structure proceeds from the number of service categories aka streams on the vertical axis and the number of management layers on the horizontal axis. If no exceptional circumstances arise, there is a correlation between both axes. Indeed, a limited number of categories does not require multiple layers of management and, conversely, multiple service categories raise complex integration issues which require arbitrations exceeding the prerogatives of a sole project manager. The practice establishes the following:

- Type One outsourcings require only project management at the execution level. The engineer who manages the project also executes the work, supervising or not a small group of engineers or technicians.
- Type Two outsourcings require a two-level structure: project management and project execution. A project management layer is added to Type One.
- Type Three outsourcings require a three-level structure: project steering, project management and project execution. A project steering layer is added to Type Two.
- Types Four and Five outsourcings require ad hoc structures. Additional project management or execution layers are added to Type Three to absorb the complexity and/or the volumes.

Figure 41 illustrates a possible structure for a Type Five outsourcing including all service layers, takeover of personnel and operations of legacy systems during the project. The structure functions as follows, in decreasing order of decision power:

*Level One: Arbitrage* Characterised by a steering committee presided over by one of the parties, normally the provider. This committee is made up of executives from both sides, including project managers. Its role is to make strategic, project-related decisions as well as to approve significant changes to the project scope, costs and deadlines. Each party has equal voting rights.

*Levels Two and Three: Management* Characterised by a project committee presided over by the provider. This committee comprises the project managers on both sides

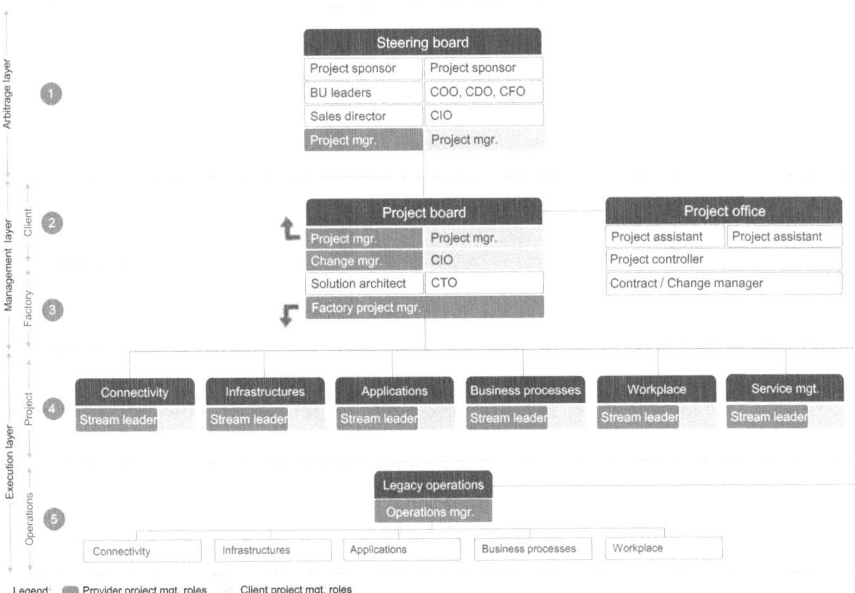

**Fig. 41** Example of five-level governance structure

who ensure that all operational and technical activities comply with the project's mission. A solution architect supports the project board. Two project managers represent the provider: one who faces the client and the other faces the factory. The former handles the relational complexity and manages the stakeholders, the latter handles the technological complexity and organises the delivery of the services.

*Level Four: Execution* Characterised by the streams (working groups organised by subject area) and composed of technical personnel from all the parties. The role of these working groups is to execute the project tasks. Each stream is led by an engineer or a project manager who has extensive knowledge of the area in question. Each stream manager reports to the factory project manager.

*Level Five: Legacy operations* Represents the existing IT structure of the client, reinforced, as the case may be, with resources from the provider. The team is led by an operations manager from the provider. This construct is needed when the client wants or needs to delegate its operation during the transformation. In such a case, the operation of legacy systems and the transformation towards the target systems run in two separate streams, each led by a separate manager. To make sure changes requested by the client during the project and performed on legacy environments are executed by considering the impacts on the systems being transformed, the operations manager is subordinated to the project committee.

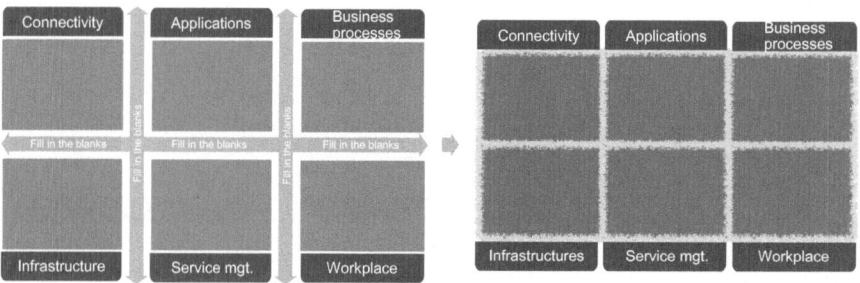

**Fig. 42** Clear versus broad roles definition

The grey boxes in Fig. 41 represent project management or project management-related roles. Not surprisingly, the more complex the project, the higher the cost of the project management. On average, count with 10% for Type One projects, 15% for Type Two, 20% for Type Three and up to 30% for Types Four and Five. At this point, the project usually reaches its absorptive capacity,[9] i.e. the capacity to assimilate information and efficiently apply it to the sought ends. Should the project need to absorb more complexity, the parties would be well advised to think of structuring the project into a programme with several independent yet interrelated projects. It might not be always possible, however, because of the multiple dependencies between each stream.

## Define Roles

Contrary to popular belief, clear role definition is not optimal. If roles are too clearly defined, each person looks after their set of activities in their domain and it is up to the project manager to "fill in the blanks" between the domains as represented in Fig. 42. For example, the security specialist correctly installs a security system but does not open the communication ports needed for a given application. The result is that the security system works, but the application does not communicate. When roles are more broadly defined, each person feels compelled to constantly search for the appropriate boundary that applies to their given activity. This does not solve all problems, but it transforms wide white spaces into smaller grey zones.

The main characteristics of the roles composing the Type Five outsourcing illustrated in Fig. 41 are, from the top to the bottom of the structure, as follows:

*Project sponsor and other executives*  Each party shall appoint a senior executive to take responsibility and accountability for the project. On the provider side, the executive who bears the biggest proportion of services comes as the natural choice. On the client side, the issue is more delicate. The executive who has the biggest

---

[9]The higher the need for coordination, the higher the need for communications, and the higher the number of communication channels, the lesser the efficiency of the overall communication structure.

stake, e.g. the COO in organisations with a solid IT tradition, is the most appropriate. When no such position exists, the client needs to nominate the executive who is the closest from the subject or, better still, an executive who is interested and willing to act as sponsor. There is nothing worse than a sponsor who does not attend the steering committees on the base of allegedly priority commitments.

*Project manager* Each party shall appoint a project manager to orchestrate the execution of the project and ensure a smooth interaction between the teams on each side. Finding the person with the right combination of hard and soft skills is no easy task. Project managers are not industry-independent: in addition to being experienced in project management as such, the person needs to be highly knowledgeable in the various matters of the contemplated outsourcing. As illustrated in Fig. 42, they act as the glue between the different domains and are solely responsible for aggregating all the bits and pieces into a consistent whole. The corollary of such an underlying complexity is having to manage high-flying personnel. Some of the senior individuals embarked in the adventure may have a very clear idea of how things should be done, while more junior ones may have a strong wish to show they can handle their task by themselves. Both represent a risk for the cohesion of the project, especially bearing in mind that the project manager is not a line manager and has no hierarchical power. On the flipside, other individuals may feel more comfortable in the back seat. They will do the job, but upon clear instructions only. They represent another kind of risk for the project. Handling this diversity requires a person with a great deal of social awareness and influential power. This is at least in theory, because in practice it is nearly impossible to find a person who concentrates such a wide range of skills to their full extent. The choice of the project manager shall then be carried out by considering the most predominant factor in the given context: technical, social, political, etc. If the project is challenging in multiple aspects, it may be wise considering a duo, as represented in Fig. 41: upwards, one project manager manages the stakeholders, and downwards, another manages the factory.

*Stream leaders* The structure of the streams derives from the services taken over which derive, in turn, from the structure of the provider. Indeed, as explained in section "Get the Big Picture" in Chap. 2, the essential characteristic of an outsourcer is its capacity to allocate the needed specialists in quality and quantity horizontally in each service layer. By grouping together, in a single stream, the experts, the processes and the tools belonging to a given service, the provider can ramp up large numbers of identical items in a short period of time. Reaching this efficiency calls for a timely coordination within the stream itself—many different experts executing many different actions in sequences—as well as with the other streams—each sequence triggering the start of other sequences in subsequent layers. Example of sequence: the connectivity team prepares a secured network zone in the data centre, the infrastructures team provisions the servers in this zone, the applications team installs the business applications on the servers, the connectivity teams opens the communication channels for the applications to communicate, the infrastructures teams migrates base data, the applications team starts parameterisation.

This example shows that all streams run in parallel but do not follow an even workload over time. Mobilising in time the needed resources in a stream requires the stream leader to be aware at all times of the upstream and downstream dependencies and needs to be one step ahead in the coming sequence. Missing an internal deadline may force them to temporarily release planned resources, which could have cascaded consequences. Stream leaders are true project managers who sometimes need to deal with matters that are even more complex than the project itself.

## Select Staff

Once the roles have been defined, they need to be filled. Since an outsourcing project is a long adventure with a complex environment to digest, it is worth spending time so that the right person is on board right from the beginning and thus not having to replace them halfway down the line—which may anyway happen, complex projects usually burning at least one project manager. If the opportunities to choose, on the client's side, between various individuals for a given role are very limited, if not non-existent, there may be many more options on the provider's side. So much the better because each project comes with its own context, and it is the latter that should guide the selection. Key elements of the selection include:

*Acquaintance* When staffing the team, experienced project managers search their network and solicit the persons they would like to work with directly instead of asking line managers to provide resources. Fair enough. When under pressure, people are more efficient if they know what they can expect from the people they are working with.

*Personality* Leaders shall be like a beacon for their team and this applies to all levels of the governance structure. Real leaders show the way. They manage to create trust just thanks to who and how they are. And trust is of major importance when enrolling into a long-term trip. In stormy times, team members who do not feel unfailingly supported by their manager start acting inappropriately.

*Resilience* If the project is to meet strict deadlines because of business constraints and is already late on schedule, it is likely that the last months will be very difficult. Late hours, busy weekends, frozen vacations, etc., will place a considerable strain on people. If the project is postponed, the situation may last for a very long time. The weakest members may run into serious health problems and be forced to stop working, possibly at a very critical stage. To avoid any such situations, the parties need to fill critical positions with persons who can cope with a high level of stress.

*Flexibility* Or inflexibility, according to the context. When both the source and the target information systems are mastered and the success of the project largely depends on the strict application of proven recipes, rigorous persons are well suited. However, when things are unclear, the project needs people who can cope with uncertainty and take decisions accordingly. This sounds trivial, but it is not. People who think rationally do not know what to do with the unknown parameters in an equation. In such cases, one cannot expect them to find the solution on their own as well as take responsibility for it. This is upper management's duty. Here again, appointing the leader fitting the context is key.

*Experience* Appointing experienced people is not as obvious as it seems. On one side, experienced people may be very sought-after and not available. On the other, younger people may be very eager to learn and motivated. Even in a critical project, some positions tolerate a certain level of discovery. In virtue of the preceding topic regarding flexibility, the right attitude sometimes has more worth than the right skills.

*Culture and language* Multicultural/multilingual teams may be enjoyable and efficient, but they could be risky for a trial run.

## Dos and Don'ts

Figure out requirements
- At the time of negotiating the contract, the provider should communicate to the client their estimates in terms of skills and number of persons required on the client side for the execution and the coordination of the project. This will probably be not sufficient to actually have these persons appointed, but at least the client will have been informed.

Set governance structure
- Limit the number of streams to the minimum. This concentrates the responsibilities on fewer persons, which mechanically increases the awareness per person. This allows to keep technical matters at the streams level as much as possible, in reference to the concept illustrated in Fig. 42.

Define roles
- At the streams level, align roles on both sides according to the technical knowledge of the persons. At the steering level, align roles of executives according to their capacity to influence or decide.
- Empower people thanks to an imperfect role description and a certain degree of flexibility.

Select staff
- Carefully consider egos, especially on the client side. At the steering level, beware of selecting persons on both sides who hold a similar rank in their own organisation. Failing to consider egos properly may lead executives to not join the board.
- Select staff according to the context. Technical versus Social orientation, Innovation versus Conservatism, etc.: no two projects are the same.

## Plan the Project

Attention which each party should pay to this topic: Client: ●○○ Provider: ●●●

## Objective

Set the baseline to guide project execution.

This section focuses on the conceptual phase of the project. It describes how to figure out, structure and organise the work products to be delivered.

## Description

Planning the project aims at formalising the common understanding of the parties about the ins and outs of the project. It tackles the following key questions:

- What exactly is the project to deliver with respect to the services/products (content) and deliverables (outcome)?
- When is the project going to happen? Which milestones conclude which phases, and, finally, what is the overall duration?
- How is the project going to be executed with respect to the transformation of the systems and to the shift from present to future mode of operation?

## Process Overview

Figure 43 positions the planning phase within the whole project life. On average, it accounts for 20% of the total project duration. It depends, of course, on the delta between the source and target environments. In a complex business transformation such as a major change in the core application, the preliminary analysis may take a year or more and last longer than the project itself.

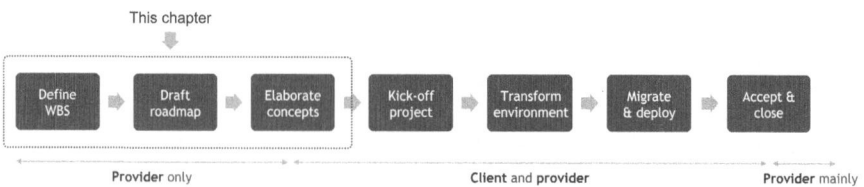

**Fig. 43** Plan project process

## Define WBS

The work breakdown structure (WBS) is a decomposition of the project into small, manageable pieces that can be attributed to identified individuals who shoulder the responsibility. It constitutes the backbone of the project schedule and serves for the elaboration of the road map.

## Draft Road map

The road map is the high-level project schedule. It positions the work elements on the timescale of the project and groups them into phases concluded by milestones.

## Elaborate Concepts

Concepts are of two kinds: solution type and project type. The former aims at defining the exact shape of the target information system and the latter the way to go.

## Practical Implementation

## Define WBS

*What* The WBS is a breakdown of the project into smaller elements named work packages. It stands as a hierarchical decomposition of the work in layers where, in an outsourcing project, Layer One represents the project itself, Layer Two the streams, Layer Three the work packages and Layer Four the detailed activities. Figure 44 illustrates this concept.

*Why* The principle is to divide the work into manageable pieces to better control it. The resulting work packages are attributed to the prospective stream leaders who shoulder the responsibility for all dimensions, including scope, time and costs. The latter element is critical given the high degree of function segregation in each service layer and the risk of cost overrun increasing with the number of specialists booking hours on work packages.

*Who* Under the general guidance of the project manager, it is the stream leaders, supported by a limited number of subject matter experts (SME), who define the work packages. The sales team provides explanation of all the peculiarities that do not clearly emerge from the contract.

*How* A solid WBS is carried out in two steps: top-down then bottom-up. Top-down: the project manager performs an initial subdivision of the project in streams and the stream leaders divide their respective streams into work packages. This leads to a clear hierarchical structure, but leaves on the side elements which do not naturally fit in the structure. Bottom-up: the team brainstorms about all the big and smaller elements that would normally be required for such a type of project. If the new elements can form stand-alone work packages, they are inserted at the right place

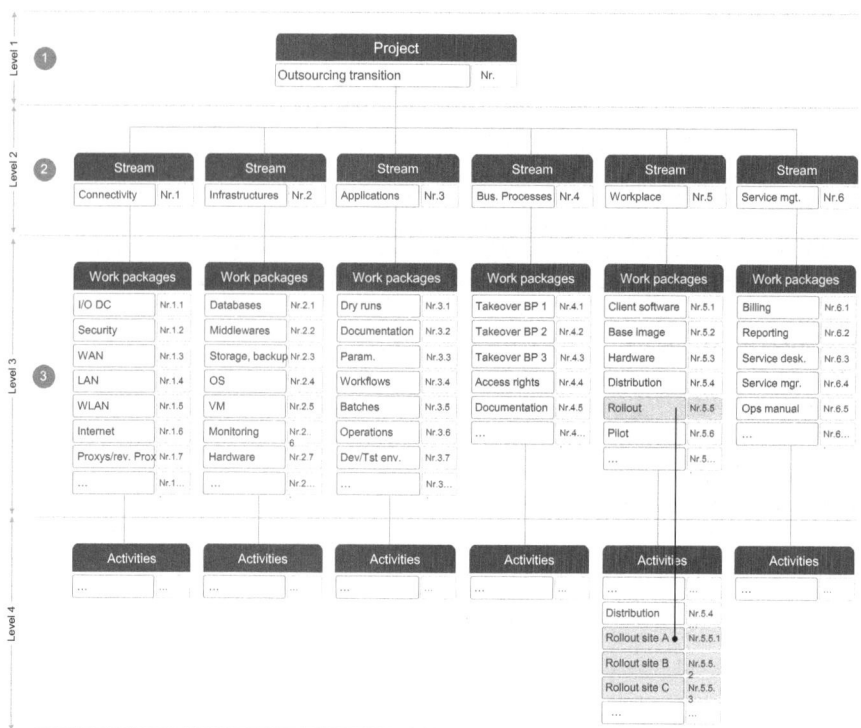

**Fig. 44** Example of work breakdown structure

into the structure and the structure is adjusted to accommodate them. If the new elements only represent activities, either these deserve their own place in Layer Four as constituents of work packages or they are left out. The WBS is meant to represent the scope of the project, not the thousands of activities that will need to be executed.

*How much*   Given the complexity of an outsourcing, one may expect ending up with thousands of work packages. It is not the case. Like Russian dolls, work packages are in fact aggregates of more basic work packages, delivered as black boxes by the provider's factory. For example, a work package that aims at provisioning a server is constituted by several sub-work packages including provisioning the hardware, installing the operating system, configuring the connectivity and activating the monitoring agent. When sub-work packages are delivered by distinct teams, they are usually coordinated by internal systems and processes that are coded to handle confluent work orders and guarantee an SLA at the work package level. This brings us back to section "Get the Big Picture" in Chap. 2 and the importance of processes in an industrialised organisation. The practice establishes that work packages should not be smaller than a week and not bigger than twice the duration of the project's reporting period. This is to limit the administrative overhead for reporting on one side while being able to keep a close eye on the advancement on the other. With respect to the number of levels in the hierarchy, three is optimal, unless some work packages need a closer attention because of complexity, dependency, risks or repetitive actions. For example, in Fig. 44, work package 5.5 concerns the rollout of new computers for a multi-site corporation and is subdivided into as many distinct locations: 5.5.1 for Site A, 5.5.2 for Site B, 5.5.3 for Site C, etc.

## Draft the Road map

*What*  The road map is the layout in time of the work packages and their organisation in phases marked with milestones.

*Why*  Firstly, to determine the project total duration, because the longer it lasts the more it costs. Secondly, to determine the phases and milestones, the end of a phase releasing the corresponding payment and triggering the start of the next phase. Finally, to determine the chaining between work packages to know when to involve the different teams. Unlike development projects, where the teams are allocated for a significant part of the project, outsourcing projects strongly rely on the timely involvement of a large number of people, most of whom are only called upon sporadically to contribute. Time management in outsourcing is key.

*Who*  Under the general guidance of the project manager, it is the same stream leaders who defined the work packages who also contribute to the layout of the road map. The difficult situations they obviously suffered in previous projects make them well suited for establishing a realistic schedule. The sales team fosters the discussion with its assessment of the client and its capacity to follow the pace.

*How*  Instantiating a road map that integrates the lessons learned of previous similar outsourcing is the starting point. On this base, stream leaders organise their work packages and determine the red path. They discuss the internal and external dependencies, where internal relates to upstream and downstream activities surrounding each work package and external relates to all factors on the client side that could jeopardise the schedule. And these are many: outdated documentation, lack of governance, absence of users for testing, unclear instructions, missing source code, shadow IT, etc. Whatever the capacity of the provider has to deliver, they are always conditioned by the capacity of the client to receive. Once ordered, the work packages are grouped into phases.

*How much*  On average, an outsourcing without business transformation lasts from 6 to 16 months and, with business transformation, up to 24 months. The longer the project, the less financially efficient. Indeed, clients almost never reduce their level of CtB on the existing environment during the transformation, with the consequence that the project inflates correspondingly and suffers an increasing volume of adjustments and rework.

## Elaborate Concepts

*Solution-type*  Defining the target starts with a sound assessment of the source. It is the duty of the client to describe as precisely as possible its current environment, with the support of an external firm if needed. If it is unable to do so, it will be up to the provider to (re)build this knowledge against appropriate remuneration. This can take on various forms from provider's templates to be filled by the client, up to a complete reverse engineering performed by the provider. Whichever party executes the work, the minimal outcome should be a systems landscape with a focus on the relations between the systems for a lift and shift outsourcing and detailed systems parametrisation on top for a business transformation. In parallel to the assessment of the existing environment, the provider starts designing the target architecture. This results in technical blueprints that include systems layout, sizing, configurations, interfaces, security and process flows, to name but a few. When both the source and the target are known, the parties compare them and identify so-called gaps. Gaps are missing functionalities that need to be developed. The development may take on the form of an integration and configuration of off-the-shelf products or real software development. The risk increases with the number of gaps. The riskiest gaps are those involving software development because of the instability they engender in the solution and the delays they cause to the project. Another important risk to mention pertains to the DB and AO layers which stand at the border between systems and applications. In addition to ensuring up-and-running applications, AO encompasses the middleware systems, processes and business logic that allow the applications to exchange data in an orderly and timely manner. Depending on the complexity of the information system, it can range from a simple file exchange between two applications to the processing of thousands of batches between dozens of applications. Although AO belongs to the application category, it heavily relies on infrastructures. Sometimes, the exchange logic is even entirely built on the batch scheduling capacity offered by the operating systems. Whatever the scope of the outsourcing, these two layers shall always receive a special focus (Fig. 45).

*Project-type concepts*  The goal is to lay down a transition plan that minimises business impacts and segments the project into phases to avoid the tunnel effect. Transition is defined as the changeover from one equilibrium regime to another, where regime stands as the combination of operating model and information system. The set-up of the target operating model is described in section "Enforce Operational Governance" in Chap. 4. With respect to the systems, there are three main challenges:

1. Building the target information system.
2. Migrating the data.
3. Switching over from the existing systems to the new ones.

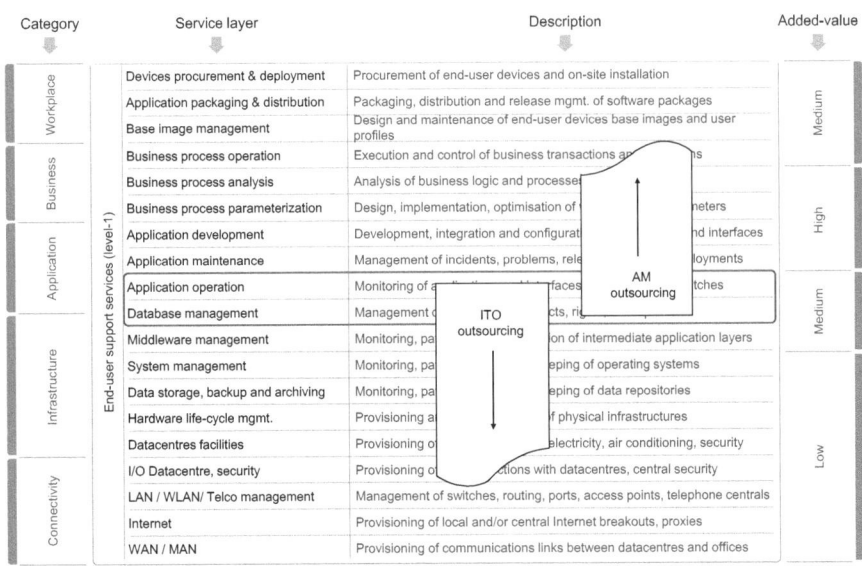

**Fig. 45** DB+AO as critical layer between ITO and AM

1. While moving or rebuilding one single system already raises a lot of considerations, moving or rebuilding an entire information system brings the problem to another dimension. It is like assembling a car from spare parts and requires extensive integration testing.

2. Extract, Transform, Load (ETL) is the underlying principle on which any data migration is based. Migrating data from system A at the client site to the same system A at the provider site is no big deal: the client extracts the data and the provider uploads it. Migrating data from system A to system A', where A' is a more recent version of A, requires a little more attention as the data structure may have evolved and could need adjustment. In this case, the parties need to ensure that no transformation is required. Migrating from system A to system B requires maximum attention because it certainly involves a data transformation. Depending on the volumes, the necessity to re-index documents and the obligation to guarantee that the content will not be altered during the transformation for audit purposes could become a project in itself.

3. If the number of systems is limited, e.g. a maximum of 20, the cutover can probably be executed as a big bang. In larger environments, the ramp-up will need to happen gradually, in lots.[10] In that case, it may run over a period of several weeks or months. During this time, old and new systems need to cohabit, possibly leading users to enter business transactions into the two environments. Cutover strategies depend on the given application and technological landscapes. Detailed strategies go beyond the scope of this book.

---

[10]Groups of applications that should not be dissociated because of their close interrelations.

## Dos and Don'ts

WBS
- Respect the "100% rule" that establishes that the WBS shall capture all work elements required to deliver the project. This applies at each level of the hierarchy, e.g. the sum of the work packages in a stream must equal 100% of the work to be delivered by the stream, and to all parties involved in the project. This is undoubtedly the most critical element given the myriad of third parties, e.g. client, provider, outgoing provider, software vendors, etc., that will contribute to the project. The client must ensure that the WBS elaborated by the provider encompasses external activities.
- Limit the level of detail to what the human brain can absorb without losing the context. A WBS which spans over several pages is not appropriate and must be simplified. Remember that it should not be an exhaustive list of actions.
- Use the coding scheme of the provider organisation. The WBS represents work elements which rely on established organisational/procedural structures to be delivered. Going away from the structure may trouble the allocation of work orders and subsequently their tracking and billing.

Road map
- Develop a critical path that contains as less dependencies as possible with the client organisation. For example, if user testing is on the critical path without any float, the project has every chance to drift.
- Beware of specific time constraints on the client side such as month/quarter/year ends, budget season, etc. All activities may be periodically or seasonally frozen.
- Be particularly aware of summer vacation. Even though they last two weeks on average for a given individual, validations or signatures usually require at least two persons. It is safe to consider that during summer, nothing important should/can/will happen.
- These recommendations lead to consider involving the client in the concepts and to force it expressing its constraints.

# Building Phase: The Project

**4**

**Abstract**

In this chapter, you will learn how to actually perform the required transition and/or transformation, how systems are operated during the project and what contractual regime applies to them, how to create a positive human dynamic around the transformation, how to address the people dimension with professionalism and humanity in case of personnel transfer, how to set up the operational governance given the complexity of the outsourcing and, finally, how to switch over from the transition to the future mode of operation.

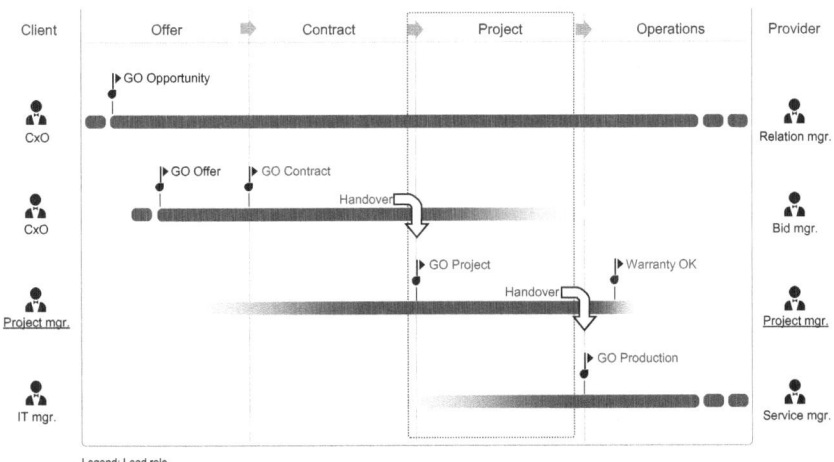

**Fig. 46** Building phase in the outsourcing life-cycle

## Execute Project

Attention which each party should pay to this topic: Client: ●●● Provider: ●●●

## Objective

Perform the required transition and/or transformation.

This section recalls the project management disciplines involved in controlling the execution of any project and explains how they apply in the context of an outsourcing. It is not intended as a project management guide.

## Description

A project is a unique endeavour with a beginning and an end. One may ask what is so unique about outsourcing projects where the target environment is mastered by the provider which already reproduced it dozens of times during previous projects. Knowing that at least half of outsourcing projects run over budget and schedule, the question is worth consideration.

Whereas any project involves the construction of a target environment, outsourcing adds another dimension: the transformation of the source.

- The source, represented by the client's environment, represented in turn by the client's information system and operating model, is altered in many ways and to varying degrees according to its own complexity and to the magnitude of the contemplated change. In addition, as if the complexity was not enough, the source continues to evolve during the transformation because the client does not stop doing business.
- The target, represented by a new, extended environment, is a direct function of the complexity of the source. And since the source is a living whole, it triggers as many on-going changes to the target with the consequences increasing as the project proceeds. Indeed, whereas at the beginning a change usually has a 1:1 impact ratio (one change in the source triggers one change in the target), nearing the end each change has a 1:$N$ impact (one change in the source forces to consider cascaded effects in the target because of the interrelations between systems)—hence the reason the progression rate slows down as the project reaches the end.

An outsourcing transformation being similar to operating a walking patient, it requires top-notch skills in all project management disciplines in addition to a healthy dose of adaptability.

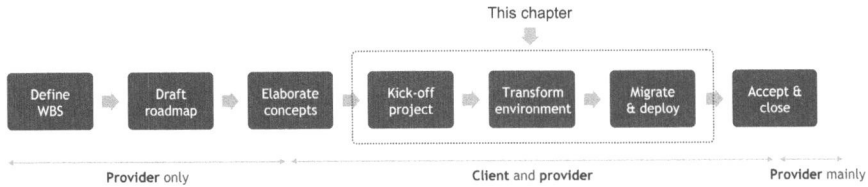

**Fig. 47** Execute project process

## Positioning

Figure 47 positions the execution phase within the whole project life.

The execution of the project starts with the kick-off where the parties' teams officially meet and align on the terms and conditions of the delivery.

Then follows the transformation, encompassing the construction of the target environment and the corresponding modification of the source environment.

Once the new environment has passed the user acceptance tests, it is ready for deployment. Data has been migrated and a pilot deployment has been performed on a limited population of users, e.g. a department or a subsidiary is organised. The pilot enables malfunctions which can only be detected in a live environment to be removed.

The end of the pilots triggers the mass rollout. It is at this moment that the target environment becomes productive for all users. The project can start the formal acceptance and handover processes described in section "Handover to Operations".

## Practical Implementation

The section shows how to apply the key project management disciplines to an outsourcing transformation.

### Scope Management

Figure 48 illustrates the building blocks that helped to precisely define the scope of the project at the time the contract was written up and on which the project managers will have to keep a close eye on during the delivery. These are:

- The services to be delivered by the provider, including its subcontractors.
- The obligations and services to be delivered by the client, including third parties, e.g. the outgoing provider and software vendors.
- The limit of the services, which, by default, is everything that is not expressly stated in the contract (although it would be risky to solely rely on such a statement). Here the parties need to identify all borderline topics which could reasonably be interpreted as being part of the project.
- The assumptions on which the project is based, e.g. metrics communicated by the client used for the design of the solution.

**Fig. 48**  Scope definition and management

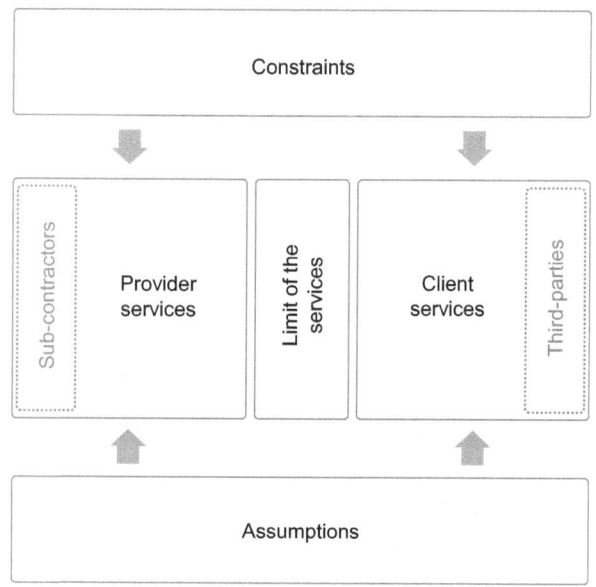

- The constraints applying on the project, e.g. users' availability, frozen zones and legal constraints.

## Requirements Management

It is the process of documenting, analysing, tracking, prioritising and agreeing on requirements, where requirements are defined as the functional and/or technical needs of the client. Figure 49 positions the requirements as a base constituent of the scope. To explain in simple words the difference between scope and requirements, let us say that scope is the container and the requirements are the content.

---

**Example**

Scope: The client asks the provider to develop an e-payment module to integrate in its website.

Requirements: The module shall be constituted of five different screens representing the five steps from the client identification to the payment confirmation. Screen One shall encompass features $a$, $b$, $c$; Screen Two features $x$, $y$, $z$, etc. The module shall interact with the website based on technology X.

---

The need for requirements management is limited in lift and shift projects where the bulk of the work consists in moving/rebuilding the information system on the provider stack of services without changes extending beyond the configuration of the variants and options proposed by the target services. In such cases, the standard

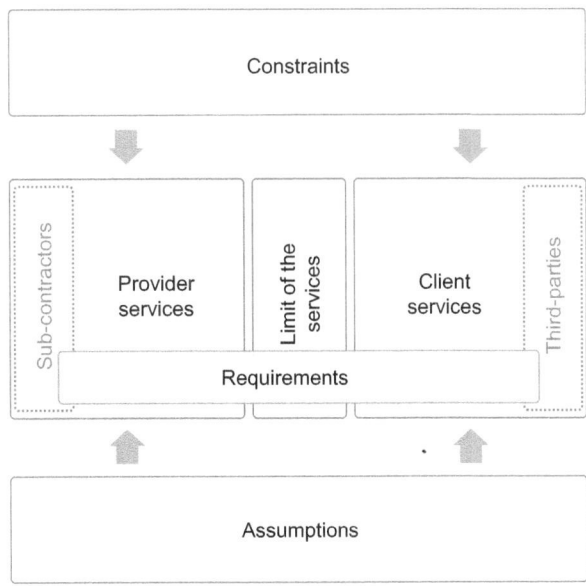

**Fig. 49** Requirements definition and management

change management procedure is sufficient to track configuration changes which could substantially affect the project.

In transformation projects which affect the technical or the application layers more deeply, e.g. rewriting a mainframe-based suite of applications with a modern development language or implementing an enterprise resource planning (ERP) involving a complete re-engineering of the client's processes, the story is different. For changes in transactions, batches, performance, parameters, decision trees, workflows, gaps, etc., requirements must be captured in a dedicated system for the entire project life cycle, from the initial costing down to the further identification of changes and the final user acceptance. Failing to adequately maintain requirement changes may have dramatic consequences going from preventing completely the parties from running the acceptance process, with all the consequences this could have. The complexity of the system to track requirements depends on the complexity and on the volume of requirements. It ranges from a simple text document to a real application.

## Schedule Management

Somewhat surprising is the almost generalised absence of professional scheduling tools in outsourcing companies or, in other words, the absence of institutionalised, corporate-wide scheduling tools. Even more surprisingly, the level of detail in the schedules appears inversely proportional to the complexity of the projects: the more complex the project, the broader the schedule.

There is one major reason for this: the level of decomposition and automation of the work in an outsourcing company is such that it renders as impossible as useless the tracking of all individual activities. Bear in mind that the activities (fourth layer of the WBS) in each work package are executed by service units through semi-automated work orders. The persons executing the orders work in production areas and report in their own systems, not in any project scheduling tool. Consolidating the information at stream level and then at project level in a Gantt chart would represent a massive overhead.

Schedule management within the provider organisation is already a challenge, but nothing compared to the difficulty in remaining on time when the delivery bears dependencies with the client organisation. Maintaining close, constant and personal contacts between both project managers is mandatory.

## Financial Management

Here again, the large number of persons and activities involved complicates the already difficult task of financial controlling. People execute several activities per day but do not report their time continuously. The most conscientious ones report it every day, but the less diligent ones do it solely on a monthly basis, rendering the internal booking approximate. Just like an accordion where the sum of the small moves of the bellows creates a large shift in the end, the accumulation of suboptimal if not erroneous booking entries distort the reality. However, this distortion tends to compensate between different work packages within a same project and, at a higher level, between the different projects within the company. It is also limited by the fact that some activities are billed internally at a fixed rate. This does normally not affect the client, however, as outsourcing projects are usually billed at a fixed price.

## Resource Management

In outsourcing, resources management has a lot to do with anticipation and networking. Anticipation refers to ensuring that the right persons will be available exactly when needed to execute the next sequence of activities. This is a challenge even in an industrialised organisation because processes are limited by the capacity of the organisation to absorb the work. Networking refers to activating those colleagues who proved in past projects to be reliable and keep promises. We all know that personally asking someone to execute an order has much more impact than placing the order in a system and waiting for the result. The order shall still be placed in the system, but it has a better chance of getting a different priority.

The IT industry has not reached (and will probably never do given the profound changes continuously affecting it) the level of automation of other industries like that of car manufacturing. While activities are increasingly automated, the assembly of a complex information system still heavily relies on humans.

## Stakeholders Management

When talking about project stakeholders, one immediately thinks of high-ranked individuals with power or influence who could jeopardise the project if not satisfied. These exist, but they are not the only type. A stakeholder is any person who is concerned by the project in one way or another to varying degrees of interest and influence. Figure 50 divides them into four categories:

**Fig. 50** Communication
needs per stakeholder type

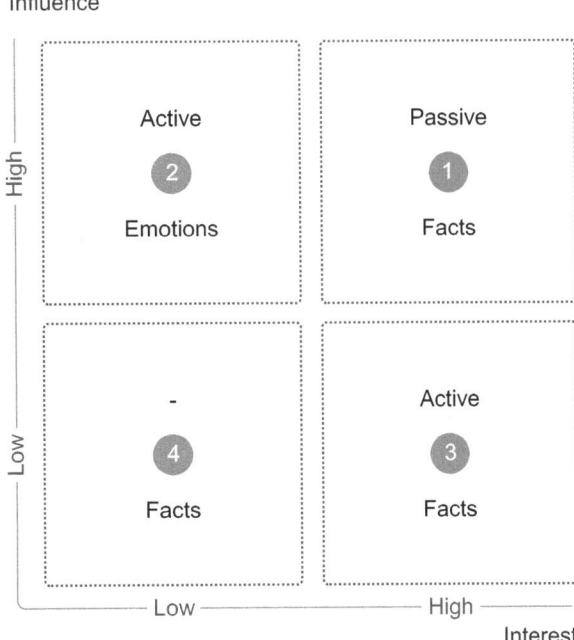

- Category One with high influence and high interest: They are already fully committed and just need to be kept well informed with facts through passive communication, e.g. status reports.
- Category Two with high influence but low interest: They could help the project by becoming evangelisers but would need to be emotionally involved for this, e.g. workshops.
- Category Three with high interest but low influence: They could also help the project, but to a lesser extent, e.g. by creating a positive noise in the organisation. They need to be kept informed.
- Category Four with low interest and low influence: Taken individually, their impact is negligible. However, the latter—either positive or negative—increases with the number.

Project managers on both sides shall ensure that stakeholders of Category One are always satisfied to limit the risks, capitalise on stakeholders of Categories Two and Three to turn them into active sponsors and keep a distant eye on stakeholders of Category Four.

Section "Accompany Organisational Changes" explains how to turn down opponents and transform stakeholders into real project evangelists.

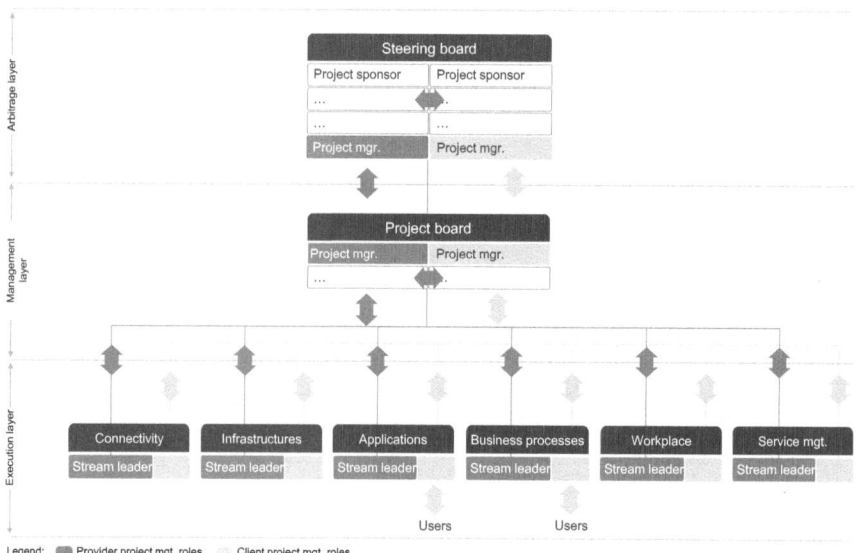

**Fig. 51** Communication structures based on three-layer governance

## Communication Management

Once the appropriate structures are in place, properly handling communication is almost a routine activity. Considering a three-layer governance, as the one outlined on Fig. 51, a reasonable yet efficient communication scheme is:

- Arbitrage level: monthly steering meeting between the selected executives on both sides, including a written steering preparation report and concluding steering minutes.
- Management level: weekly meeting between the two project managers, including a written status report to a wider audience.
- Execution level: weekly meeting between the provider project manager and the stream leaders to report on work package advancement and verbally exchange; if the client has set up a team on its side, it is well advised to do so also.

## Project Change Management

The parties need to enforce a change control process to keep track of changes occurring during the project. A solid change control process shall describe how changes are:

- Initiated, analysed and processed.
- Accepted or rejected.
- Tracked in a log with a unique identifier.

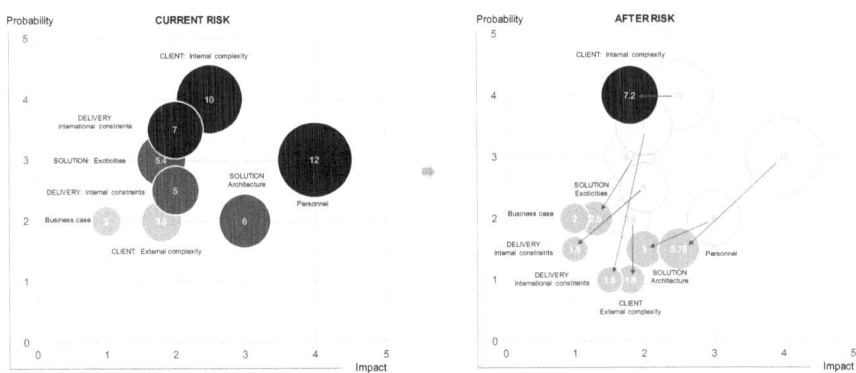

**Fig. 52** Example of risk assessment and mitigation

The aim is to be able to reflect all the changes consistently in the contract at the end of the project.

Changes should take the form of simple one- to two-page documents with mandatory fields such as, for the requesting party, the requestor, description, reason, timing, supporting documents, decisions and signatures and, for the provider, the proposed solution, impacts scope, time, costs, risks, consequences if not executed, decisions and signatures.

## Risk Management

In theory, risk management is a constant process that applies throughout the whole project. In fact, it is an activity that is often performed at the beginning of the project and that gives rise to special provisions which are incorporated in the plans, but that are not actively monitored anymore afterwards. This is suboptimal, but at least risks have been identified and addressed.

One method to assess risks is to combine the probability of occurrence and the impact in case of occurrence. For a situation identified as at risk, rate the probability of occurrence on a scale from 1 to 4 and the impact in case of occurrence on a scale from 1 to 4 as well, then multiply the two factors to get the importance of the risk, i.e. the theoretical level of attention it requires. On Fig. 52, the importance is represented by the size of the bubbles.

When this is done, address the most important risks by either reducing the probability or limiting the impact, or both. Then do the maths again and plot the resulting risks by order of importance on a second graphic. Figure 52 shows the before and after situation with black risks as the most important.

## Dos and Don'ts

Scope
- Set the scope, and especially its limits, in an unquestionable and non-misleading way. What is obvious for one party may not be for the other. Go through the scope line by line when discussing the contact and figure out what the service really encompasses. In case of possible misunderstanding, describe the activity in one of the corresponding sections: scope, limitations of the scope, client obligations.

Requirements
- Identify, evaluate and track the evolution of requirements with utmost precision. The lack of formalism may have dramatic consequences on costs or, worse, on the acceptance process. If important deviances are not documented, the target information system may become at odds with the contract.

Schedule
- Due to the dependencies on so many persons—most of whom are not directly involved in the project—project managers should always be one-step ahead, ensuring the availability of the next required resources.

Financial
- Project managers should request internal personnel booking hours to report daily and team leaders to control them weekly.

Quality
- Have quality checks run by persons outside the project at least at the end of each phase. The checks should focus on the respect of the processes and ensure that the project actually follows the contract. Important deviances between how the project was thought and how it is executed are common. While the contract is a complex arrangement of conditions constraining the scope/budget/time triangle, the operational reality leads the team to concentrate their efforts on the scope and time dimensions only, without paying any more attention to the conditions.

Resources
- Keep an eye on how people cope with stress. When embarked on corporate-wide adventures, they try their best to meet the expectations, but when the resistance of the organisation becomes too strong, they burn out. Only a close, personal contact can help detect symptoms. Small social events like a weekly after-work drink are important to release the pressure.

Communication
- To provide for communication speed and avoid the accordion effect where every non-response generates a cascade of consequences, the contract shall foresee specific communication-decision mechanisms. For example, if the provider

does not receive an answer from the client to a request within a given time frame, it is entitled to decide or act while informing the client in parallel.

Changes
• Project managers on both sides should literally chase changes and get them formally approved or rejected. Experience shows that verbally approved changes can raise unfair discussions at the end of the project.

## Operate Systems During the Project

Attention which each party should pay to this topic: Client: ●○○ Provider: ●●●

## Objective

Keep an operational eye on the systems during the project.

This chapter explains how to keep services under development in a reasonable state of operationality and progressively put them into production.

## Description

When the outsourcing requires an initial transformation, in most cases, the contract distinguishes two phases: the project, where the services are under construction, and the operations, where they are used productively.

The switch from project to operations aka business as usual (BaU) follows the special process called handover to operations illustrated by Fig. 53 and further described in the chapter of the same name.

This instantaneous switch between project and operations works for simple transformations and when the duration is limited to a few months only, but it does not work for complex transformations lasting for a year or more, because it is simply impossible changing the state of potentially dozens of new services from not supported to fully operational overnight. Such handovers take months. This time constraint, illustrated in Fig. 54, asks the following questions: in which state of operationality are the systems during the ramp-up phase and what contractual regime applies to them?

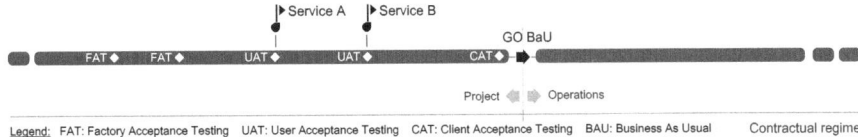

**Fig. 53** Handover to operations basic principle

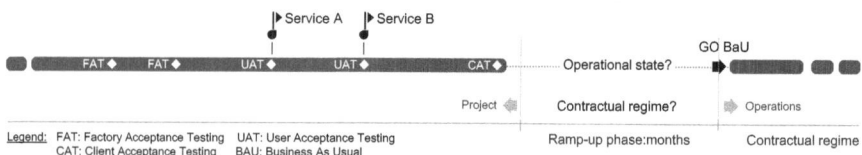

**Fig. 54** Handover to operations time constraint

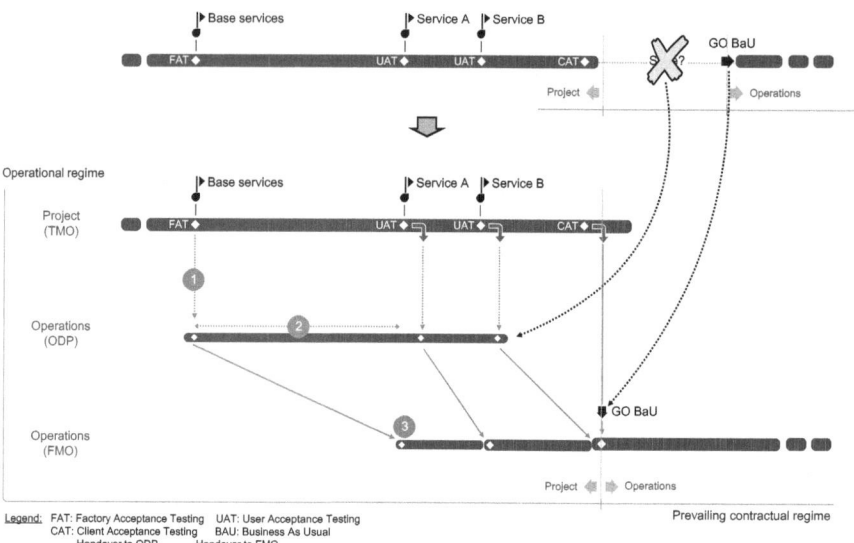

**Fig. 55** Operations during project principle

The answer to these questions lies behind the introduction of an intermediary regime between project and operations: operations during project (ODP).

## Process

To gradually ramp up services to their operational state and ensure they are covered by an appropriate contractual regime during that period, ODP applies in parallel with the project as represented by Fig. 55.

The principle is to have services under construction (1) operated by the target operation teams under a light contractual regime (2) until the moment the target operations' regime enters into force (3).

This allows the project and operation teams to stabilise the services and prepare themselves progressively for target conditions, including guarantees, processes and reporting. As shown in Fig. 55, critical services or services bearing critical dependencies with other services—whether under development or already productive—need to enter the target operating regime [future mode of operation (FMO)] before the end of the project.

## Triggers

It is the provider that decides when to transfer services from the transition mode of operation (TMO) to operations during project (ODP) and then from ODP to FMO, although in the latter case they normally invite the client to agree with the consequences. This section lists the main factors triggering the need to transfer services to ODP or FMO; the section "Practical Implementation" addresses the consequences.

*Complexity* Upper layers of the service stack need lower layers to work, e.g. applications need infrastructures that need data centres. The more the accumulation of layers in a project, the more complex the transformation and the longer the time span from installing base infrastructure components to deploying business applications. This means that a year or more can elapse between the moment servers are installed and the moment applications are ready for production. During this year, a lot will happen: hardware and software vendors will issue patches to correct defects of their systems, new security threats will come out, client parameters will change, etc., and although the systems installed will not yet be productive, they cannot get stuck in time on suboptimal configurations. The provider would have to catch up on the accumulated arrears anyway at the latest before going live. In addition to the risk incurred during the project, this would impose a massive global retesting at the end.

*Continuity* As the project progresses, systems accommodate an increasing volume of data. Whether it be configuration parameters or preloaded productive data in anticipation of the final delta migration, a loss could have severe impacts on the project.

*Dependencies* Some new services to be deployed during the transformation cannot coexist in reasonable conditions with the productive services they are to replace. For example, running two separate LAN in parallel, including duplicate passive cabling from the patch panels down to the user workstations, is rather exceptional. Since replacing a LAN on multiple sites is usually an operation that takes place over several days or weeks, during the ramp-up the client will work on both legacy and new LAN components. As the LAN is the communication backbone, the provider needs to support it under conditions close to target operations during this phase.

*Volumes* The more the services to migrate, the longer the duration of the transformation. From a risk perspective, one could not envisage going live in one stroke with an information system made of hundreds of applications. Instead, applications go live progressively and that is to say by lots, to give users enough time to test and proceed to acceptance. The same causes producing the same effects, during the ramp-up phase users will use business functions running on both legacy and new environments. The number of applications used productively will grow to a point where the provider will have to ensure a reasonable level of service in order not to put the client at risk.

## Practical Implementation

Such a construct involving three streams running in parallel whereas project acceptance has not taken place yet requests clarification with regard to a number of matters. Here are the three main ones.

*Operational* While FMO represents target operations with guaranteed service-level agreement (SLA), ODP generally provides for reaction and intervention times on a best-effort basis. The services include minimal functional, technical and security patching levels as well as data backup and regular operational checks. For outsourcings involving a transformation of the application layer, ODP is an integral part of the TMO without which the transformation could not take place. It includes regular release management, database (DB) cloning and job scheduling activities to keep the various application environments[1] constantly in line.

*Contractual* At first sight, Fig. 55 may appear misleading with respect to those services falling under the FMO operational regime, but still considered under the project contractual regime. How can a service be covered, at the same time, by two different regimes? This is an important question that calls for extreme precaution when structuring the contract. The vertical axis tells the nature of the services that apply to a bestowed service at a bestowed moment, freed from most of its legal obligations and consequences. The horizontal axis reminds us of the legal regime that applies to the service at this moment. In other terms, (1) a non-achievement of SLA does not bear any consequence, and (2) at any time during the project, a service may be operated under the TMO, ODP or FMO conditions, but until the final client acceptance test (CAT) is successfully passed, the whole construct remains a project in the sense that, if the CAT fails, the client can terminate all services, including those already operated under FMO conditions. If the final acceptance is achieved, then all services enter the BaU mode and are ruled by the target operation contracts.

*Financial* Each provider will value (approximately) ODP according to the services provided. As a rule of thumb, consider 20% of FMO costs for ODP, both considered on the same duration. For example, if FMO amounts to CHF 5 million/year and the TMO is expected to last 1 year, then ODP could represent a surcharge of one million on the TMO. This is an average: mere technical projects may not require any ODP at all while transformations of the application layer like those mentioned above could

---

[1]For example, development, integration, testing, training, data warehouse, etc.

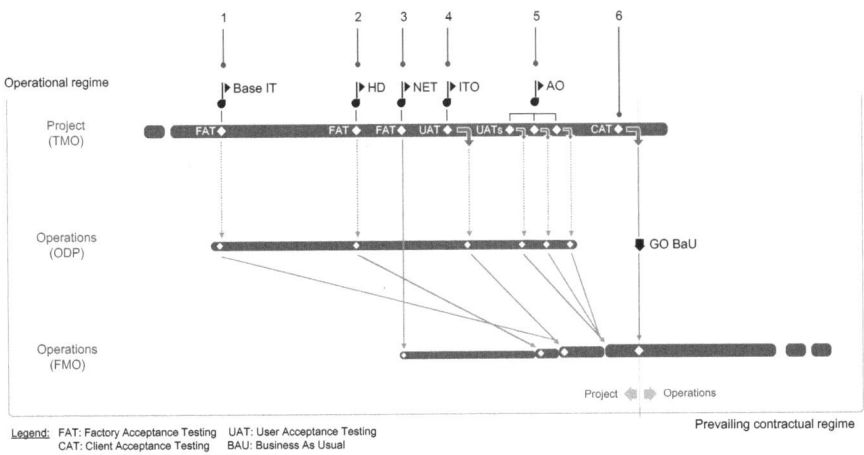

**Fig. 56** Handover to production example

need up to 30%. With the exception of those cases where ODP is mandatory, choosing between ODP or FMO costs is a trade-off between guarantees and costs that is governed by the criticality of the systems and the risk appetite of the client. The costs for ODP are normally deemed to be included in the fixed price of the TMO whereas FMO are to be paid in full as soon as the services become provided under FMO conditions and benefit from the corresponding guarantees.

The following example illustrates how services move from one regime to another and the underlying motives.

---

### Example

Consider a lift and shift outsourcing involving the transformation of the network and infrastructure layers and the move or reinstallation of 200 business applications on the new infrastructures. Figure 56: Example of ODP and FMO operations for a complex transformation positions the introduction of the new services on the time scale and the successive regimes they are subject to.

1. Base IT: The provider prepares the base networking, security and directory functions in the data centres as base for the other services. The base IT quickly moves to ODP and is maintained under this regime until the introduction of ITO services (4), where it moves to FMO because of the sudden global impact a downtime may have.
2. Helpdesk: The parties decide to implement an ad hoc helpdesk structure to handle project-related incidents as well as operations-related incidents for the network, which will be the first set of services to go live. This light structure will not be able to absorb the volumes induced by the introduction of ITO

services, hence the reason they decide to execute the handover from ODP to FMO before reaching this milestone.

3. Networks: When the LAN and WAN are installed and put into production, they instantly replace the corresponding legacy environments. They move directly from TMO to FMO because the client could not afford an unlimited downtime nor security issues.

4. IT infrastructures: The provider provisions OS- and DB-ready servers on the new infrastructures to accommodate the applications. The services are not critical and thus maintained under ODP, until the first application is deployed where they move to FMO.

5. Applications: The provider ramps up progressively the 200 business applications by lots of 10 per week, each lot being subject to user acceptance tests (UAT). After a few lots, the number of productive applications has pushed the criticality to a point that all previously installed applications are transferred to FMO. After the last application is deployed, all services are live but still without guarantees.

6. The parties run the client acceptance tests (CAT), which materialise the contractual transfer from the project to the BaU mode. The remaining project activities are transferred to operations through a handover protocol signed by both teams, and the project is formally closed a month after.

## Dos and Don'ts

Contract
- Make sure the project and the operation contracts are linked and the former prevails over the latter in case of discordance through an appropriate clause set higher in the contracts' hierarchy. In doing this, the project contract is the best place to accommodate the provisions ruling ODP and FMO in the project phase. State that, until final acceptance is achieved, the provider maintains the services under ODP or FMO conditions to the extent required by the TMO, but without any guarantee, irrespectively of their possible productive use.

Costs
- If the business case is financially tight, discuss with the client during the offering phase on keeping systems under ODP as long as possible. It is much cheaper than FMO. Unless the client has critical operations that call for strict guarantees, often the services provided under ODP are sufficient.

## Accompany Organisational Changes

Attention which each party should pay to this topic: Client: ●●● Provider: ●●○

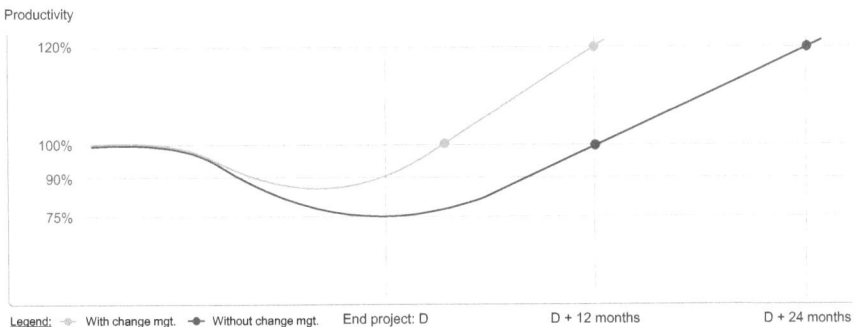

**Fig. 57** Benefits of change management

## Objective

Create a positive human dynamic around the technological transformation.

This section explains how to help people cope with the uncertainty generated by the outsourcing and turn opponents into ambassadors.

## Description

The introduction of new tools and processes upsets users' habits. Consequently, the productivity drops during the project. With proper cushioning measures, it is back to normal a few months after the end of the project and it reaches the sought productivity target in the year or so following the transformation, see Fig. 57. Without change measures, the recovery takes much longer.

The change in the ways of working is part of the problem. Resistance to change is the other. The reason lies in the fact that any change is stressful. It moves people out of their comfort zone and creates uncertainty. Since safety is the second layer in Maslow's hierarchy of needs, one easily understands that resistance is more down to a physiological reaction than to a wish.

Change management supports the process of transformation. It helps individuals to progressively overcome this resistance.

## Process Overview

Forcing people to change is one possibility. Unfortunately, it works to some extent because people need a job. They realise they cannot/should not fight against the organisation and decide willy-nilly to cope with the change. Not to say that they are not motivated and that the recourse to force generates health diseases, the most representative of which being the generational burnout.

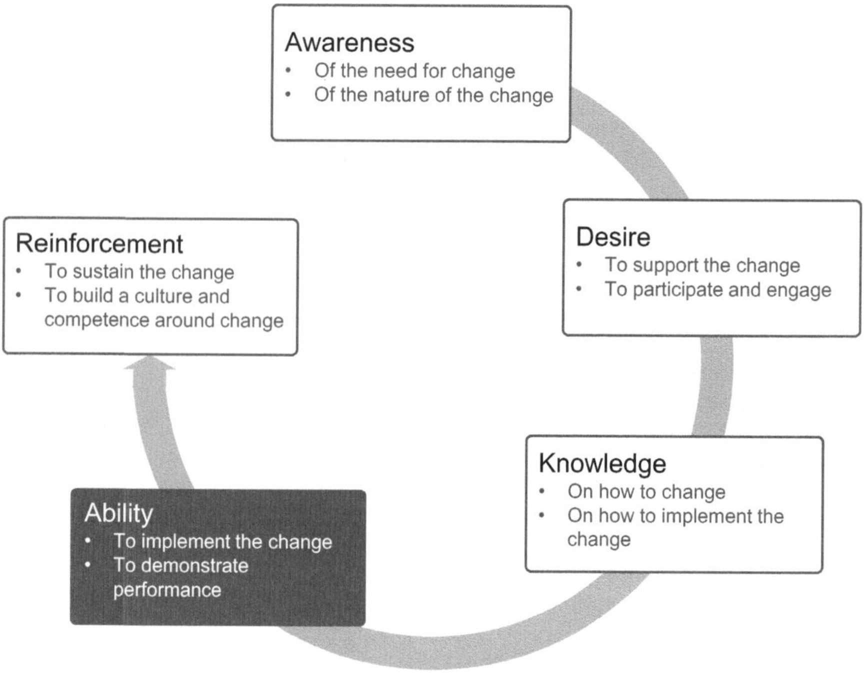

**Fig. 58**  Prosci® ADKAR model

Getting people to change follows a completely different approach. It activates the internal motivation levers that make people feel deeply involved and intrinsically convinced that change is necessary. If everyone has been secured a place in the new setting, it results in a feeling of relief which radiates throughout the whole organisation.

Any good top manager with a small sense of humanity would consider the second option, which appears more expensive at first sight, but turns out to be far more efficient in the end.

One model to explain how to trigger intrinsic motivation at a personal level and transform it into a positive dynamic is the ADKAR model shown in Fig. 58.

**Raise Awareness**

Represents a person's understanding of the nature of the change, its reason and the risks involved in not changing. Awareness also includes information about the internal and external drivers that led to the change.

**Fuel Desire**

Represents the willingness to support and engage in the change. Desire is ultimately about personal choice. It is influenced by the nature of the change, the individual's personal situation and the intrinsic motivators which are unique to each person.

## Develop Knowledge

Represents the materials supporting the change, i.e. the information, training and education supports that make the change understood. Knowledge includes information about behaviours, processes, tools, systems, skills, job roles and techniques that are needed to implement the change.

## Develop Ability

Represents the execution of the change. Ability is about turning knowledge into action. Ability is achieved when a person or group has demonstrated the capability to implement the change at the required performance level and to successfully transfer the knowledge to the next group requiring it.

## Reinforce the Dynamic

Represents those emotional and technical factors that make the change sustainable. Emotional reinforcements could include recognition, rewards or internal satisfaction that are tied to the realisation of the change. Technical reinforcements are supporting measures like training that extend beyond the project when the change is too profound and requires a long-term accompaniment.

---

**Case study: how change management can transform oppositions into enthusiasm**

The client is a nationwide administration, with all the appertaining stereotypes of resistance when it comes to innovation. To follow the pace of technological changes, top management nonetheless decides to go away from the legacy phone infrastructure in favour of a modern voice over IP solution. But whether calling with any type of device has become natural for most people in their private life, removing the traditional wired phone at work raises concerns beyond reason.

At the beginning of the project, most departments reject the change, trying to postpone it to the end of the 4-year rollout plan. The client calls on the provider's expertise to accompany the technological transformation with specific measures to foster users' acceptance. As a preliminary measure, the change manager of the provider requests the client to name a so-called executive sponsor from top or deputy level in each department.

Raise awareness. Executive sponsors are given a personal introduction to the solution, followed by a presentation and then the opportunity to discuss the possible use cases applicable to their department. Risks and fears are equally debated and ideas on how to reach users' acceptance exchanged.

Fuel desire. Additional workshops are organised with the sponsors to identify the business goals they could achieve with the new solution. The workshops are specific because they are tightly linked to the nature of the departments. For example, sedentary persons do not have the same communication needs as travelling users. Executive sponsors are motivated in the sense that they feel served by a solution that responds to their unique needs. They decide to shorten the rollout plan from 4 to 2 years.

Develop knowledge. The workshops lead to develop tailored training and communication materials for the different departments and user profiles. Executive sponsors are, once again, solicited to learn their role before, during and after the implementation.

Develop ability. Once they gained enough maturity about the solution and the approach to have it accepted, the executive sponsors start pitching in their departments. The word quickly spreads across departments, which see emerging ambassadors. The new solution creates a buzz and, all of a sudden, wired phones have become old fashioned.

## Practical Implementation

### Raise Awareness

*Analyse impact*  A problem which is well defined is a problem half solved. And here, the problem lies in (1) understanding the nature of the change and (2) understanding how the change will affect the users.

1. The analysis starts with the client's customers and how these will be impacted with respect to the services or the way they interface with the client. It is followed by a drill down into the organisation, including the impact on the culture, structure and employees. It ends with processes and tools.
2. As represented in Fig. 59, the closer the change from the user, the more the fears and the higher the resistance. For each component of the analysis, rank the impact according to the proximity from the user. Every topic that touches the user or their close working environment directly shall rank highest. They are the most difficult to address. Note that the barriers tend to move from psychological to technical as the distance between the user and the matter increases.

---

**Example**

Figure 60 shows an example of how such analysis could look like according to the type of outsourcing. The example considers an outsourcing of technical layers (ITO), an outsourcing of technical and application layers including a business transformation (AM), a simple outsourcing of business processing functions without change of the business logic (BPO) and an outsourcing of the workplace environment including the introduction of a modern mobility and communication concept (WPL).

In the latter type, the acceptance of the new communication solution (1), its efficient usage (2) and the changes to the working environment induced by mobile offices (3, 4) touch the users directly in their everyday life. They rank

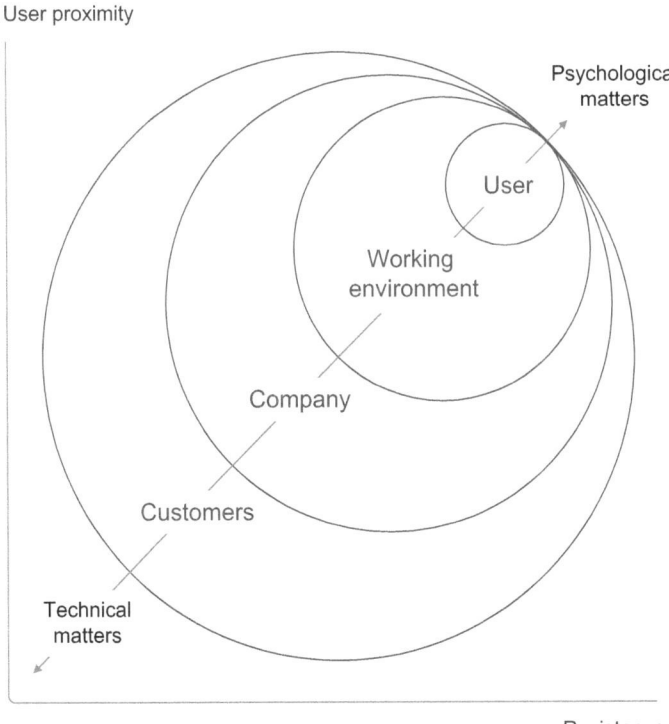

**Fig. 59** User proximity versus level of resistance

first and shall therefore receive maximum focus in the change management plan. The new type of working relations with colleagues in the same department (5), with management (6), and peers in adjacent units (7) follow close behind.

*Draw sponsors map* Once the impacts are known, identify the individuals in the organisation who may embrace them, the so-called executive sponsors. Picking the right persons mainly depends on two factors: the capacity of the persons to reduce the risk of rejection of the solution and/or their capacity to actively promote its acceptance. Such persons are likely to be influential individuals who should then be used to inspire the cultural change upwards towards peers and higher management as well as middle managers of departments who should thus be used to spread the word downwards towards the mass of employees. Since persons with high influence and high interest (Category One in Fig. 50) will probably do the job by themselves, even indirectly, the sponsors map should primarily concentrate on individuals of Category Two with high influence but low interest and then, to a lesser extent, on those of Category Three with high interest but no influence. Furthermore, the map should distinguish two profiles: one representing sponsors who need emotions to *stimulate*

| User proximity | Impact | ITO | AM | BPO | WPL | |
|---|---|---|---|---|---|---|
| Customers | Customers positioning vs. the company | | • | | | |
| | Consumption of the services | • | •• | | | |
| Organisation | Interfaces with clients | | •• | | | |
| Culture | Provision of the services | • | •• | •• | • | — 9 |
| | Governance, leadership model | •• | •• | • | •• | — 6 |
| | Working together | | •• | | •• | — 5 |
| | Costs consciousness, cost distribution | •• | •• | •• | • | |
| Structure | Internal organisation, internal interfaces | • | •• | • | •• | — 7 |
| | Sourcing model | •• | ••• | ••• | • | |
| | Jobs descriptions (retained organisation) | • | •• | | • | |
| | Dismissal/Redeployment/Transfer of personnel | •• | ••• | ••• | • | |
| Employees | Roles, responsibilities, skills (retained organisation) | •• | ••• | | • | |
| | Solution acceptance | | ••• | | ••• | — 1 |
| | Solution optimal usage | • | ••• | • | ••• | — 2 |
| | Working conditions | | | | ••• | — 3 |
| | Empowerment, self-mgmt. | | | | •• | — 4 |
| Processes | Introduction of new processes | • | ••• | • | | |
| | Change of existing processes | • | ••• | •• | • | — 8 |
| Tools | Client-facing tools | | •• | | | |
| | Business internal tools | | ••• | | | |
| | Technical/Support tools | • | • | • | • | — 10 |

Legend:        No impact  •     Limitied impact   ••  Medium impact   •••  High impact

**Fig. 60**  Change impact analysis

*their* enthusiasm, the other representing those who need factual materials to *structure* their enthusiasm. Ideally, each executive sponsor should be treated as individually as possible, although developing as many individual contents is not reasonably possible.

## Fuel Desire

Given that humans are 80% driven by emotions, fuelling desire is about activating the internal levers that trigger positive emotions. These levers are identical among humans; only the proportions differ. Expert Dr. Hans-Georg Häusel identifies dominance, innovation and harmony as the three main dimensions of the human emotional system. Bearing in mind that negative emotions are twice as strong as positive emotions, recognising the prevailing factor is mandatory to activate the right levers and generate positive emotions. However, the task is not as arduous as it seems.

The position the person holds in the company gives a first indication:

- Management, sales, project leaders: dominance.
- Research and development, IT, marketing, communication: innovation.
- Human resources, back office, administration: harmony.

The gender provides a second indication:

- Men: dominance and then innovation.
- Women: harmony and then innovation.

For the rest, a minimum of empathy and psychology should do it. The way the person stands, moves or talks, the level of emotion and passion, the level of confidence or reserve they demonstrate, etc.: just letting the person speak for 5 min about their perception of the company and their own position should be enough to give an idea about their personality and their needs.

Fuelling desire is thus talking to the prevailing dimension of each person's character. For a dominant person, it may be by showing them how the solution may help them achieve business goals, increase productivity or show accomplishment to higher management. For an innovative person, it may be explaining how the solution will ease the introduction of further innovations and make them feel part of a dynamic system in which they already are in their private life. For risk-averse persons who need harmony, the case is a bit more difficult. It involves explaining how the solution will help the company to maintain its position or demonstrate to them that the solution is not a risk by confronting them progressively to the fear, the ultimate goal being to increase their safety level.

The context influences the form—one-on-one conversations, workshops with small groups, presentations, etc.: the only thing that matters is that each message is tailored and reaches its audience.

When the target solution leaves enough room for customisation, the human-centred design (HCD) method proves to be efficient. HCD places the users at the centre of the problem and involves them in the thinking of potential solutions. This can only work with a limited number of persons, namely executive sponsors (Fig. 61).

## Develop Knowledge

*Develop concepts* To structure and formalise the mission, the change manager develops a change management plan comprising coaching, communication and training concepts:

1. The coaching concept outlines how the change manager will engage the executive sponsors into the change process and ramp them up from no knowledge about

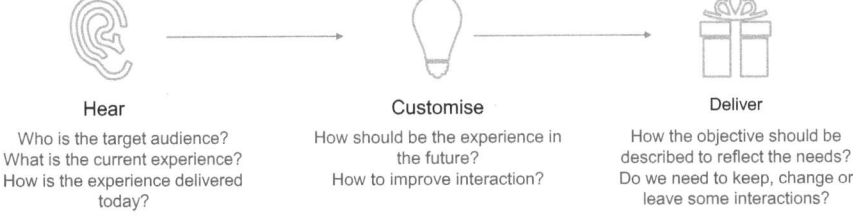

| Hear | Customise | Deliver |
|---|---|---|
| Who is the target audience? What is the current experience? How is the experience delivered today? | How should be the experience in the future? How to improve interaction? | How the objective should be described to reflect the needs? Do we need to keep, change or leave some interactions? |

**Fig. 61** Human centered design

the solution to ambassadors. More particularly, it sets out the terms of the collaboration between the change manager and the sponsors during the first two steps of the ADKAR process. The sponsor job description, which details their expected role and responsibilities (see next paragraph), rounds off the concept.

2. Communication concept. It describes the content, audience, timing and frequency of the communications. It pursues two major objectives: dispense technical information about the solution (raise awareness) and stimulate the wish to establish contact with it (fuel desire). For this, it shall distinguish the various audiences according to their needs and articulate key messages correspondingly. Technical messages should come from the communication department, countersigned by top management. They are deemed company-wide and, as such, are likely to be sent through the client's regular communication channels, e.g. newsletter or intranet. Emotional messages should come from the executive sponsors. They are meant to be entertaining and thus need to be adjusted to the target departments with respect to content and form. Whenever possible, prefer intranet videos or, better still, roadshows with live demonstrations.

3. Training concept. If communication is about absorbing the change, training is about digesting it. The concept shall adequately prepare the employees for D-day. Beyond the form and content of the training, timing is key. If taken too late, it may not leave enough time for people to familiarise themselves with the solution. Taken too early, people will tend to forget the content. Since the funding for the whole change process is limited, it may not be possible to run catch-up sessions. Introductory training sessions, based on the corporate e-learning system and taking place halfway through the project, should be followed by classroom sessions 1 or 3 months before the cutover.

*Explain roles* Maintain a close relationship with executive sponsors all along the project. Creating this relationship starts with a one-on-one personal conversation with each of them. The objective is to gauge their current level of responsibilities, prerogatives and sphere of influence to further assess the extent to which they could support the project.

Once the sponsors accepted the mission and have committed to allocate sufficient time to it, the change manager discusses their contribution with them. Although the latter obviously depends on the specific needs of each project, executive sponsors are required to at least provide the following services:

- Formulate by themselves the sought business objectives of the solution and the positive/negative impact of implementing/not implementing it.
- Communicate the objectives to their team (s) and organise workshops to openly discuss doubts and resistances.
- Ensure a presence during the execution of change management activities like demonstrations and trainings.
- Liaise with project stakeholders and other executive sponsors to coordinate internal actions and align messages.

**Fig. 62** Prosci® project
change triangle model

* Support the changes brought by the project in their department. Act as a relay for the project team with respect to communication and organisation.
* Update regularly team members about the project's progress, e.g. 2-min message in weekly team meetings.

## Develop Ability

Developing ability is turning the knowledge developed into concrete achievements. Referring to the Prosci Project Change Triangle illustrated in Fig. 62, where project management, change management and sponsorship represent the three vertexes of the balanced triangle that should rule the implementation of any complex change, this phase focuses on preparing each actor to play his role: employees to use the solution, sponsors to promote it.

*Train employees*  Getting acquainted with a new solution, whatever the complexity, is not rocket science. In the end, it is almost always down to the three following factors. To varying degrees, employees need:

* Practice, to confront themselves with the real solution through hands-on training. This is certainly the main difference with the knowledge phase where the solution was explained in abstract terms.
* Time, to digest the acquisition of knowledge. From beginners to practitioners, they will likely need to attend several sessions and, between two sessions, go about their daily business.
* Support, to not get helplessly stuck in front of the solution due to mishandling. Real-time feedback and assistance allow them to keep the momentum and relieve the frustrations.

*Coach sponsors*  If project management represents the solution and change management the users, sponsorship represents the catalyst that fosters the change by supporting and binding the two sides. In this respect, training is very different from coaching. As represented in Fig. 63, training tells a person what to do whereas coaching helps them to ask themselves what to do. Based on the principle that a

**Fig. 63** Training versus
coaching positioning

Source : Driving change with external coaching programs

person sells something better if they truly understand what they are selling, the change manager needs to provide sponsors with a broader visibility on the context so that they can take the right actions at the right time on their own. This calls for extending the scope of the regular interactions he has with them beyond the mere solution. Positioning the solution against market trends or explaining what competition does during informal discussions is an integral part of the coaching plan.

## Reinforce the Dynamic

Depending on the shift to operate, change management can be a short- to medium-term activity that takes place during the project only, e.g. accompanying the introduction of a new ERP with new processes, or a long-term endeavour that will have to be fostered over the years, e.g. strengthening a profound cultural change induced by an outsourcing. This is especially true for a disorganised or a highly reactive organisation where the rigidity introduced by the outsourcing may be a road to disaster if change measures are not thought to sustain the dynamic over the long run.

### Case study: how missing accompanying measures could kill a relation

The client is a bank that built its business model on differentiation and the quick introduction into production of tailored services targeted at high net worth individuals.

To cope with the growing complexity of its information system and the proportionally growing problem of critical mass, the client decides to outsource all layers, from ITO to BPO, of its core banking platform.

The client selects a Tier II provider known for delivering stable operations on the considered banking package. After an 8-digit, 16-month transition, the cut-over happens and the operations start.

While run-the-business (RtB) activities seem to deliver the promises, change-the-business (CtB) quickly turns out to be far below expectations. Front-office users continue requesting both important and non-important functional changes at the same pace as before, and change requests accumulate faster than the provider can absorb them.

After 2 years attempting to improve the delivery capacity of the provider, the client concludes that its business is at risk and decides to re-insource.

In the example above, the outsourcing suffered from a double conceptual misalignment. On the provide side, the parties understated, if not overlooked, the CtB capacity of the provider vs. the needs. On the client side, the client did not consider adjusting its' approach towards non-important business evolutions. Notwithstanding, appropriate change management measures could have:

- During the project, helped the front office department heads rethink the way they operate to align their expectations with the absorptive capacity of the forthcoming service model. For instance, the departments could have introduced a concept of super users responsible for channelling and prioritising important changes while discarding those whose return on investment was questionable.
- During the operation, led to install a regular committee between the IT department and the super users to focus on demand and capacity management. This takes us back to the first section "Get the Big Picture" in Chap. 2 and reminds the necessity to adequately position the IT against the business. See section "Drive Outsourcing" in Chap. 5 for a practical implementation of such committee.

The case below shows how the parties anticipated the cultural shock and implemented compensating measures for both the project and operation phases.

---

**Case study: how accompanying measures and services best support each other**

The client is a holding which buys companies of similar nature and integrate them to release synergies. It reacts quickly upon market opportunities when companies are potentially on sale.

The client has no IT culture, no IT governance in place, no CIO. At one extreme, top management buys companies, and, at the other, an IT manager supported by a small IT team of 20 runs an ever-increasing number of systems. The communication between top management and IT, between IT and users and, to a large extent, between top management and users is virtually inexistent. An order to take over the operations of a newly acquired company, to be executed without delay, can reach the IT department at any time.

Since IT navigates by sight, it has no other choice than to operate in a pure reactive mode, with the consequences described in Fig. 8 in Chap. 2, that is to say, a massive transfer of workload from the back end to the front end. Over years, the problem has grown to such an extent that half of IT members work in user support. The compelling counterpart of an exaggerated number of incidents being an ultra-fast reaction time, a corporate-wide VIP culture has been installed.

When the question of outsourcing arises, everybody is doubtful. How a provider, whose business model precisely lies on planned production, could deliver a good service in a state of continuous emergency? To answer this question, the provider worked along several tracks:

1. Culture: accompany the switchover to the new service model with appropriate change measures.
2. Governance: help the client to implement an IT governance structure at the group level to foster internal communication and better plan projects.
3. Services: deliver a mix of standard and ad hoc services, respectively with and without SLA.

The solution came from a combination of the tree approaches. The parties decided to:

1. Allocate 120 man/days of a change expert to raise awareness and develop knowledge of the target situation[2] within the organisation. The expert worked out a comprehensive communication plan in close collaboration with executive sponsors, key users, and the communication department. In addition to regular written communications, she ran a series of roadshows to humanise the project.
2. Appoint a CIO and install a weekly meeting between top management and IT to align business objectives with delivery capabilities, along with a quarterly meeting between key users and IT to ensure appropriate demand and capacity management.
3. Reinforce remote user support with dedicated field supporters, at least for the first two years following the cutover, allocate a full-time service manager with on-site presence to maintain proximity with higher management, and offer a VIP service for 60 of the most influent users.

## Dos and Don'ts

Plan the change
- Always start with a sound analysis of the existing organisational context before anything else. It is the gap between the source and target situations that defines the magnitude of the change.
- Assess which dimension of the client organisation is more likely to raise resistances and determine measures accordingly. Deep cultural changes may

---

[2]Fuelling desire and developing ability do not really apply in an iso-functional outsourcing.

call for psychologists, structural and process changes usually need business experts and office tools can be satisfied with a fleet of interns. In all cases, empathic persons.

- Do not believe that it is the change manager who achieves the change by themselves. The change manager only activates levers, the most important of which being committed executive sponsors.
- Do not launch the mission before the prospective executive sponsors have committed to take on an active role.

Raise awareness
- Recognise early on those sponsors who may not be able to efficiently play their role because of limited capabilities or lack of influence. Do not hesitate to replace them with other persons. The number two man in each department may be the best bet.
- Work with sponsors until the moment clear business goals stand out; otherwise no change management goals can be set.
- Explain the drivers of the change. Telling people why things are done is a formidable generator of intrinsic motivation.
- Anticipate acts of resistance and be prepared. Take arguments seriously even though they have no rational ground.
- Communicate, communicate, communicate.

Fuel desire
- If the change leaves enough room for it, involve people in the thought process to define the needs, customise the solution or coordinate the implementation.
- Communicate successes across departments. It generates a positive noise that cuts down on negative emotions.

Develop knowledge
- Get close to people. Always prefer face-to-face meetings whenever possible.
- Tell people what is expected from them.
- Align the timing of the communications with that of the project.

Develop ability
- Set short-term, achievable targets in the execution to avoid the tunnel effect. People need intermediary milestones and, at each milestone, time to recover before moving on to the next stage.
- Accept the change curve that each person needs to go through emotionally. The slope being particularly steep between raising awareness and fuelling desire, do not expect people to reach the same stage simultaneously.
- Be tolerant with employees going through a major transformation. They cannot perform at 100% in their current position and, at the same time, absorb the change to be productive at 120% at the end of the project.
- Concentrate on those employees who really need support.

Reinforce the dynamic
- If the project budget allows for such things, organise small group celebrations after important milestones like the last training session. This reinforces the feeling of accomplishment and belonging to the group.
- Always look further into the future.

## Transfer Personnel

Attention which each party should pay to this topic: Client: ●●● Provider: ●●●

### Objective

Address the people dimension with professionalism and humanity.

This chapter describes the so-called rebadging process in outsourcings involving a transfer of personnel from the client to the provider.

### Description

Outsourcing raises a social question: "what will become of the existing staff after the transition?" Unless the client has already lost most of its personnel and this, initially, was the reason that precipitated the decision to outsource, the client shall answer this question of fundamental importance as early on as during the business case analysis. Not only because it is the duty of any respectable employer to care for its people—some of which who served it loyally over a lifetime career—but also because it has multiple implications on the viability of the deal. To mention just the main aspects:

- *Legal.* Some countries have a strict employment framework and carefully scrutinise any action that could mask a mass lay-off or illegal dismantling.
- *Operational.* Although possible, once the transfer has been executed, the way back for the client would be, at best, extremely painful and costly.
- *Financial.* Salaries being the largest budgetary item in IT services, adding, removing or valuing differently resources can have massive impacts.
- *Risk.* Whether outsourcing is an opportunity to lower risks, the latter increase during the transformation because of the possible loss of key personnel.

Back to the question "what will become of the existing staff after the transition", one basically distinguishes three possibilities: dismiss, reallocate or transfer of personnel. In simple outsourcings, reallocation is almost the norm. In complex ones, it turns out to be a combination of the three: reallocate the best elements, transfer the bulk, dismiss the weakest.

### Process

Transferring personnel is no straightforward activity, mainly because of complex regulations ruling employment conditions in general and the transfer itself in

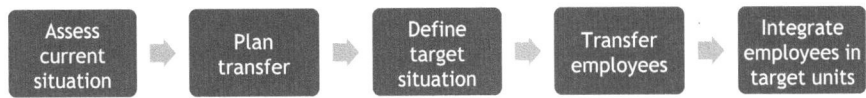

**Fig. 64** Reallocate or transfer personnel process

particular. To ensure a transfer in the best possible conditions for the client, the employees and the provider, the parties are well advised to follow a structured process as the one presented below (Fig. 64):

### Assess
It starts with a joined assessment of the current human situation with respect to the concerned people, their job description, salaries and employment conditions.

### Plan
The parties plan the next steps of the process and figure out the details of the communication plan towards the employees.

### Define
The provider projects the employees in the target organisation and analyses the deltas with the same items analysed before: job description, salaries, employment conditions. The parties negotiate these deltas on the basis of the client's expectations and those proceedings from the legislation. The phase ends with sending out employment contract proposals to the employees.

### Transfer
The provider meets the candidates to discuss the proposals. The candidates accept or reject them. The provider and client human resource (HR) departments execute the on-boarding (hiring), respectively the corresponding de-boarding (termination) activities for those who accepted.

### Integrate
The provider integrates the employees by following its standard post-hiring integration process.


## Practical Implementation

### Assess

*Identify concerned employees* Among staff members currently running the operations to be taken over, the client figures out which ones are candidates for transfer and which ones it would like to keep as retained organisation. For those to be transferred, it needs to provide the corresponding job descriptions and, if these do not exist, develop them. This may not be trivial, however, given the likely multidisciplinary nature of functions spanning vertically several service layers as represented in Fig. 6 in Chap. 2. In such a case, it would be well advised for the provider's further analysis of those activities which best represent the employees' skills.

*Analyse employees' current package* The parties assess together the candidates' current compensation package, including the fixed and variable parts of the salary, as well as other advantages like fringe benefits, out-of-pocket expenses, special employer contributions and allowances of all kinds. Working conditions like number of holidays, working time, training days and other types of paid leave shall be considered as part of the global package as well. The purpose of the exercise is to assure employees optimal transfer conditions, whether these are based on ethical or regulatory grounds.

*Analyse regulations and policies* The above-mentioned regulatory constraint applies in some jurisdictions where the legislator imposes a strict legal framework to such transfers. Detailing the mutual obligations of the parties in such a context is specific to each country and situation and thus not part of the book. The only recommendation here is that each party must individually duly assess the situation to avoid subsequent legal proceedings from aggrieved employees.

## Plan

*Elaborate transfer road map* The parties set together a prospective road map for the transfer like the one presented in Fig. 65. Since the transfer is an integral part of the deal and they both influence one another, it must be planned by involving the deal managers on both sides and considering the time required by each party to process their own steps under the possible regulatory constraints.

*Elaborate communication plan* Communicating effectively and timely is undoubtedly the most crucial aspect of any transfer for employees who have lived in doubt since hearing the first rumours months beforehand. The parties work out together the details of the communication plan that will give employees the required visibility about the transitory and target situations. When the plan has been communicated to employees, any deviation or correction to it must be transparently communicated: employees live better with changes than with uncertainty. Uncertainty generates rumours which in turn induce risks.

*Present provider organisation and business units* The first communication, run jointly by the top management of the parties in the presence of the concerned employees, is the most important. It serves the following purposes: (1) Hold harmless employees who obviously feel guilty of the situation. (2) Provide them with a clear road map for the transfer. (3) Give them visibility about their future. In this respect, the provider should present, on the one hand, its company to raise interest and, on the other hand, its employment conditions to reduce individual fears.

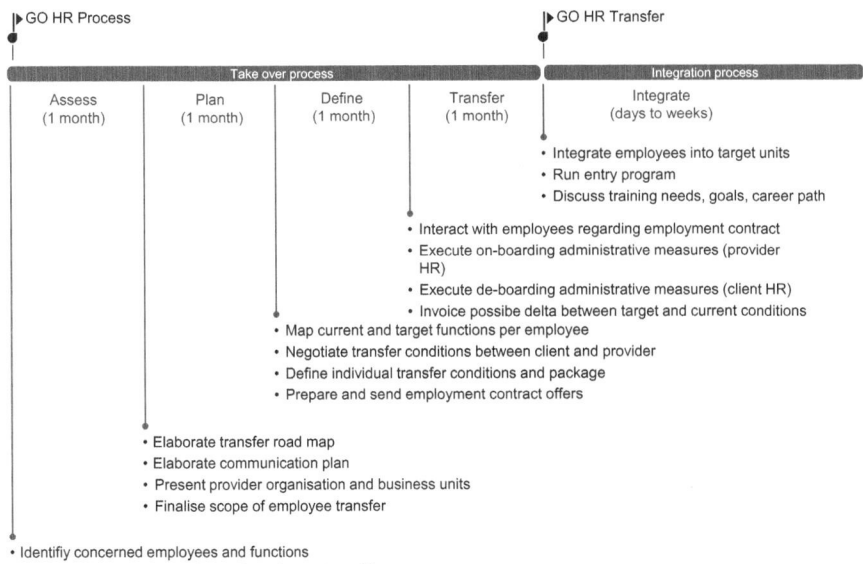

**Fig. 65** Rebadging process

*Finalise scope of employee transfer* In average, approximately 5–10% of the employees resign between the time the first rumours were heard till the decision to outsource is communicated. During this same time frame, the parties have worked out the target operating model and the client has fine-tuned its retained organisation. This means that until the present phase, the number of candidates for transfer has fluctuated—and will continue to do so until the effective transfer takes place. This is normal and unavoidable. The objective of finalising the scope of employee transfer shall be understood as setting the baseline for the forthcoming transfer negotiations.

## Define

*Map current and target functions per employee* This step is usually a delicate issue because of the 90° rotation it imposes between the generalist functions of the client job nomenclature and the specialist functions in the provider nomenclature. The problematic is amplified by the level of seniority. For the client, an expert usually refers to a senior person whereas for the provider, it refers to the highest degree of specialisation on a given subject. These two factors influence the target job role and the corresponding salary bands. In case of deadlock, the parties need to determine the best approaching skills set for the concerned employees, ideally with one alternative, and openly raise the possibilities with them during the interviews.

*Negotiate transfer conditions between client and provider* When the client or the applicable legislation requires protecting employees' acquired rights and these outmatch the provider's standard employment conditions, the provider will want to charge back the extra costs to the client. The problem is that the amounts are directly linked to the duration of the employment contracts and are thus not known beforehand. Reasonable practice: the parties agree on a grandfathering clause limited from 12 to 24 months that the client finances in full. Beyond this, the provider is freed from any obligation, and it becomes their responsibility to either maintain the same conditions at their own costs or adjust the employment contracts.

*Define individual transfer conditions and package*  In addition to the global transfer conditions applying to all transferred employees, the parties may want or need to have a closer look at the specific situation of selected individuals. Most common examples include the takeover by the provider of contractual commitments initially taken by the client towards some employees, e.g. long-term trainings, along with special incentives decided by the parties to secure key members during the transformation phase.

*Prepare and send draft employment contract offers*  The provider prepares employment contracts offers based on the corporate and individual conditions discussed in the previous step. When not imposed by law, the contracts usually take into consideration the years of service and do not include any probationary period. Apart from this, they resemble any other employment contract and contain elements such as job description, salary, place of work and employer insurances, to name but a few.

## Transfer

*Interact with employees regarding employment contract*  Until that point, employees probably had no individual, face-to-face contact with their future employer, hence the advice to organise at least one intermediary informal encounter between the employees and their prospective team leaders if the plan phase is expected to last more than 2 months. Among other benefits, it creates proximity, provides employees insight about their future assignment and allows them to address personal issues they would not dare raise otherwise. Depending on the number of employees to be taken over, these encounters may represent a few days of effort on the provider side, but the benefits are unquestionably worth the time invested.

*Execute on-boarding administrative measures*  The provider's human resources department executes the administrative activities related to its regular hiring process as well as any activity proceeding from legal provisions applicable to the transfer.

*Execute de-boarding administrative measures*  The same applies to the client human resources department by analogy.

*Invoice possible delta between target and current conditions*  From the effective transfer date, the provider invoices the client all items proceeding from legal obligations recalculated on the base of the target salary, e.g. holiday and overtime balances and pension funds adjustments, as well as those items proceeding from the negotiations, e.g. off-band salary adjustments and long-term training courses. In terms of responsibility, the client assumes all claims arising before the transfer, the provider assumes those arising after the transfer and the parties assume jointly those resulting from the transfer itself.

## Integrate

Integrating employees into target units, running an entry programme and discussing training needs, goals and career path are standard activities not related to the transfer and thus not detailed further. What is interesting to mention here is that they may happen long after the effective transfer date. Indeed, if the outsourcing involves a present mode of operation (PMO) as explained in the following section, then the transferred employees are likely to be affected by it until the end of the transformation which lasts a year on average. If they are affected by it, during this phase they will very likely continue working exclusively for their former employer and have little contacts with their new business unit.

## Timing

The timing of the transfer influences the deal and vice versa. Unless the transfer happens exactly when the provider starts providing the target services (FMO), it leaves the client without staff for running its current operations and thus calls for a temporary operations contract (PMO). This boosts the overall level of complexity and risk of the deal.

The following paragraphs distinguish the four most common variants and their consequences.

### Takeover Without Transformation

The HR takeover happens at the start of the FMO as shown in Fig. 66. The provider takes over the personnel and, immediately after, starts running the client's operations with the latter, without transforming the operations—or more likely with a transformation happening later under its full control.

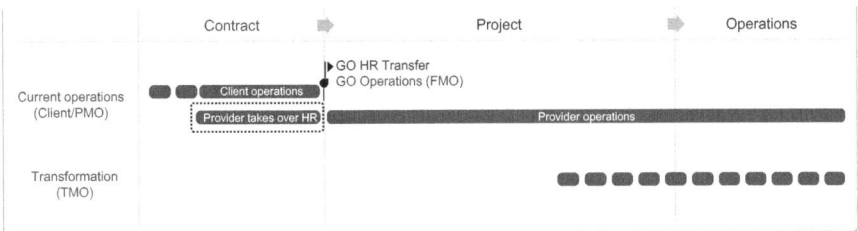

**Fig. 66** HR takeover at start of target operations

**Fig. 67**  HR takeover at the beginning of the project

This construct applies best for heavy, multi-year transformations when the personnel taken over is critical for the continuity of the business. For example, the provider wishes to enter a new market and needs the personnel to build its own knowledge base.

The main advantage of the construct resides in the smooth transition from the client to the provider, both for the client's business and employees. The main drawback lies in the economics of the model. All other things being equal, outsourcing is more expensive than internal operations meaning that, to generate efficiency gains without a major transformation at the beginning, the deal needs to span over a much longer period of time, e.g. 10 years.

### Takeover at the Beginning of the Transformation

The HR takeover happens at the start of the project (TMO) as shown in Fig. 67.

This construct applies best when there are chances that the deal may collapse before signature. In this case, no activity should start before both the technical and human situations are clarified. For example, the provider wants to run a due diligence to assess the current environment before confirming the deal and taking over the personnel.

The main advantage of the construct is that it allows the provider to plan the reallocation of personnel in advance before the end of the project and integrate it progressively as it decommissions legacy environments operated under the PMO. The main drawback is that a failure of the project (extremely rare) would place the employees and the client in a disastrous situation.

### Takeover During the Transformation

The HR takeover happens at any time during the TMO as shown in Fig. 68.

This construct is the most common. It applies when the parties have built a high level of trust in the deal, want to go forward as fast as possible and see the early transfer of personnel as a risk limitation measure.

The main advantages of the model are its swiftness and its capacity to optimise the costs. Indeed, alone at the controls, the provider can ramp down the PMO as it

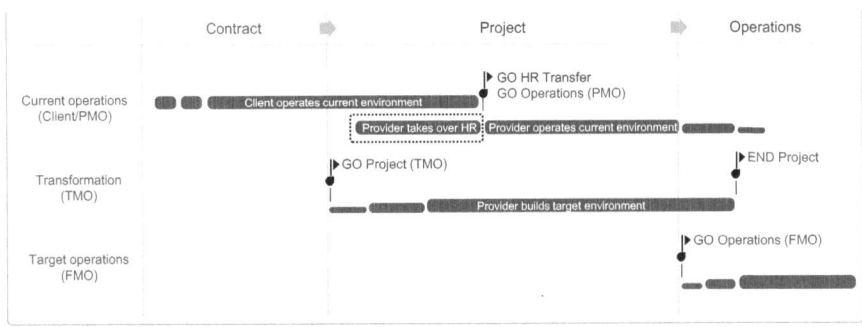

**Fig. 68** HR takeover during the project

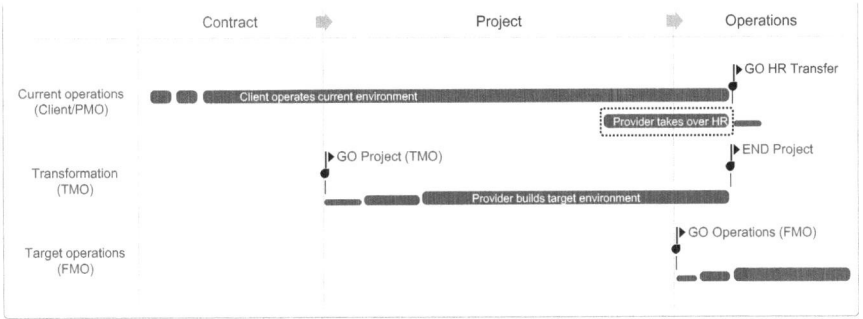

**Fig. 69** HR takeover at the end of the project

ramps up the FMO. The same drawback as stated before applies: a failure of the project would engender a disastrous situation.

## Takeover at the End of the Transformation

The HR takeover happens at the very end of TMO as shown in Fig. 69.

This construct applies best when the client sees a risk or constraint of any type transferring its current operations to the provider. For example, the client owns confidential client data that it needs to extract from the systems before being able to entrust its operations to the provider.

The main advantage of the model is the capacity of the client to continue operating as before in case of project failure. The main drawback generally lies in the economics with the client paying both current and target operations costs for a few months before the cutover if the systems are introduced progressively into production.

## Dos and Don'ts

Assess
- Job descriptions are the number one element for the provider's analysis. If they do not exist or are not of sufficient quality, the client should start listing the employees' main activities as early as the beginning of the process and try to map them with layers of the service stack.
- The parties need to assess separately the regulatory framework to limit the risk of misinterpretation regarding its applicability given the contemplated deal structure. For example, some legislations consider differently outsourcings with and without transformation and, consequently, have different sets of measures.

Plan
- The parties shall recognise communication towards the employees as one of the key success factors of the transfer and plan regular information meetings accordingly. They should set at least one individual, face-to-face exchange between each candidate and their future line manager halfway through the process to humanise the takeover and allow people to address personal topics.
- Each party should agree not to communicate anything to the employees in relation with the transfer without the approval of the other party during the whole rebadging process. Non-concerted communications may place the faulty party in a difficult situation and generate a trust deficiency among the employees when the wrong communication is invalidated.

Define
- Consider special long-term training programme as part of the individual conditions to be negotiated for employees whose current function cannot be mapped with any function in the provider job architecture.

Integrate
- Whenever possible, the provider should consider allocating the employees taken over to missions for other clients as soon as possible. In addition to training replacements for the client environment, it provides for maximum efficiency with respect to resource utilisation. It is a fact that rebadged employees who are allocated full-time to the client—what is more, if they stay on its premises— have special acquaintances with former colleagues and are tempted to support them on the fringes of the contract.

---

## Enforce Operational Governance

Attention which each party should pay to this topic: Client: ●●● Provider: ●●●

## Objective

Install the bridge and the major communication routes between the parties.

This chapter explains how to organise the governance of the relation according to the complexity of the outsourcing.

## Description

Governance is the human interface between the parties that steers the contract. It is deemed to be a symmetric structure which relies on roles, bodies and rules:

- *Roles.* The parties define the required functions and allocate the key persons correspondingly.
- *Bodies.* The persons meet regularly within the context of meetings with predefined form and content.
- *Rules.* The roles and the bodies have voting rights and follow escalation and arbitrage procedures.

Simple outsourcings may be satisfied with little or no bodies at all and function well with direct communications. More complex outsourcings require a more rigid framework and a higher level of the formalism.

## Prerequisites

### Client Side

The staffing of the governance structure constitutes an important driver of the business case and shall thus be carefully thought through as early as the offering phase. Since it relies on a combination of several factors, it can be difficult to assess both in terms of functions and number of full-time equivalent (FTE). If it does not impose by itself naturally, the client would be well advised to seek external expertise.

Reasons calling for a thorough analysis include, per dimension:

- *Strategic.* The client decides to preserve its know-how and expertise that it considers a competitive advantage.
- *Structural.* The client organisation is widely spread geographically, and the delivery of the services requires the coordination of many—even small—remote locations.
- *Functional.* The client has a pronounced appetite for change, which requires a lot of interactions with users for requirements definition and acceptance testing.
- *Technical.* Two or more providers contribute to deliver a unique final service, e.g. provider A delivers application management (AM) services and provider B the infrastructures on which they run.
- *Operational.* The provider's services are incorporated into a broader chain of services and have upstream and/or downstream dependencies.

- *Risk.* The client imposes restrictions on the way the services shall be delivered on personal grounds such as security or confidentiality.
- *Legal.* The regulatory framework to which the client is subject, e.g. banking, healthcare, army imposes strict conditions of supervision of the outsourced services.
- *Audit.* Internal or external auditors consume an annual effort amounting in days when not weeks to assess the relevance of IT controls in place that outsourcing will not eliminate.
- *Financials.* The client seeks to post-process the provider's bills to break down, analyse and invoice costs internally on a tailored accounting base.

## Provider Side

The governance structure is something inherent to the delivery of the services and thus normally already included and detailed at the stage of the offer. However, although providers are more than familiar with all governance topics, it is not unusual that they underestimate either the complexity of the client and/or the volumes it will generate. This often originates in an incomplete or even non-existent analysis of the business of the client at a time when the provider is more concentrated on trying to sell his services versus solving the problems of his prospect and, sometimes, an insufficient involvement of the service delivery service unit during the design of the solution. Since governance is deemed to be a symmetrical arrangement, some factors affecting the client will affect the provider.

Examples of how factors affecting the client could lead the provider to adjust its staffing[3] afterwards at their own cost:

- *Structural*: Limited to no impact.
- *Functional*: Very high impact. The number and pace of changes placed by the client in production lead to massive bottlenecks and an ever-increasing backlog of unrealised changes.
- *Technical*: High impact. Suboptimal multi-provider situations on the client side have consequences on the services of the provider and consequently rise to the surface through the governance team.
- *Operational*: Medium impact. If the client is not able to properly manage a chain of services, this may lead the provider to reschedule services and will generate unpaid overhead.
- *Risk*: Limited to medium impact depending on the expectations of the client. Non-standard processes or ad hoc reporting may have to be maintained and overload the governance.

---

[3] Addresses here only the need for strengthening the governance and excludes the consequences that the various situations may have on the services themselves. For example, a multi-provider context (technical factor above) generates governance issues but may also have operational consequences on the services if the client does not assume properly his coordination role of the various providers.

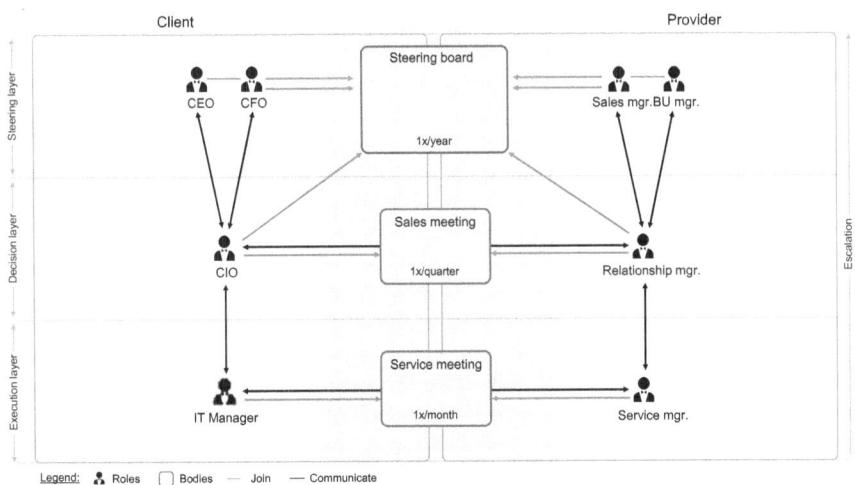

**Fig. 70** Simple operational governance

- *Legal*: Limited to high impact depending on whether the provider has already incorporated in its services the requirements of the regulations. If not, all questions and issues will flow through the governance team.
- *Audit*: None to medium depending on whether the provider has already incorporated in its services conformity reports[4] of its own internal control system.
- *Financials*: Limited. Governance team may have to provide detailed explanations on services from time to time.

## Practical Implementation

A governance organisation is a fully standing organisation between the two companies it brings together. Most governance implementations are architectured around the same principles:

- Three-layer layout: execution, decision, steering.
- Horizontal interactions between the parties within each layer through the roles and the bodies.
- Vertical, bottom-up escalation path crossing the layers.

### Simple Outsourcing

Although defined on paper like in Fig. 70, simple outsourcing governance organisations are characterised by a reduced number of interlocutors—namely,

---

[4]Formerly known as SOS, ISAE reports seem to become the worldwide standard commonly accepted by clients.

two on each side (the couples CIO–relationship manager and IT manager–service manager), and direct communication routes ignoring bodies and their formal rules.

In a simple outsourcing, the satisfaction of the client usually comes from the quality of RtB activities, in other terms, from the capacity of the provider to ensure stable operations with a low level of incidents. Since the stake lies in the execution layer, it is the IT manager and the service manager who are the key players.

This kind of organisation works well as long as the IT manager on the client side (supported by one, max two other team members) and the service manager on the provider side can handle both the complexity and the volumes of the outsourcing.

### Complex Outsourcing

Here the complexity and the volumes can no longer be absorbed by single individuals, hence the need to shift from a person-oriented to a process-oriented governance structure. Complex outsourcing governance organisations are thus characterised by a higher number of interlocutors acting under a more rigorous segregation of duties and a higher level of formalism arising from a more systematic use of the defined bodies.

In a complex, strategic outsourcing, the quality of RtB activities is deemed to be a given fact, meaning that experiencing stable operations will usually not be the main source of satisfaction for the client (but unstable operations will indeed be a source of great dissatisfaction). It is rather the capacity of the provider to accompany in quality and quantity the development of the client's business that leads the client to consider the outsourcing successful. It is consequently the whole CtB sub-organisation that has the focus as highlighted in Fig. 71, where the main activities of such sub-organisation include:

- *Requests managers*. Submit/take, quote orders and project requests.
- *Sales meeting*. Discuss and authorise non-automatic orders; decide contract changes.
- *Change meeting*. Analyse, prioritise and organise orders execution.

### Dos and Don'ts

The parties should
- Lay down the details of the organisation in the service operation manual during the project and raise early enough with top management potential issues with the staffing foreseen.
- While in production, organise as many encounters between the persons or the bodies as required although it exceeds the corresponding financial provisions foreseen in the contract. Saving costs on the relationship is a bad investment.

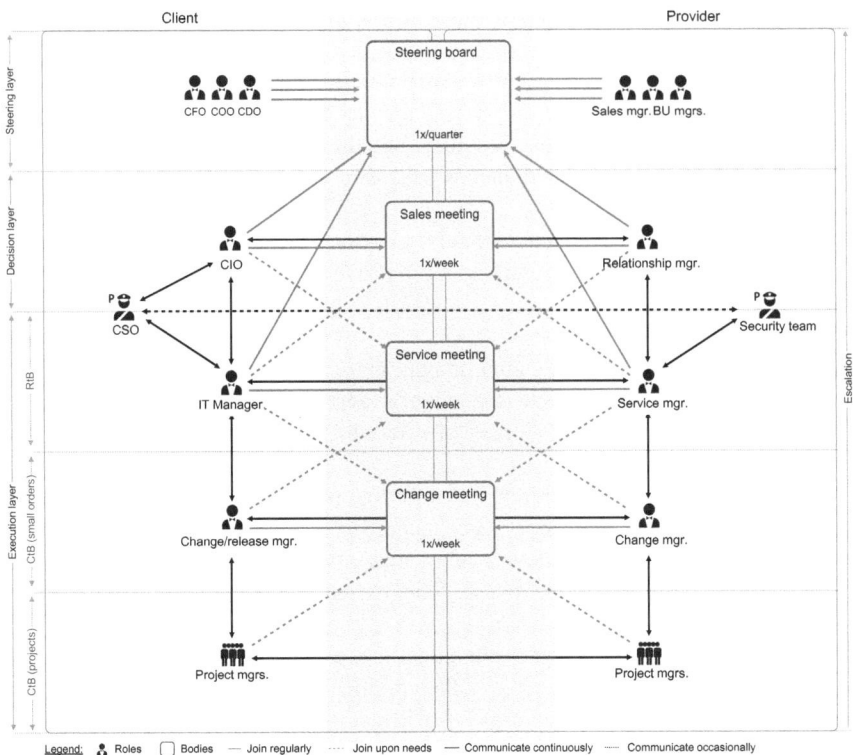

**Fig. 71** Complex operational governance

- Prepare, run and close the meetings in a structured way with appropriate formalism to avoid discrepancies and misunderstandings. It is good practice to have the minutes of the meeting finalised and ready to be sent at the end of the meeting.
- Pay attention to teams' morale on each side, in particular to front-line members who have regular and close interactions. For these persons, organising an initial internship into the other's party organisation would help to create links and have a better understanding of the constraints of that party. On a more regular basis, spending a day per week or per month in the other party's offices would also help.
- Organise punctual encounters between the members on each side who bear the same roles, e.g. service desk process owner (client side) with service desk manager (provider side), even if this is not foreseen in the governance framework.
- Regard each other as part of a truly balanced relationship and adopt a respectful attitude at all times. The provider is not a slave and the client is not the cash cow. Overconfident behaviour and inappropriate words should be banned.

The client should

- Carefully select the persons who will constitute the team. Good engineers do not necessarily make good managers. The persons should be able and willing to change from hands-on to hands-off and from a technology- to a service-oriented role. For those persons who previously considered staying in IT, but would want to change jobs in a more managerial position, it could be an excellent opportunity. In contrast, forcing existing staff members to occupy a role against their nature would lead to problems: not only would they try to do things on their own instead of having them done by the provider, but they would also sometimes try to understand useless technical details and direct the provider with respect to technological choices.

- As the case would be with an internal IT, give the provider a reasonable amount of time to adjust its own organisation and improve its services.

The provider should

- Understand fully the client's environment before bidding by paying attention to the business complexity and the client's appetite for change. The business complexity determines the number of roles and the appetite for change and the workload per role.
- Figure out early enough during the offering phase if on-site presence of the service manager or other governance team members is needed. Highly demanding clients or those with a low level of maturity require close contacts, at least during the first part of the phase. The closer the parties, the smoother the relationship.
- Adjust the governance team to the client's expectations. Should the client feel uncomfortable with one member of the provider's team—especially the relationship or the service manager—the provider should not hesitate to replace the individual concerned. Unfortunately, the same principle applies if it is one member of the provider's team who does not feel comfortable with his/her counterpart on the client side: here again, the provider should not hesitate to replace the concerned person on its side.

## Handover to Operations

Attention which each party should pay to this topic: Client: ● ● ○ Provider: ● ● ●

## Objective

Move into the new home.

This chapter explains how the switchover from project to operations takes place and what the consequences are.

## Description

Handing over to operations is shifting services from the project mode to the operations mode and transferring the responsibility from the project to the operation teams.

The shift happens in sequences and depends on the type of service. If standard, e.g. the factory provides an OS-ready server from its virtualised infrastructure, the handover is straightforward with reduced, if no, formalism. In this case, the operation team mainly expects the project team to state the delivery conditions agreed with the client, e.g. SLA. If not standard, e.g. the factory takes over non-supported technologies from the client, or requires a deep understanding of the client's environment, e.g. prepare the service desk to be SPOC, the handover requires much more preparation.

The shift can take place when the services successfully passed the tests that characterise them: factory acceptance tests for standard services, user acceptance tests for tailored services, client acceptance tests as agreed between the parties.

User and especially client acceptance tests call for client sign off in a contractually valid form.

## Process

For most services, the shift follows the basic principle described below:

1. The provider prepares the services.
2. Once ready, it makes them available to the client for testing.
3. The client tests them against predefined criteria and confirms acceptance.
4. The provider prepares the target operational conditions.
5. The provider hands over to operations.

Services subject to ODP or requiring a long handover preparation are on-boarded before they are made available to the client for testing. Upon acceptance, the provider may have to perform some minor adjustments to prepare them for the FMO as represented by Fig. 72 (Fig. 73).

**Fig. 72** Handover to operations process

**Fig. 73** Handover to operation process with preliminary on-boarding

## Practical Implementation

### Tests

Among the many denominations used in IT literature to qualify tests, in outsourcing one distinguishes two main categories: factory tests, which are the responsibility of the provider, and acceptance tests, which are the responsibility of the client.

Factory tests are further broken down into:

- *Unit tests*, executed by the production units when delivering the individual components of the solution, e.g. team A of the factory delivers OS-ready servers, team B operational workstations and team C security control mechanisms.
- *Integration tests*, executed by the project team when integrating together the various components of the solution, e.g. the project team checks that client applications running on the workstations reach the servers without being blocked by security.

Acceptance tests are further broken down into:

- *User tests*, executed by key users for applications involving business workflows and parameters and by the IT staff for the others.
- *Client acceptance test*, executed by the IT staff or IT management or, as is often the case, not executed at all. Instead, the client mentions that the project is accepted in the last steering board minutes.

Other main test types encountered:

- *Continuity tests*, to ensure the capacity of the information system recover from major disaster. It is usually the provider that runs the test on dry infrastructures and the client to confirm its successful execution.
- *Security penetration tests*, when the systems require a high level of protection. The client almost always expects the test to be executed by an external, specialised company.
- *Load tests*, when the new systems are expected to process large volumes of transactions. Such tests are rather difficult to set up because they require the systems to be preloaded with volumes of data close to those of the target production environment and the transactions to be executed simultaneously by large numbers of concurrent users. Often, the tests are executed during the dress rehearsal when dozens of users are invited over for a week-end to prepare for the cutover.

### Acceptance

Acceptance refers to the action of testing the services against predefined criteria commonly agreed between the parties beforehand and formalising whether the tests passed or failed. If the criteria have been properly formulated, test results should be unquestionable. Properly formulating criteria is difficult however, particularly due to the parties' diverging views about the services to be delivered: service-ready for the provider vs. function-ready for the client. The SMART technique described below helps structuring the thought process.

*Specific* In outsourcing projects where the resulting information system is made of a countless number of foreign components, the criteria should be set to exclusively measure the services delivered by the provider, excluding any services from the client or third parties. If this is not possible, the parties should at least be able to reasonably isolate such foreign components or limit their influence.

*Measurable* It seems obvious to say, but there must be a technical mean to check the criteria. Both the means (nature) and the volumes (quantities) should be clearly defined.

*Assignable* A defined person (or category of person) or eventually a system should be identified to perform the test.

*Realistic* The criteria must be obviously achievable, ideally benchmarked against similar market services.

*Time-related* When the test is to be executed or when it is supposed to produce its results can be decisive in some situations.

---

**Example**

The outsourcing is about transforming a mainframe hosted in the client's premises and running four distinct applications into a distributed architecture of four smaller servers hosted in the provider's data centres and each running one application. The components of the new architecture shall meet the same performance levels as before, during office hours when the workload is the highest.

The parties wish to agree on performance criteria and discuss what is acceptable (OK) and what is not (NOK):

- Specific. NOK: the new architecture shall... | OK: application x shall....
- Measurable. NOK: ... process x transactions of y type per minute | OK: ... process x transactions of y type per minute by using tool z and measures being taken at the exit of application x.
- Assignable. NOK: [nothing] | OK: the processing shall start upon activation of module x by any user of department y.
- Achievable. NOK: the latency between applications x and y [now distributed on a network] shall not exceed that of the same modules on the mainframe | OK: [either leave blank or agree on acceptable values in ms including how these would be measured].

- Time-related. NOK: [nothing] | OK: the test shall be executed at any time between 10 a.m. to 4 p.m. during a working day [to best represent peak hours].

## On-boarding

Establishing the bridge between project and operations is the responsibility of the service management stream within the project governance structure. The stream leader, who represents the FMO, first establishes the overall framework for the operational services by preparing the service and operation manuals. They then liaise with the various service units in the factory to prepare them individually, as a minimum to implement the basic service delivery conditions agreed with the client, e.g. the SLA. Units that need a deeper understanding of the client to provide their services need to follow a reinforced on-boarding process and usually have their own dedicated on-boarding structure. The example below describes the on-boarding relation between project and operations for the most representative of them: the service desk.

---

### Example

When, during the project, it comes to delivering the service desk work package, the service management stream leader establishes contact with their counterpart in the operations, the service desk on-boarding team leader, as illustrated in Fig. 74. After collecting the relevant information from all project streams, the service manager discusses them with the service desk on-boarding manager. Together, they prepare:

1. The internal and external processes that will allow the service desk to route incidents and service requests to the right business units.
2. The support scenarios for complex incidents which are most likely to occur so that by day one service desk agents can rely on a pre-coded logic.
3. The knowledge base for incidents which are likely to repeat regularly. Initially empty or nearly empty, agents will constantly populate it with new cases.
4. The tools to handle incidents and service requests, along with those required to support users remotely.
5. The contact names database including the details of regular users, VIPs and client managers.
6. The service levels agreed including hours of service, pick-up rate, target resolution rate and languages spoken.
7. The content and structure of the regular service reports, including incidents opened, closed, pending, trends, mean time to resolve, etc.

Furthermore, the on-boarding manager prepares the service desk in general, team D in particular, to the forthcoming handover.

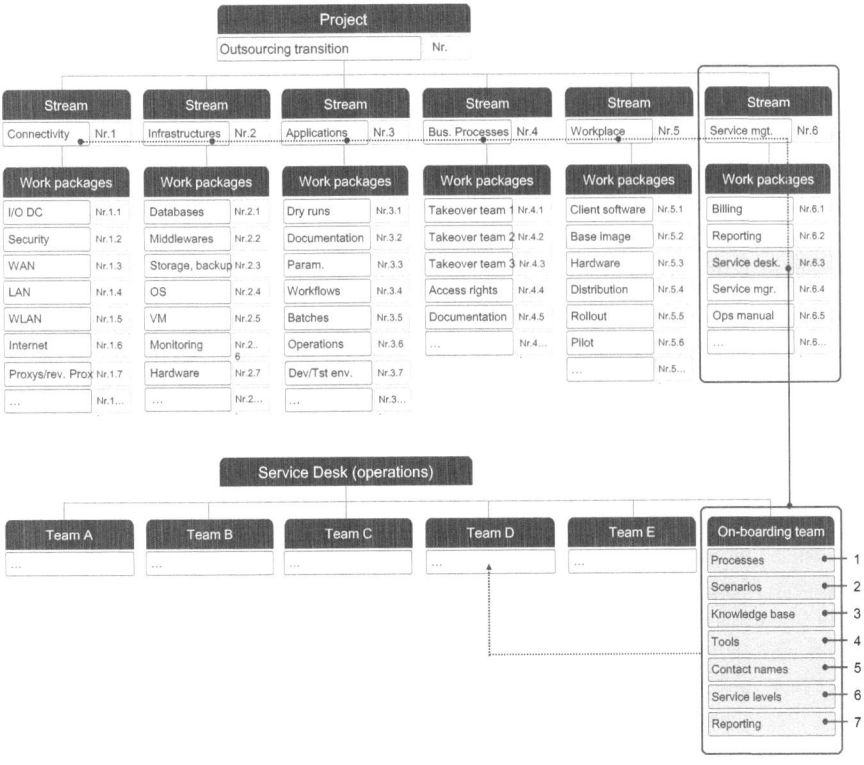

**Fig. 74** Example of service desk on-boarding

To ensure a smooth ramp-up, the service desk will absorb the new services gradually. For complex incidents, it will be able to count on the active support of project stream leaders during the project.

## Handover

The project may have passed the final acceptance without necessarily being fully completed. Services accepted with reserves; services not properly working, but not subject to any acceptance tests; minor configurations requiring fine-tuning; etc.: the list of small to bigger imperfections may be long, but not sufficient (legally or operationally) to postpone the start of the systems' productive use. The parties then agree to go live and have the defects corrected while in production.[5] For this, they establish the delta between services contracted and delivered and attach the list to the go-live protocol. At this stage, the services are considered productive and the project can start closing down.

---

[5]Either under the warranty regime of the project contract or the conditions of the operation contracts, as agreed between the parties during the negotiations.

In parallel, the provider's project and service manager ensure the same internal handshake on the basis of the said list. If they do not agree, as is often the case because, e.g., the list contains too many elements that fall out of the capacities of the production teams, the services still go live but the provider may need to maintain a reduced project structure for weeks or even months to correct the defects. However, these are internal matters which would be transparent to the client.

## Dos and Don'ts

Tests
- Plan user acceptance tests long in advance and leave enough float in the planning to have users prepare and execute them. Pay particular attention to winter and, above all, summer holidays, where no significant testing activity will happen due to the lack of personnel.

Acceptance
- When the outsourcing includes a transformation or a major move of the upper layers, it goes without saying that UAT represent a key element of the project and both parties shall consider it with due care accordingly. In all other cases, such as lift and shift outsourcings, try to limit the involvement of users through UAT to critical functions or applications that may have been altered. A complete retesting of the business logic for all functions is not relevant; smoke tests or application integration tests are sufficient.
- Pay attention to how changes occurring during the project may alter previously agreed acceptance criteria. In projects involving heavy configuration work of business applications, requirements evolve over time as key users discover details they could not figure out before. If the chain requirements (client) → configuration (provider) → acceptance (client) is not maintained in line at all times, UAT may be complicated.

On-boarding
- Whatever the complexity of the outsourcing, always foresee a stream representing the operations and, by extension, the target operating model, as an integral part of the project governance. Limiting the project to the sole set-up of the systems would only postpone other necessary activities to a later date at a moment where the parties are busy running daily businesses and the project structure no longer exists.
- Preparing the handover to operations takes months. Involve the target business units, at best, right from the beginning of the project and, at worst, at the latest halfway through. The parties may, otherwise, be assured that the months following the handover will be chaotic. Unresolved incidents, ping-pong communications, manual processing of service requests, missing reports, missing documentation, etc., will add up to all other unavoidable post-cutover problems that characterise a complex outsourcing.

Handover

- To compensate for all kinds of fuzzy situations where acceptance has not taken place as it should have, e.g. lack of time, lack of diligence, misalignment between requirements and acceptance criteria, but the client uses the systems productively, the parties shall agree on a clause of automatic acceptance. In other terms, once the systems are used productively, they are deemed automatically accepted without any reserves within the meaning of the contract, irrespectively of whether tests have been performed or not.

# Running Phase: The Operations

**5**

**Abstract**

In this chapter, you will learn how to expand the operational governance structure within the client organisation to foster communication and compensate the loss of flexibility induced by the outsourcing, how to align multiple operating models in case of a multi-provider management situation, how to anticipate up front an inexorable end of the contract to avoid bad surprises.

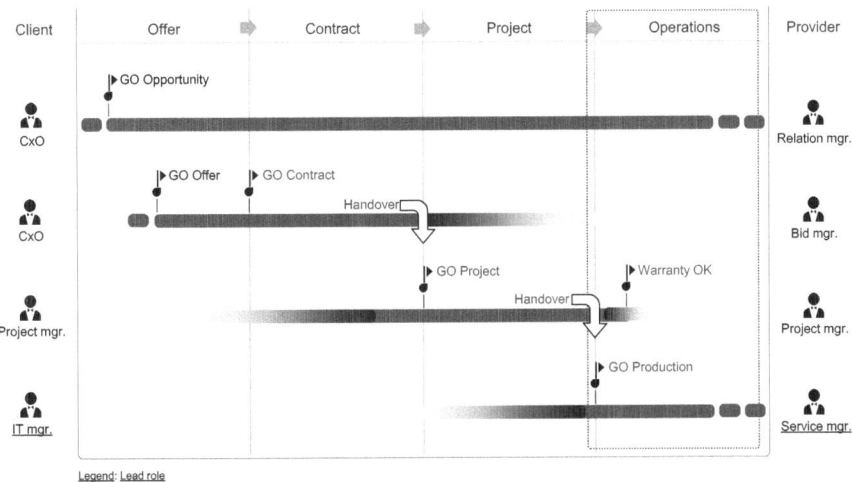

**Fig. 75** Running phase in the outsourcing life-cycle

## Drive Outsourcing

Attention which each party should pay to this topic: Client: ●●● Provider: ●●○

## Objective

Expand the outsourcing governance structure within the client organisation.

The section "Enforce Operational Governance" in Chap. 4 explains how to structure the communication between the client and the provider. This chapter explains how to expand this structure upstream in the client's organisation to get the provider even closer to the client's business.

## Description

It will take at least a year for the parties to embrace smooth collaboration, from service units producing the services to end users receiving them. During that time, governance teams will have to adjust and optimise their own internal processes along with the processes at the junction between them.

However, how fluid the processes between the parties are, an outsourcing is never as flexible as an internal IT (whether such flexibility is detrimental to other aspects is something different). This forces the client to operate a profound shift of paradigm, from reactive to proactive, where proactive means anticipating as much as possible the evolution of the information system. Anticipating is made possible by properly managing the sources from where the evolutions can emanate. Basically, these are:

- *Management*, which sets the business strategy and expects the information system to adequately sustain it.
- *Users*, who report on the delta between sought and actual capacities, i.e. the gap between what the systems should ideally allow versus their limitations.
- *IT*,[1] which maintains existing systems constantly in line with the market and introduces new systems proceeding arising from internal or external requirements.

Depending on the industry, other factors such as audit, security or compliance expand the list of sources triggering evolutions.

Since the sources are all interrelated and influence each other, they need to be connected and form part of a common communication platform ruled by hard structures.

---

[1]Including services delivered by the internal staff and the provider.

## Communication Structure

The most efficient communication structure is the one that stands as a natural extension of the governance structure which rules the outsourcing relationship as illustrated in Fig. 71. Following the same perception with regard to the flow of the communications and the prerogatives entrusted at each level, one can define three layers: steering, management and execution, the latter distinguishing between run-the-business (RtB) and change-the-business (CtB) activities. Each layer is further characterised by the corresponding ITIL processes at the interface between the parties.

### Decision Layer

This layer is materialised by an IT steering committee comprising members from top management like the CEO, CFO, CDO, etc., and is driven by the COO or the CIO.

Its' role is to keep in line the business and the IT strategies. It is the place where corporate-wide and off-budget decisions are taken.

The committee meetings should take place, at a minimum, on a monthly basis.

### Management Layer

This layer is materialised by a users' committee comprising key business users, each member representing a key business function, process or system and is driven by the CIO or their deputy.

Its' role is to keep in line the needs of the users (who follow the business strategy) and the capabilities of the information system (which follows the IT strategy). It is the place where business needs and IT constraints are openly discussed.

For a complex information system, the committee should meet quarterly. In other cases, one or two committee meetings per year could be enough.

### Execution Layer

This layer is materialised by two committees:

- A service committee, comprising the internal IT staff as well as the members of the provider' governance. The committee is driven by the IT manager. Depending on the volumes, the meeting can be subdivided into several meetings, e.g. incidents, problems, service management.
- A change committee, also known as change advisory board (CAB), comprising the project managers as well as other persons of the organisation who have a stake in the changes, e.g. the organisational change department if there is one. The committee is driven by the change manager.

The roles of these committees are, respectively, to run and change the services according to the decisions taken in the above layers as well as to feed back the management and decision layers with technical information affecting the strategy or its execution.

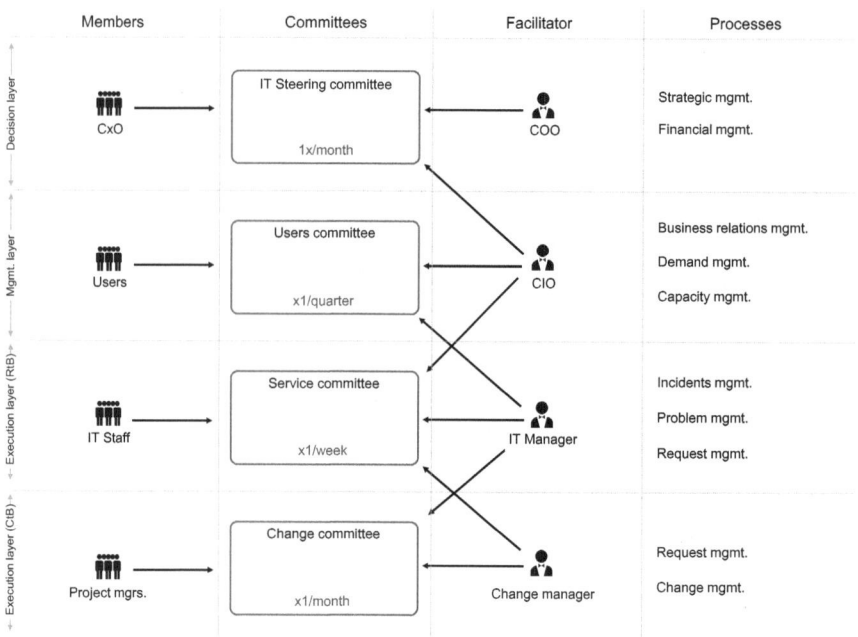

**Fig. 76** Client internal driving structure

The service committee meetings should take place weekly; the change committee monthly or weekly when in high-volume environments.

## Practical Implementation

Figure 76 shows the possible implementation of such communication structure with, on the right, the key ITIL processes applying to each layer. The accompanying case study tells how the structure can help the client to cope with suboptimal processes.

**Case study: how an optimal driving structure can help cope with suboptimal processes**

The client is a universal bank with a growing wealth management division targeting customers who have an excess of cash that calls for financial investments. As opposed to the former generation, though, those customers from the new economy are both aware and active with respect to the management of their money. As a consequence, they rank modern investment tools as number one driver when it comes to choose between two banks.

The bank wishes to bolster this segment and takes the necessary steps to implement an adequate strategy, including a complete review of its investment fee base and an adapted communication. After 18 months, the bank records a double-digit growth in this business but at the same time experiences a growing misalignment between front activities and back capacities. The information system is not any more in line with the daily reality.

This misalignment originates in a flawed capacity management process. But even though the bank failed to anticipate the technical consequences of business expectations, it could count on a solid internal communication platform to tackle the problem reactively.

*Users committee.* The key user representing the bank frontline reports that client managers face an increasing number of requests from clients, who expect real-time valuation of their fortune, including cash accounts in addition to market assets, and who are not any more willing to wait 24 h as in the past for this. The key user representing portfolio management informs his colleague that the portfolio management application—that contains the market assets, feeds the core banking application—that contains the cash accounts, only daily through the end-of-day batch. They then turn to the key user representing the core banking application to discuss the possibilities and consequences of transforming the batch interface into a real-time one. The three of them agree to analyse the matter in detail and work out a functional requirements definition document for the CIO.

*IT management committee.* The CIO discusses with the IT staff the technical consequences of transforming a high-volume batch interface into a real-time one on the core banking and portfolio management applications. The team amends the functional requirements elaborated by the key users with technical and service delivery considerations. Based on this requirements document, the CIO requests two quotes, one to the core banking software provider for the development of the interface, the other to its service provider for the implementation of the interface and the consequential adjustments of affected infrastructure components.

*IT steering committee.* The CIO and the COO expose the matter to the board of directors: business requirements and consequences, IT requirements and consequences, total cost of the recommended change. The board decides to go forward as soon as possible. The CFO releases the corresponding budget. The board asks the CIO to report on the details of the project in the next steering.

*IT change committee.* Through the IT manager, the CIO entrusts the change manager to define the project requirements. On the base of the proposals received from the software and service providers, the latter analyses the impact on the project portfolio, resets the priorities of other projects as required and sets up the project structure that will be responsible for delivering the project.

## Decision Layer

*Strategic management* The mission of the IT steering committee is to define an IT strategy and keep it in line with the business strategy. For this, it shall consider the needs of the market (demand), the service offering of the providers (offer) and the capacities of the company. Note that this is true for any company, whether in the case of outsourcing or not. However, in the context of a strategic outsourcing, the parties

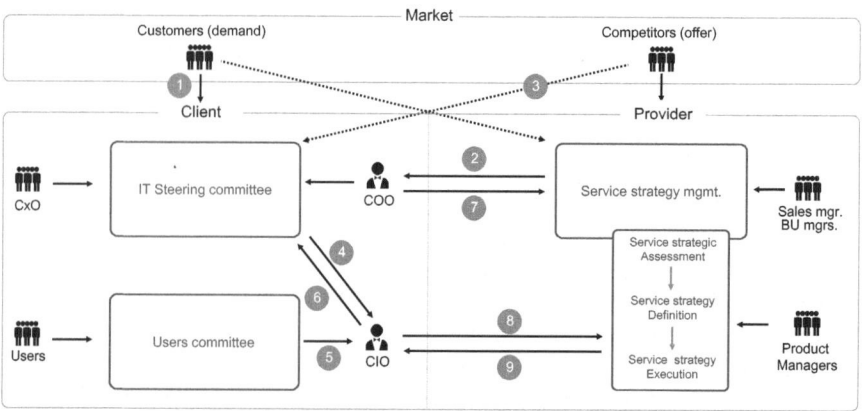

**Fig. 77** Strategic management

can draw mutual benefits from interfacing their respective strategies. The client can influence the development of the services and the provider can access insider, first-hand information in return. Figure 77 shows an implementation of such alignment at a strategic level, which the client can replicate with its key software vendors and outsourcing providers, as the case may be.

The client collects market requirements from its customers (1) and looks at the provider's service offering to meet them (2). At the same time, it analyses the competition's offering (3)—something that the provider obviously also does to develop and benchmark its services. The client then defines an IT strategy (4). To ensure the latter is consistently declined at an operational level, it collects feedbacks from key users (5) and IT (6) and then realigns it as needed. By doing this, it feeds back the provider with actual market demand (7) and actual user needs (8). Such exchange can happen through the regular steering boards illustrated in Fig. 71 in Chap. 4 or ad hoc strategic meetings. The provider adjusts the services and informs the client on the improvements (9). The steering committee can play its full role when working in symbiosis with the users' committee.

*Financial management* This process serves three objectives: (1) allocate the budget required for the services, (2) understand how the budget is distributed and (3) control how it is actually used:

1. Outsourcing somehow eases the CIO and CFO's jobs because of its OPEX nature, but the fact remains that a certain level of CAPEX for new projects is always required and depends on the client's appetite for change. To avoid the usual bottleneck created by a massive number of requests for quote (RfQ) coming on top of the ongoing CtB quoting process during the budgetary phase, the client would be well advised to issue RfQ evenly during the year and as soon as needs arise.

2. Understanding how the costs are structured and then how they can be distributed throughout the organisation to reflect the total cost per user is no easy task, if it is possible at all. It vastly depends on the capacity of the provider to provide granular invoices and in such a format that the client can post-process them. This activity should be given a large amount of thought and attention from the parties during the initial transformation when the provider creates the billing structure into the invoicing system; otherwise, it may be very difficult to review it afterwards.

3. Controlling how the budget is spent is straightforward for fixed price services. It is not for complex projects billed on a T&M basis. If the provider does not compute the costs using the earned value approach, it reports monthly hours without knowing whether these were used efficiently or not, resulting in a late detection of a possible slippage. Although it is its duty to warn the client when the project starts to exceed budget by more than an agreed percentage, e.g. 10%, it is very common for warning signs arising when the gap has become so important that it becomes noticeable without having to be computed. The discrepancy between how the deliverables are presented in the offer, how they have been structured in the provider's system and how they are reported monthly, complicate even further the controlling. Financial management requires a significant contribution from the CFO during the budgetary phase, but for the remainder of the year it is mainly an activity under the responsibility of the CIO.

## Management Layer

*Demand management* This process is best known for being the means by which to understand users' needs throughout the business life cycle and detect new needs as they arise: IT invites users to provide their feedback on the services made available to them and to communicate their expectations with respect to significant changes they would recommend introducing, with the further objective of improving the services. In order for this platform of dialogue to not turn into meetings where whines about existing services mingle with unrealistic expectations regarding future services, the process must be two-sided. Not only does IT have its own constraints, but the budget is not endlessly expandable. The CIO or their deputy shall duly explain the former and challenge the latter. In the end, the goal is to align mutual expectations between IT and business. It is good practice to structure the meetings into three parts: the first one reserved for IT, the second for users and the third for a third party proposed either by the IT or the users. Demand management reaches maximal efficiency when backed by communities, e.g. the super user of an application is also member of an external community of clients using the same application.

*Business relationship management* It is the soft part of demand management and aims at maintaining a close and trustful relation with key users. It is primarily a social process: the CIO and their deputy shall go out of their offices and visit regularly key users to build a personal relation with them. There is no need to further detail the many benefits they will draw from it. The technical side of the process is to maintain the map of application super users up to date. When it comes to introducing new application releases, IT must know who to involve in the testing process. This takes on its full meaning in large organisations with hundreds of different applications. Here, a simple list with names and details maintained up to date upon personnel turnover perfectly makes it.

*Capacity management*  Match IT resources with business demand. IT resources can be of hardware type (e.g. components, size, performance), software (e.g. applications, modules, options) or human (e.g. staffing, training, support). Most organisations manage capacities responding to specific events, but very few anticipate them. This is precisely what capacity management is all about: understanding how and how much the company's business is developing to anticipate the extra needs and have them ready within a reasonable time frame. If demand management is run as described above, then capacity management should flow out of it naturally. One hour from the users' committee once per year to go over the main business trends and understand how these may affect the information system could be enough for the IT to collect the requirements.

## Execution Layer

*Incident management*  Incident management aims at restoring normal service operations as quickly as possible after an incident to minimise business impact. However, if solving each incident individually as it arises is obviously important, the client satisfaction index is measured by the development in the situation over the long term. Development being determined by the observation of the trend between two points in time and the situation representing the overall volume of incidents during that period, trend analysis is the means to measure the performance of the service to further optimise it. Performance may mean different things to different clients, but generally speaking, fewer incidents per period, a higher resolution rate and a lower resolution time are the main factors. How does one improve the performance on a large number of items? By determining repetitive patterns and optimising the underlying processes. This brings us back to section "Get the Big Picture" in Chap. 2 and the necessity to have supporting tools properly set up and allowing to draw on useful statistics.

*Problem management*  Focus on root cause analysis of errors instead of spending too much time on troubleshooting. This should be the motto. Problem management aims to resolve the root causes of incidents to prevent recurrence of additional incidents related to the same underlying reason. Problem analysis can be complex because the root cause may be caused by many factors and located far away from the incident. Each problem being unique, there is unfortunately no magic nor generic solution. The recommendation here concerns the way the process should be handled: maintain the links in the incident–problem–release chain, ideally through an ITIL-based integrated suite of tools and thus determine, upstream, what actions lead to problem analysis and, downstream, what actions proceed from the analysis.

Upstream, a granular classification of incidents that allows drawing up detailed statistics definitely helps; downstream, a pointer on the corrective measure, whether it is a temporary workaround or the final solution, allows to keep track of the correction and inform the various persons who opened the incidents at the origin of the problem accordingly.

*Request management* Requests are small needs originating from users or the IT governance team. They can take the form of requests for information when the requestor seeks support on how to perform a certain function, e.g. execute a macro in a text processor, or the form of requests for services when the requestor asks for the execution of an activity usually referenced to as IMACD. IMACD are minor standard changes, where minor means a small amount of money (from 50 to 200 € in most cases) and standard means precoded, risk-free and billed at a fixed price. IMACD are specific to each service category. Examples of workplace IMACD include *I*nstalling a software, *M*oving a workstation, *A*dding a right on a share, *C*hanging a password, *D*isposing a printer. The parties shall anticipate the standard requests which are likely to happen in production and prepare them during the project. Preparatory works include identifying the types of requests, inserting them into the request management system, coding the workflows from the users to the factory unit that will execute them and defining their cost. When a request does not meet the minor and standard criteria, it is a request for change. In that case, it requires more attention from the parties and thus invokes the change management process.

*Change management* As opposed to requests, changes are not standard. They theoretically call for requirements definition from the client, to which the provider responds with an offer. In high change volume environments, such formalism would rapidly clog the business, hence the need to foresee a contractual mechanism that offers an optimal speed/risk ratio. To this end, it is good practice to distinguish between small and bigger changes. Small changes may be, for instance, services which do not require more than a few man days, e.g. five, and which can be carried out by a single person. These can simply be managed without formalism on either side. Among the hundreds of small changes the parties may handle per year, the benefits drawn from the absence of formalism largely offsets the few discussions proceeding from changes inadequately described and/or executed that may arise. It is good practice to foresee in the contract a pool of hours with the persons on both sides who have authority to request and execute changes. If the client knows the approximate volume of changes it may place per year, it is advised to discuss a prepaid pool. In exchange for a commitment regarding a minimum number of hours, the provider offers a discounted hourly rate. Larger changes such as projects, especially if they affect recurring services, shall be formally contracted through offers. All changes must be identified with a unique number and tracked in a tool.

## Dos and Don'ts

Decision layer
• If the client's level of maturity in IT matters is low, it may be difficult to mobilise top management for the steering committee. Unfortunately, there are very few other options other than forcing at least a member of the board to have regular exchanges to align IT with the business. If successful, keep in mind that executives think holistically. Be synthetic and keep away from annoying details. With respect to operations, present only the trends and the big figures; in projects, stick to one page per critical project. Prepare precise questions for decisions.

Management layer
• Involving users is almost as hard as involving management. Plan the committee way ahead of time and at a time when all key users can attend. Since the committee aims at discussing key functions of the information systems, do not accept second cutters joining for representation purpose only. Well-chosen topics involving product demonstration from third parties normally help.

Execution layer
• Execution does not mean executant. The CIO deputy and the change manager shall be empowered with prerogatives allowing them to take important decisions such as how things are done like introducing new or changing processes, modifying tools and also have a budget for this.
• Set up a change advisory board and hold weekly discussions about the production plan including all changes likely to affect the production environment.

## Manage Multiple Providers

Attention which each party should pay to this topic: Client: ●●● Provider: ●●○

### Objective

Align multiple operating models.
    This section presents the consequences of working with multiple providers and explains how to streamline the various operating models to mask the complexity to the client.

### Description

Working with multiple providers can either be a wish when it proceeds from the IT strategy or a requirement when one provider does not offer all the sought-after services. Depending on where the client made the cuts, the consequences can

**Fig. 78** Level of attention required per type of multi-provider situation

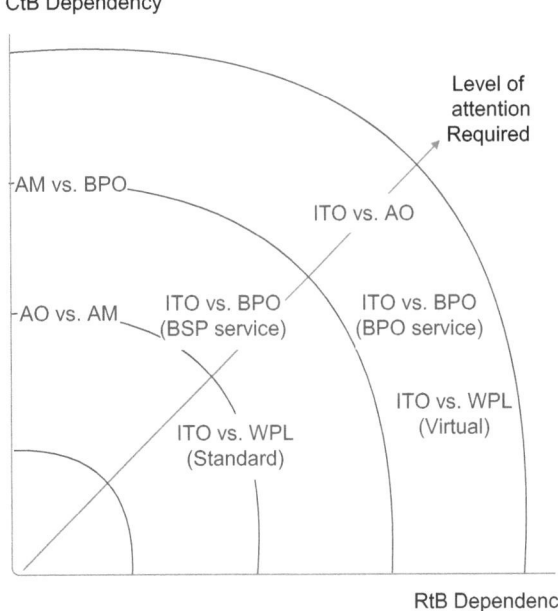

CtB Dependency

Level of attention Required

AM vs. BPO

ITO vs. AO

AO vs. AM

ITO vs. BPO (BSP service)

ITO vs. BPO (BPO service)

ITO vs. WPL (Virtual)

ITO vs. WPL (Standard)

RtB Dependency

range from keeping an eye on the interfaces between the outsourced services to actively managing them.

One way to determine the level of attention required is to observe their dependencies on the RtB and CtB axes, where RtB determines to what extent they dynamically rely on each other to run and CtB to what degree they influence each other during a change. The higher the dependencies, the higher the level of attention required.

Figure 78 represents common multi-provider situations and positions them in relation to the others with respect to the level of attention required. The positioning shall be understood in general considering a complex information system; some systems taken individually may lead to completely different results.

It comes as no surprise that the most problematic cut is between the IT operation (ITO) and application operation (AO) layers, business applications running on technical systems. On the RtB axis, the unavailability of an interface hosted on a system run by the ITO provider may, for example, block the whole end-of-day batch process run by the AO provider. On the CtB axis, each maintenance window of one or the other provider requires extensive coordination to reach the up-and-running state.

On the other extreme, cuts that usually go well together concern the ITO and workplace (WPL) layers. Client-only applications run on workstations and have little or no RtB dependency with back-end infrastructures. Client–server applications have dependencies, but do not affect back-end components dynamically. When they do, it is usually in a predictable way, e.g. office automation applications consume increasing storage volumes, but at a speed that should not endanger daily operations. As per Fig. 78, virtualising the WPL layer boosts the level of dependency on the RtB axis up to its maximum if the virtualisation systems are run by the ITO provider.

---

**Case study: how the absence of multi-provider management can lead to chaos**

The client has a complex information system comprising 30 business applications interconnected with a central ERP through interfaces. The ERP heavily relies on the data received from the applications during the night to run the end-of-day batch. The information system is outsourced to a Tier I provider that provides the whole stack of services, including ITO, AO and application management (AM).

The client is satisfied with the RtB capacity of the provider but seeks a higher level of business expertise with respect to CtB. At the end of the contract, it decides to leave the ITO layer for all applications with the current provider (A) and transfer the AO and AM layers to another Tier I specialised provider (B). For this, it negotiates two separate contracts with strict borders of responsibilities: A is responsible for providing the infrastructures and B for running the applications.

Both providers showing the highest degree of professionalism in their respective areas, the sum of the two contracts could only lead to an up-and-running information system with the highest possible guarantees. This proves to be true, at least for the RtB part that fully delivers the promises. CtB is a completely different matter, though.

Weekly, A and B send to the client their respective production plans with planned maintenance windows. The client being unable to understand the dependencies between the various items in the plans and their consequences, it requests B to align with A and sort out the potential conflicts. B having no contract with A, this is followed by endless tripartite ping-pongs leading in the end A and B to go repeatedly through their internal change advisory boards (CAB) and reschedule activities. When maintenance windows are finally agreed, the execution of joined activities require even more coordination: each server restarted after maintenance has cascaded consequences on the applications and each deployment of a new application release calls for infrastructure and security adjustments. Given that maintenance windows take place at night or on Sundays, specialists on both sides are sometimes unreachable.

During the 3 years of the contracts, the coordination between ITO and AO/AM is left to chance. The functioning of the information system only relies on the goodwill of both providers, each of them spending per month dozens of extra, non-remunerated hours, and in a global atmosphere of permanent chaos. Upon termination, both providers set the record straight: should the client want to renew the contracts, it needs to enforce a new organisational set-up and compensate all costs induced by this multi-provider situation.

## Consequences

This section assumes that the client installed a multi-provider situation without consistently aligning the respective operating models between all involved parties. Based on this the consequences, per business dimension, are:

*Functional* In addition to a reinforced governance organisation, the client needs to maintain technical personnel to liaise with the providers. The persons must understand the interactions between the layers at a technical level to orchestrate the production and to ensure end-to-end consistency.

*Operational* Of all the production matters, let us mention those that have ongoing consequences. (1) Production. The client needs to consolidate on a weekly basis the providers' production plans and align them to prevent conflicts. According to the dependencies between the outsourced layers, they must be at all times prepared to react immediately upon production issues. (2) Incidents. The client attributes incidents pertaining to each provider outside its organisation. This causes a disruption in the incident processing chain with cascading consequences on their capacity to follow up, inform, analyse and report on those incidents. Add to this that it should be prepared for periodic ping-pong incidents. (3) Major incidents. The client needs an on-duty organisation comprising of at least four persons to coordinate major incidents whose analysis or correction spans several layers. (4) Changes. The client attributes changes pertaining to each provider outside their organisation. Single changes that each turn into several changes placed to different providers, e.g. moving a user workstation, require the WPL and LAN providers to coordinate their actions and call for post-processing activities to execute them completely.

*Technical* Aside from their own tools, the client needs to place incidents and changes in the tools of each provider. If not, they are likely to log incidents over the phone and changes through e-mails. In all cases, they experience disruptions in the processing chains and suffer an overhead in proportion to the volumes.

*Financial* Although a single provider applies a financial surcharge for internal coordination when providing multiple services, managing multiple providers is more expensive because of the proliferation of communication channels and the multiple leakages described above.

*Security* Multiple access points between the client and the providers call for as many protection measures. While this has an impact on costs, once security is implemented, it is usually not a topic for further discussion in normal conditions. In critical environments requiring a centralisation of the security function, things can get complicated, if possible at all. It is, for example, the case when the client implements an intelligent data loss prevention tool to prevent leakage of confidential data from all exit points of the information system (systems, databases, Internet, e-mails, USB ports of workstations, etc.).

*Risk* There are several schools of thought on this subject. Some say that concentrating all services on one provider increases the risk in case of default, others say that multiplying the number of providers increases the risk of operational issues and, furthermore, others still who say that one provider has a greater chance to restore the services alone after a disaster than if it is the client who coordinates several providers. All these affirmations can prove to be false or true according to the circumstances. In the end, it is the given context that shall have the final say. In general, one can say that the complexity to establish, test and activate a DRP in case of major disaster increases with the number of providers. The likeliness to restore business-ready functions at the level of the entire information system decreases correspondingly.

*Audit* Audits are complicated because of the multiplication of providers and processes. Audit tracks of business functions spanning several layers may either suffer disruptions difficult to reconcile or simply be impossible to establish. This may raise serious concerns in regulated environments.

*Contractual* Hours of service, hours of support, service levels, maintenance windows, contract durations, maturity dates, etc.: although all providers are presumably aligned on industry standards with respect to the provision of services, the possibilities of contractual misalignments between them remain many. Keeping them approximately in line requires solid providers' management.

*Legal* Each provider is responsible for its own services, the client for the orchestration.

## Practical Implementation

If the client can afford the extra costs to orchestrate the providers, standardise the processes and interface the tools, they can decide to manage the situation on their own. Whether yes or no, they would do well to consider delegating this activity to a third party, normally the provider that bears the biggest proportion of services.

Figure 79 illustrates such delegation where the client entrusts the main provider with the management of the others. On the upper part of the figure, the client addresses up front the situation with triplicated communication channels, processes and tools. On the lower part, they are back to a standard client-provider operating model with the complexity moved backstage (Fig. 79).

For the purpose of the service, the main provider implements a so-called integration layer, consisting of a combination of organisation, processes and tools which interfaces its own operating model on the left with the operating model of second-line providers on the right. A multi-provider management (MPM) service includes the following minimal characteristics:

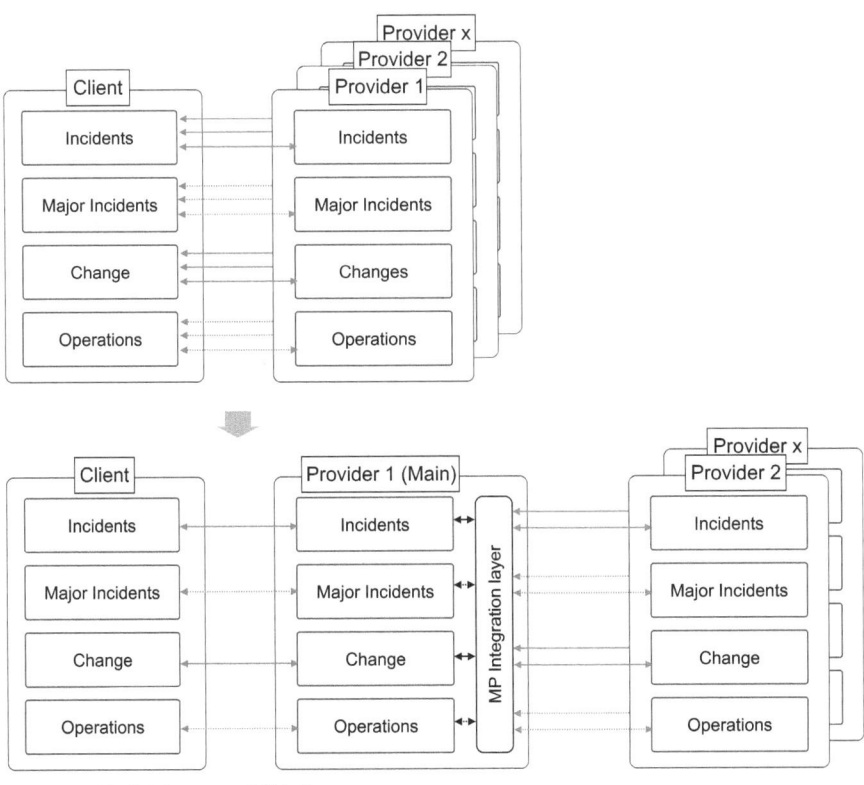

**Fig. 79** Multi-provider integration layer

*Organisation* A specific organisation, whose central figure is the providers' service manager. This organisation is normally distinct from that responsible for delivering the services to the client, the main reason being a question of role. The client service manager is the orchestrator of all the services constituting the contract with the client and MPM is only one of these. Obviously, both service managers have tighter interactions than between any other service. The role of the providers' service manager encompasses the implementation of the processes listed below and the execution of the corresponding activities.

*Processes* The minimal set of processes required to ensure smooth operations include the RtB processes (production, incident and major incident management) and one CtB process (change management). Main activities include: (1) Production. Drive service meetings with the providers; consolidate, analyse and report service performance of providers; consolidate metrics with own service performance indicators. (2) Incidents. Implement a SPOC and establish contact with other providers' L-1. (3) Major incidents. Provide the escalation point and war organisation with competences to interface with each second-line provider.

(4) Changes. Participate in the client's CAB. Check, allocate, track and closes request for change tickets.

*Tools* The unification of the second-line providers' tools is a key element of the integration layer. Without business-to-business and real-time interfaces, at least for incidents and changes, it is hardly imaginable that the service could be offered. For this, the provider is more likely to use an integrated service framework such as those mentioned in section "Get the Big Picture" in Chap. 2.

Most significant benefits and limitations that the client can expect from an MPM service are, per dimension:

*Functional* There is no need for technical persons to steer the services any more. The client can stick to a pure governance structure.

*Operational* The client gets a unique production plan with all potential conflicts sorted out that the provider can even consolidate with the client's internal plan for a marginal price increase.

*Technical* The client gets a unique set of tools for incidents and changes—its own ones or those of the provider. In both cases, they benefit from a consolidated view on all items. The integration of the tools prevents disruptions in the processing chains.

*Financial* The few dozens of thousands of euros per year that the service costs largely offset the direct, indirect and hidden costs the client would incur in doing the job on their own. The initial set-up may be the only hurdle if the tools of the providers do not offer easy interfacing capabilities.

*Security* The service does not change the technical set-up, meaning the client should not expect any changes with respect to security.

*Risk* The service slightly reduces the risks because of the technical expertise it brings to the coordination of the providers. This proves especially true in case of major incidents.

*Audit* MPM slightly alleviates the client's workload for responding to audit checks in a sense that it transfers, to the main provider, the questions of the auditors. The costs however remain, as the service excludes any audit costs which are, by essence, unpredictable.

*Contractual* The service should not affect existing contracts. However, the client and/or the provider may want to renegotiate specific provisions in existing contracts. The client may expect the provider to take on additional responsibilities because of its central role, while the provider may want to refine the boundaries of existing clauses, especially those pertaining to responsibility and liability. See legal consequences below.

*Legal*  At first sight, the service does not generate any legal obligations beyond the service itself. Although the master agreement between the parties may state that the provider's responsibility is limited to the provision of its services and the provider does not guarantee the services if not laid down otherwise, there may be situations where the responsibility of the provider could be engaged, for example, if the provider is supposed to coordinate crises but is unreachable when a major incident arises and this prevents the client from restoring operations. In such a case, the client may invoke a gross negligence of the provider and engage its responsibility in an unlimited way.

## Dos and Don'ts

Before considering a multi-provider situation:

- Unless decided otherwise for strategic reasons, consider multiple providers as a source of pain rather than a source of gain. During the bidding phase, segmenting the deal in lots attributable to distinct providers is no guarantee for better conditions on each individual lot. Quite the opposite in fact, cumulated lots would allow for operational and then financial synergies between the services. Once in production, the effect of competition is only negative: each provider stays in its own perimeter and pushes back to the client, more vigorously than normal, any activity that falls out of it.
- Notwithstanding what precedes, as the case may be, consider two distinct providers jointly providing a single solution through an MPM layer as an alternative to a single provider subcontracting part of the services. Co-sourcing may allow for better prices, particularly if the single provider subcontracts critical services and charges the client a significant risk premium for it.
- Assess all dependencies between layers before outsourcing them to distinct providers. Some layers that may seem to have nothing in common sometimes do. For example, moving a computer (devices deployment layer) that involves re-cabling in a distribution cabinet may require granting access to that computer on the target switch if Network Access Control is enforced (LAN management layer). The two distinct layers would then have to be coordinated to make the computer usable again. Though in absolute terms these two tasks are trivial, their combination calls for extensive coordination and induces delivery delays.
- Consider providers of ASP or BSP solutions as fully fledged actors of a multi-provider situation. Such solutions are not as transparent as their vendors pretend when they are part of a global information system. Interfaces, incidents, changes, etc.: from a governance perspective, they deserve almost the same level of attention as systems operated in a more traditional way.

Setting up multi-provider management:

- The client shall get extensively involved in the design of the new, global target operating model, not only because they are, in the end, the final receiver of the services, but above all also to be given enough representation authority to the MPM provider.
- The client shall ensure that their expectations towards the MPM provider are contractually backed by corresponding SLA with the other involved providers.

## Terminate Relationship

Attention which each party should pay to this topic: Client: ● ● ● Provider: ● ● ○

## Objective

Anticipate up front an inexorable end to avoid bad surprises.

This chapter describes the causes and consequences of the contract termination by pointing out the topics with most weight in the exit cost.

## Description

All contracts end one day or another. If the parties decide to continue their relationship, they are obviously the best placed to figure out the conditions of the renewal which are important for them. If they do not, there are a few other situations where the contract becomes as important as at the end of the relationship, when the parties can no longer expect anything from a common future. Depending on the conditions of the termination, the dialogue can range from cordial to completely broken off and the corresponding importance of the contract from limited to decisive.

Whatever the reasons, it would be a risky gamble to fly over the reversibility clause during initial contract negotiations.

## Causes

There can be many reasons for the contract to end, but these fall into one of the two following categories: ordinary and extraordinary.

*Ordinary termination* The contract reaches its natural end and the parties do not renew it. The decision usually comes from the client, who is not fully satisfied with the services and decides to re-insource or transfer the services to a successor supplier. Another reason may be that, on grounds of internal instructions, the client is compelled to change supplier after several renewals, irrespectively of the quality of the services.

*Extraordinary termination* It is wise here to distinguish between fault, convenience and force majeure. Fault first. These are the most problematic cases, yet rare in proportion. They proceed from events that render the pursuit of the relationship obviously impossible. For example, one party repetitively fails to fulfil its obligations, e.g. the provider breaches SLA, the client does not pay invoices. Other reasons may include mergers, acquisitions, dismantling, change of control, bankruptcy, to name but a few. In such cases, the faulty party usually assumes the consequences of the breach and a large part of the associated costs. Convenience applies when one party wishes or needs to leave the contract, but not as a consequence of a fault of the other party. For example, the headquarters of the client decides to close down operations in the country where the subsidiary outsourced its IT. In such cases, the leaving party usually assumes the consequences of the breach and a large part of the associated costs which may include penalties for unrealised gains on top. Force majeure applies when one party is not able to fulfil its obligations as a consequence of extraordinary events out of their control, e.g. earthquake.

## Practical Implementation

### Services

*Transfer and run-down services* Whether the client retains a successor supplier or re-insources, they require the provider's support to execute an orderly transfer of the services. The latter shall cooperate reasonably with the client for the development and execution of the exit plan. Although the corresponding activities do not stand in the same order of magnitude with respect to complexity and volume than those to be executed by the client for the new transition, they must be planned enough in advance, long before the new transition starts. Indeed, one of the very first activities to be executed by the provider is the interconnection of its network with that of the client or the successor.

Figure 80 positions transfer and run-down services in the context of the existing contract and shows the interrelation between these services and the ramp-up services of the successor.

The situation is as follows:

1. The client decides to transfer operations to the successor. It informs its provider 18 months in advance and requests an offer for assistance services from it.
2. The client launches the transformation with the successor through a project planned to end 3 months before the end of the current operation contract. This leaves enough float to recover from possible slippages without having to extend the contract.

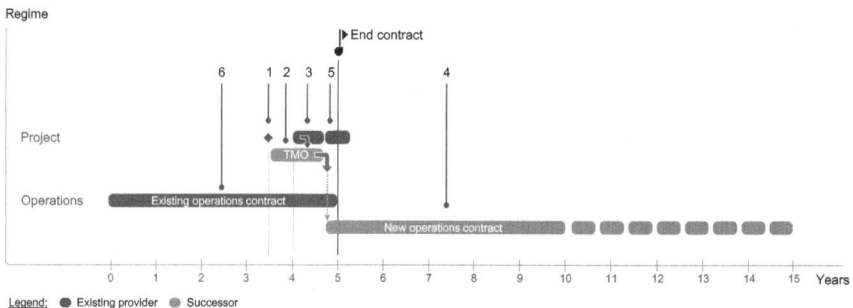

**Fig. 80** Transfer and run-down services

3. The provider delivers its services upon instructions given by the successor. Beware that at this stage of the relation, the provider does not take any initiative. It stands in a pure reactive position, waiting for precise instructions.
4. The new operations contract starts slightly before the end of the existing one. The negative lag between the two is deemed to be the fallback plan in case of serious issue with the new services.
5. The provider starts running down and decommissioning non-critical services. Unless the client opted for an early start of the new services, i.e. months before the end of the existing contract, the activities normally extend beyond the end of the existing contract.
6. The provider continues billing operational services at least until the ordinary contract term. Between the beginning of the new contract and the end of the existing one, the client pays double operation costs. This is almost unavoidable.

*Post-contract services* While Fig. 80 represents the ideal case when services between the provider and its successor barely overlap, situations involving services from the provider extending far beyond the end of the contract are not unusual. This especially happens when running down the services involve complex migrations of legacy systems.

**Case study: how heavy data migration from legacy systems can weight in the business case**

The client is a big corporation that handles large volumes of data which are subject by law to retention periods extending up to 20 years. The information system is architectured around a central mainframe, whose core application, in-house developed, evolved significantly over the last two decades. The client is outsourced to a provider.

The client decides to leave the mainframe and move to a modern, open architecture. It selects a successor able to execute the transformation and then run the services afterwards.

The problem that arises is the following: in 20 years, the mainframe application generated hundreds of millions of documents that it stored in an archive.

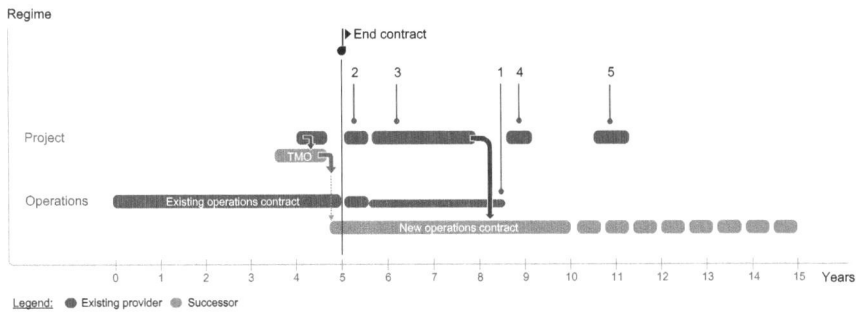

**Fig. 81** Example of post-contract services

These data can only be accessed through the application running on the mainframe. Extracting the data from the archive through the mainframe without impeding the daily performance is a 3-year endeavour.

Basically, the client has two options: freeze in read-only mode the mainframe in its current status, including the archive, for the next 20 years or launch a project to retrieve historical data, transform it and load it into the new archive. The first option forces it to maintain a 20-year operation contract; the second forces it to have only a temporary operation contract but calls for a contract representing a massive amount of work amounting to millions.

The client opts for the archive transformation. The situation, illustrated in Fig. 81, is as follows:

1. The client and the provider agree on a specific operation contract for the estimated duration of the transformation. The contract comprises the full range of services, namely, the operation of the mainframe and the archive with limited updates, connectivity, security, helpdesk, crises management. It is divided into two phases: read-write to cover the period required for the activities detailed in point 2 below and read-only for the rest of the contract.
2. Archive data not being easily accessible, the successor supplier will likely migrate only the last 6 months of transactions from the mainframe to the new platform. Consequently, the client needs to execute the annual closure of accounts on the mainframe and on the new platform at the same time, and the provider to execute the related set of services.
3. The archive transformation takes place. It is a rolling project between the provider and the successor, data being continuously extracted by the former, and then transformed and loaded by the latter.
4. At the end of the transformation, the provider runs down and decommissions all remaining services.
5. If the client had chosen the option to freeze the mainframe for 20 years, it would have taken the risk of a major project impacting the mainframe or its environment before the end of the term, e.g. the mainframe vendor could have ceased support, the provider could have changes premises, etc.

## Fees

In addition to the termination fees and/or penalties agreed in the individual contracts, the client is liable for fees and expenses incurred for the transfer and run-down of services. Unless agreed up front—very rare—these amounts are never included in the contract. The parties can nonetheless agree on cap amounts for a given scope.

## Data

As data processor, the provider is not entitled to retain data property of the client. Therefore, the two issues of great importance for the client concern extraction costs and the remittance format. If the provider uses proprietary formats for rendering the services, the client shall ensure receiving the data in an open format and, if a transformation is required, be given a clue as to the corresponding duration and cost. The example in subsection post-contract services above clearly illustrates the situation and its potential consequences.

Whereas it is usually the client that is concerned with retrieving its data, the provider may also want to protect itself from situations where the client does not request them anymore. For this, it may impose the client to order their deletion and, if the latter fails to fulfil its obligation, reserve itself the right to delete them. This clause is enforceable as far as no valid reasons such as legal obligations concerning archiving or preservation of evidences speak against it. In the latter case, the provider would be entitled to charge the client for the corresponding costs.

## Assets

The provider normally agrees to sell, at book value, the dedicated assets used in the services. These most often concern decentral hardware like user workstations and network components. This calls for special attention from the client and further clarifications at the time of establishing the contract because it is very likely that the provider will want to wipe all configurations containing intellectual property before handing over the hardware, thus rendering the devices unusable.

For the rest, the parties shall promptly return any material provided by the other party, e.g. keys, IT and telecommunication gadgets, badges, etc., and vacate the premises.

## Documentation

Documentation is a sensitive topic as it touches the limit of intellectual property. The client will try to have the provider disclose all existing documentation, including systems configurations, designs, specifications, operations manuals, user-related documentation, subcontractors, etc., to ensure they can continue operating and developing the information system after termination. For its part, the provider will try to protect its intellectual property from being disclosed to competition. The border between what is intellectual property and what is not may sometimes be difficult to determine though, and this can have dramatic consequences if not precisely formulated, as illustrated by the case study below. Industry practice establishes that the provider discloses all documentation, including that covered by intellectual property and grants the client the right to use and sometimes modify the systems after the termination, but with the right strictly restricted to the sole use/modification by the client, thus excluding any third party.

> **Case study: why receiving documentation is not necessarily receiving intellectual property**
>
> The client has a complex information system composed of a hundred of client-server applications interconnected through as many interfaces. Daily operations heavily rely on a central middleware to execute the eight-hour end-of-day batch process. The IT is fully outsourced to a provider (A). The middleware was developed by a specialised company (B), which supports corrections and evolutions through a pluriannual maintenance contract.
>
> The outsourcing contract with A reaching its end, the client issues a global RfP. A provider (C) offering a full-featured service that includes a built-in job scheduling system which would allow to replace the bolt-on middleware wins the deal. Once the transformation and reversibility contracts between the client and A respectively C are signed, the transformation project from A to C starts.
>
> The client then requests B to deliver the detailed configurations of the middleware, so that C can parameterise its own job scheduling system using the same logic. B officially answers that the remittance of the documentation agreed in the contract grants the client the right to receive the full documentation on how to run the middleware, but not on how the business logic was implemented in it.
>
> The client attempts as vigorously as vainly to assess its rights, including by requests for provisional relief. However, given the delays, it finally orders provider C to redesign from scratch a new business logic in the job scheduling system to the terms of a multi-year, multi-million project. During the redesign, provider C runs the newly built information system with the old middleware from B.

## Immaterial Provisions

Some clauses need to survive the contract for a period of time to be agreed between the parties. The most common are:

- *Confidentiality*. The parties oblige themselves to keep confidential all information and documentation received from the other party during the course of the relation.
- *Non-solicitation*. Each party undertakes not to solicit employees who were involved in concluding or delivering the services. Public solicitations like general advertising are not concerned by this clause.
- *Warranty of title*. The provider warrants that the services do not infringe any proprietary right held by third parties. Note that this only applies if the provider granted the client the right to continue using/modifying the systems.

- *Intellectual property.* Jointly created intellectual property shall remain in force for the duration foreseen by laws according to the nature of the creations.
- *Warranty for third-party hardware and software when transferred to the client.* The provider usually does not offer any warranty on such elements beyond that offered by the vendor.

## Dos and Don'ts

Services
- The provider shall maintain an irreproachable professional code of conduct at all times from quoting to executing the assistance for the transfer of services.
- Beware of network and other security components. These are backbone communication elements that can seriously hamper the transfer if the provider opposes a resistance on security grounds. The same applies for domain trusting.
- Consider a bonus scheme for the provider to execute the reversibility on time and in budget as a good investment. At this stage of the relationship, the provider does not expect anything more than extra money.

Data
- Keep a close eye on time and cost impacts for extracting the data. Make sure data will be returned in an open, directly accessible format.
- Keep a close eye on time and cost impacts for permanently deleting the data considering the client requirements, e.g. wiping data and then destroying hard disks and/or the provider constraints, e.g. removing all data stored from incremental backups.

Assets
- Focus more on immaterial content than on the assets themselves. Assets without proper configuration are worthless.

Documentation
- Do not mix up documentation with intellectual property. It may have dramatic consequences.

# About the Author

**Lionel Haas** is an outsourcing specialist with 25 years of experience acquired with top-tier clients and IT provider organisations in key positions of the outsourcing value chain: consulting, offering, contracting, project, operations and service management. He is currently employed by Swisscom, shaping multi-million deals that span the whole stack of services from the lowest IT and application operation layers to industry-specific application management and business process outsourcings, with a special focus on banking and healthcare.

With 20,000 employees, 6000 corporate clients and 100 banks in full outsourcing, Swisscom is Switzerland's leading IT service provider.

Lionel Haas holds a BSc in computer science from the Conservatoire National des Arts et Métiers and an MBA from the University of Phoenix.

© Springer International Publishing AG, part of Springer Nature 2018

L. Haas, *Align Client and Provider Perspectives*,

https://doi.org/10.1007/978-3-319-92064-1

# Index

**B**

Business case, xi, xiii, 25, 26, 42, 44, 75, 77, 138, 161, 194

**C**

Change the-business (CtB), 10, 17, 37, 40, 44, 75, 87, 90–92, 99, 101–103, 119, 149, 164, 177, 180, 185, 186, 189
Contract, ix, xi–xiv, 30, 43, 45, 54, 55, 59ff, 67, 73–75, 78, 80–108, 115, 117, 125, 131–133, 136ff, 153, 156, 157, 160, 161, 164, 171, 173, 183, 186ff, 192–197
Critical mass, ix, 8, 9, 12, 78, 148
CtB, *see* Change the-business (CtB)

**F**

Future mode of operation (FMO), 45, 50, 135–138, 157–159, 170

**G**

Governance, xii–xiv, 23, 24, 36, 44, 50, 51, 72, 74, 83, 99ff, 107–115, 119, 120, 130, 149, 150, 160–166, 172, 176, 177, 183, 187, 190, 191
Guarantee, xi, 6, 17, 71, 78, 82, 106, 118, 121, 134ff, 191

**I**

Integration, x, xi, 23–26, 35ff, 41–44, 66, 73, 109, 110, 120, 121, 136, 155, 168, 172, 188–190

**O**

Offer, ix–xi, 5–67, 76
Operating model, ix, x, xii, xiv, 6, 7, 23, 26, 33ff, 44, 99, 120, 124, 155, 172, 188, 192, 193
Operations, x, xiii, xiv, 8ff, 18, 20, 25, 41ff, 50ff, 57, 60, 62, 65, 72–75, 79, 82, 91, 98, 101–103, 106, 109–111, 125, 133–138, 148, 149, 153, 157–159, 164, 166, 167, 170–172, 182ff, 189, 191ff, 225
Organisation, ix, x, xii, xiv, 7, 8, 12ff, 23, 25–27, 33, 37ff, 43, 45, 50, 65, 72–74, 79, 91ff, 115, 118, 119, 122, 128, 129, 132, 139ff, 147ff, 153, 155, 161, 163–166, 176, 177, 181, 187–189

**P**

Present mode of operation (PMO), 45, 50, 157, 158
Process, ix, x, xiii, xiv, 12ff, 25, 28, 33, 36ff, 41–43, 45–47, 53–56, 64ff, 70, 73, 74, 77–80, 87, 95, 97, 99–101, 104ff, 116, 120, 127, 130–134, 139, 145, 146, 148, 151ff, 165ff, 177, 179–183, 185, 189, 197, 225
Project, ix, xi–xv, 10, 12, 15, 17, 18, 37, 45, 49–52, 57, 60, 62, 65, 74–76, 79–83, 91ff, 99ff, 107–122, 124, 125, 128–131, 133–139, 141, 144, 146–151, 158, 159, 164, 166–172, 177, 179, 181ff, 193ff, 225
Proposal, x, xi, 52–58, 65–67, 80–83

**R**

Risk, ix, xiii, 8, 16, 44, 46, 55, 56, 64, 74, 77, 90, 93ff, 105, 113, 117, 120, 131, 135–157, 140ff, 149, 152, 157–160, 162, 183, 188, 191, 195

Run-the-business (RtB), 10, 17, 37, 40, 74, 75, 90, 91, 100, 101, 103, 149, 164, 177, 185, 186, 189

**S**

Service model, x, 18–21, 26, 28, 38, 46, 49, 51, 53, 59, 66, 149, 150

Sourcing model, x, 14, 18, 24, 27, 33, 36, 41, 48

SPOC, 12, 22, 23, 25, 41, 48, 167, 189

Standardisation, x, 34–36, 38, 39, 42–44, 73

**T**

Target Operating Model (TOM), 33, 43

Tools, ix, x, xii, xiv, 3, 7, 10, 15–18, 22ff, 33, 35, 36, 39, 41–44, 50, 51, 60, 72, 73, 105, 106, 113, 127, 128, 139, 141, 142, 151, 169, 178, 182, 184, 187, 188, 190

Transformation, xii, xiii, 25, 45, 48, 55–57, 59, 74, 75, 82, 91, 102, 109, 111, 116, 119–121, 123–125, 133, 136ff, 151, 152, 158, 160, 172, 181, 193–197

Transition mode of operation (TMO), 135–138, 158, 159

Trust, xi, xiv, 20, 56, 77, 80, 97, 105, 114, 158

**V**

Volumes, ix, 6, 12, 35, 39, 42–44, 50, 53, 65, 75, 79, 86, 92, 99, 100, 110, 121, 127, 135, 137, 162, 164, 168, 169, 177–179, 185, 187, 194